Max I. Dimont

THE JEWS IN AMERICA

THE ROOTS, HISTORY, AND DESTINY OF AMERICAN JEWS

Simon and Schuster
New York

LIBRARY OF CONGRESS CATALOGING IN PUBLICATION DATA

Dimont, Max I
The Jews in America

Bibliography: p.
Includes index.
1. Judaism—United States—History. 2. Jews in the
United States—History. 3. United States—Religion—
History. I. Title.
BM205.D55   296'.0973   78-13408
ISBN 0-671-24267-9

*"America saved not only our lives
but our souls."*

DR. LOUIS FINKELSTEIN
(In an address delivered in 1976
at the Bicentennial celebration
in Newport, Rhode Island.)

*This book is dedicated to the
United States of America with love and respect.
It is also dedicated to Jewish youth,
whose task will be to save future
American Judaism and preserve its soul.*

CONTENTS

7

INTRODUCTION
American Judaism: Wasteland or Renaissance?

THE JEWS IN THE UNITED STATES are the inheritors of a four-thousand-year-old culture. Into their willing—or unwilling—hands, history has placed the symbolic scepter of this heritage.

Will this Jewish culture—entrusted to the American Jews either by blind permutations of events or by a manifest destiny—wither in a wasteland of indifference? Or will there be a renaissance—a humanistic rebirth—to ensure this culture continued growth?

For those who view purist Orthodoxy as the only authentic Judaism, American Judaism is nothing but a wasteland. For those who see medieval concepts of Judaism vanishing and new modes of expressing one's ties to Judaism emerging, American Judaism offers a renaissance. Thus, American Judaism finds itself in a dilemma. Which view of itself should it accept—the former, which threatens extinction, or the latter, which offers hope?

Viewed through the lens of orthodoxy, American Judaism is in grave danger. As one Jewish leader succinctly summarized the threat: "Fewer than half of American-Jewish households belong to synagogues. Close to 40 percent of all Jews are marrying non-Jews (compared to 6 percent twenty years ago). Religious school enrollment has plummeted to 400,000 in the last fifteen years, down one-third from a high-water mark of 600,000. . . . In recent years 10,000 young Jews have been enticed into joining evangelical sects . . . and various other occult movements . . . all too often ignorant of their own rich religious and cultural heritage. It has been forecast that the forces of assimilation, lowered birth rate, and increased intermarriage will reduce today's 6 million American Jews to 4.5 million within twenty-five years." *

These are shocking statistics, but we doubt that greater fertility and more diligent religious school attendance will solve the problems confronting American Jewish youth as long as it remains indifferent to Judaism itself. Kaddish has been intoned on the Jewish people by Jews since the days of Moses for the laxity of their ways. Throughout the centuries, kings, prophets, and rabbis have railed against the tendency of the Jews to share their bedrooms with non-Jews in an amicable exchange of love and religion.

The Jews have survived friendly bedrooms, persecutions, expulsions, concentration camps. But there was always a commitment to Judaism, which permitted Jewish history to march unimpeded into the next challenge. The danger to Judaism today is perhaps the absence of such a commitment, especially among Jewish youth which is indeed "all too often ignorant of their own rich religious and cultural heritage." One reason for this is that many Jewish educational institutions tend to teach *how* to be Jewish instead of *why*. Not finding an answer to the question "Why?" Jewish youth drifts out of religious schools into rootlessness, prey to the forces of assimilation.

One way of discovering one's roots is to read Jewish history. Yet Jewish youth is reading very little of it, perhaps because all too often Jewish history is presented as a dirge of oppression. As one non-Jewish scholar observed: "One thing I could never understand about Jewish historians is why be so proud of being the victim. The sacrificial lamb does not

* Bernice S. Tannenbaum, president, Hadassah: *Hadassah* magazine, February, 1978.

taste good to itself." Jewish history is also all too often isolated from world events, and thus seems to float in a vacuum, unanchored by relevance. It also often tends to be a "public relations history," suppressing anything thought of as unfavorable to the Jews.

In this book, as in our previous works, we have discarded the concept of Jewish history as a specialized saga of suffering so that the real Jewish history may emerge—rich, rebellious, and full of intellectual adventure. We have also discarded the conventional approach to American-Jewish history and based it instead on three new concepts: that American Judaism is a unique outgrowth of the American soil, shaped as much by the American spirit as by the Jewish ethic; that the early Jewish settlers in the Colonies were not devoted Orthodox Jews who came in search of religious freedom, but came to seek new business opportunities; and that American Judaism is destined to play the same role in the future of the Jews that rabbinic Judaism played in their past. We will also contend that American Judaism will not only preserve the Jewish heritage but will serve as a vehicle for its enrichment.

As American-Jewish history has evolved within the context of general American history, it must be evaluated within that framework. Thus early American-Jewish history and early American history must be observed as related phenomena.

Generally speaking, there are two ways of viewing the genesis of American history. One school sees the Colonial experience until the Revolution as part of British history, with American history beginning after 1776. The other sees British history ending and American history beginning with the settling of Jamestown in 1607. Though both schools can use the same dates, each will come up with totally different evaluations.

Similarly, there are two ways of viewing early American-Jewish history. The prevalent one is to see it as an extension of European Orthodox Judaism, changing only after 1845, with the arrival of the German Reform rabbis. The new, modern view is that American Judaism began in 1654 with the arrival of the first Portuguese Jews. Just as it can be held that American history began at Jamestown, and that this experience set the framework for future American history, so it can be demonstrated that the Portuguese Jews and their successor immigrants in the Colonial period set the framework for a new Jewish history.

American Judaism was shaped neither by a book nor a blueprint. It evolved not out of what was said, but out of what was done. It lived itself into existence. The Hasidic saying "Judaism did not create the Jews; the Jews created Judaism" describes the American phase of Jewish history, because in America the Jews themselves created their own brand of Judaism.

Because the Jews in Colonial America, like their Christian brethren, were pioneers who grew up with the country, they learned how to innovate. Like the Puritans, the first Jews to arrive in Colonial America showed a willingness to amend the nonessentials in their Judaism but to hold on to the nonnegotiable items. This gave them the same resilience that Congregationalism gave the Puritans, and for the same reason.

The spirit of the frontier influenced the Colonial Jew as much as it did the Colonial Christian. The American historian Frederick Jackson Turner stated that each time a part of the West was conquered, America experienced a rebaptism of primitivism, a revival of strength. The frontier, in Turner's view, brought a continual regeneration of the primitive conditions the early Americans experienced. This perennial rebirth, this westward expansion with its new opportunities, unleashed the forces that shaped the American character.

"The frontier takes the colonist," Turner says, ". . . a man in European dress, with European habits of thought, strips off the garments of his civilized past, puts him almost on par with the Indians, and disciplines and changes him during his long struggle to implant a society in the wilderness."

The same forces that created the Christian colonist also created the Jewish colonist, making him unique in the history of Judaism—a Jew differing as much from the European Jew as the European Jew differed from the biblical. Just as this frontier culture stripped the European Christian of his cultural vestments, so it stripped the European Jew of his. In the same way that the Christian colonist emerged from the wilderness not as a European but as an "American," so the Jewish colonist emerged not as a European Jew but as a distinctly "American Jew." Thus, for both, the frontier meant a steady turning away from the influences of Europe.

To understand the American Jew, then, we must see him as he grew up in the frontier situation. We must assess the impact the frontier situation had on his Judaism, because this experience, rather than events in Europe, laid the psychological and physical foundations for his future Judaism.

This new approach to American Jewish history has left us open to several criticisms. Some conventional scholars still contend that the most notable characteristic of the first Jewish settlers in the Colonies was their orthodoxy and adherence to European modes of Judaism. Others, however, feel that a reexamination of the evidence clearly indicates that this conventional view is superficial, that the life style of the Colonial Jews was completely altered as a response to the radically new conditions of social and economic openness in America. We concur with this second school.

Another criticism has been that we debunk everything Jewish and extol everything Gentile. We trust the reader will find this to be sheer nonsense. We have tried to place things in perspective. We do not view every act against a Jew as incipient anti-Semitism. A stupidity does not become a virtue when committed by a Jew; we counter a stupidity with ridicule whether it is of Jewish or Gentile origin. Jewish history does not need to hide behind the pretense of sensitivity; it will float to the top by the sheer force of its grandeur and achievements, its few follies notwithstanding.

We have also been accused of being harsh with the ghetto Jew. Such is not the case. We have been harsh, not with the Jew who was forced to live in the ghetto, for whom we have the greatest compassion, but with the stereotyped image of the ghetto Jew that persists to the present day. This stereotype was created by the Christians when they imprisoned the Jews in those ghettos. The ghetto Jew does not represent the proud Jew of past history. The authentic Jew is the Jew of the thirty-five centuries preceding the Ghetto Age and of the two centuries after its fall.

The word "Judaism" means many things to many people, all of them no doubt correct. To prevent misunderstanding, however, we wish to stress that in this book "Judaism" refers not only to the religion of the Jews but to their total social, cultural, and religious behavior.

I would now like to offer several acknowledgments.

Drs. Norman and Judith Katz, two modern Orthodox scholars, critiqued the manuscript from a consistent Orthodox viewpoint, yet with total objectivity. If there are still errors in this respect, it is because I failed to heed their advice out of secular considerations.

Mr. F. Garland Russell, historian and attorney, has my heartfelt thanks for his research of all non-Jewish aspects of this book. This work owes many of its insights into American history to his broad knowledge of the subject.

I extend an especial vote of appreciation to Jeffrey B. Stiffman, Rabbi, Temple Shaare Emeth, St. Louis, Missouri, for his perceptive reading of the manuscript and for strengthening it with many cogent comments.

I am grateful to Dr. Jacob Rader Marcus, Hebrew Union College, for his pragmatic critique. Regretfully, Dr. Marcus was only able to read part of the manuscript. Though he disagreed with my views on the Marranos (which I have not changed), the manuscript has gained much from his friendly suggestions.

I am indebted to Dr. Julius Nodel, Rabbi, Temple Emanu-El, Honolulu, Hawaii. Dr. Nodel, never one to inject timidity in his views, caused me to reexamine all aspects he disagreed with. If errors still survive in the path he trod, it is because I dared to persist in views with which he did not concur.

May it be pointed out, however, that usually where one

scholar disagreed, another concurred. In heeding one scholar, I always ran the risk of disregarding the good advice of another.

And now it is time to praise two professional editors whose help has been invaluable—Martin Baron, a researcher, and Kathleen Howard, assigned by Simon and Schuster to edit this work. This book owes much of its strength to their careful attention to detail, analysis of content, and editorial advice.

And finally, I wish to pay tribute to three individuals— Mr. Gordon LeBert, who acted as the general editor for this work as he did for my two earlier books, *Jews, God and History* and *The Indestructible Jews;* my daughter, Mrs. Gail Goldey, who also critiqued her father's manuscript; and to my wife, Ethel, who was not only my amanuensis, but also a most valued adviser.

A Note to the Reader

SEPHARDI (Plural Sephardim): All Jews from Spain and Portugal, or of Spanish- and Portuguese-Jewish descent.

MARRANO (Plural Marranos): Spanish and Portuguese Jews who were at one time converted to Christianity, whether or not they later abjured it. In this work, this term is also used to describe the descendants of these Jews.

ASHKENAZI (Plural Ashkenazim): All European Jews not of Spanish- or Portuguese-Jewish ancestry. The Ashkenazim include:

German Jews—Jews who live or originated in German-speaking countries like Germany and Austria.

Russian Jews—Jews of Slavic or Baltic countries such as Russia, Poland, Lithuania, Latvia. Hungarian and Rumanian Jews consider themselves distinct from Russian Jews and are often called "East European" Jews. Adding to this confusion is the fact that Russian Jews are also referred to as "East European," and that Jews of Polish origin often prefer to be classified as Polish rather than Russian Jews.

ORIENTAL JEWS: Jews born in or living in North African countries, Egypt, Syria, Palestine (before 1900), the Balkans, and the former Ottoman Empire.

Of the 12 to 13 million Jews living today, about 10 to 11 million are Ashkenazi and the rest Sephardi and Oriental.

The words "orthodox" and "reform" will be used in two specific senses in this book. When capitalized, *Reform* and *Orthodox* will stand for two recognized denominations of Judaism, as Protestant and Catholic describe the two chief sects of Christianity. When not capitalized, *orthodox* shall merely refer to any body of Jews who are resistant to change. When not capitalized, *reform* will simply refer to reform movements in Jewish history. Thus, for instance, the priesthood at the time of the Prophets is described as "orthodox," and those Prophets who opposed the priesthood as "reformers." But this does not mean that the priests were "Orthodox Jews" and the Prophets "Reform Jews" in the modern sense of these terms.

I

THE COLONIAL EXPERIENCE
(1654–1776)
The Age of the Sephardi Jews

Grandees and Marranos

THE USUAL WAY to present the early history of the Jews in America is to tell of the twenty-three hapless, poverty-stricken faith-laden Jews who arrived one September day in 1654 on a French bark in the Dutch harbor of New York, then known as New Amsterdam, where they were met by a governor named Peter Stuyvesant, who told them to get out, presumably because he was an anti-Semite. The trouble is that, except for the year, the place, and the name of the governor, it is not quite true.

These Jews were not the first to arrive in the Colonies; there had been Jews in the Colonies as early as 1621. Those who arrived in 1654 had not always been paupers, but were educated and formerly wealthy merchants. They were not pious Talmudic Jews; some were worldly Sephardi Jews and others were the descendants of Marranos. And Stuyvesant was not an anti-Semite but an ordinary bigot who feared Catholics and Lutherans more than he disliked Jews.

This account raises some interesting questions. Where did these twenty-three Marrano and Sephardi Jews come from? How did they get there? Why did they leave? And what are Marranos and Sephardim?

The answers are even more interesting. These Jews came

from South America, where they had been prosperous entrepreneurs; they were fleeing from the Inquisition, which had
earlier forced them to leave Spain and Portugal. The Marranos were Sephardi (that is, Spanish or Portuguese) Jews
who had converted to Christianity or were descendants of
such converts.

Because this thread of Jewish history is woven into the
subsequent history of the Jews in America, we must unravel
it to find our way out of the labyrinth of events that took
the Jews from Spain and Portugal to South America, and
from there to New Amsterdam.

Jews had settled in Spain as early as the first century A.D.,
during its occupation by the Romans. It is said that St. James
himself had preached the Gospel in Spain. But this fact had no
effect on the Jews until the late sixth century, when Reccared,
the Visigothic king of Spain, added force to persuasion. The
Jews, who thought they had hit bottom with the Reccared
persecutions, had not reckoned with a later king, Sisebut
(612–620), who found a slack in the Reccared screws. He
tightened them with his edict (616) that all Jews who had
escaped baptism under Reccared must embrace Christianity
or be banished with loss of all property. Though the Jews
called this period "The First Evil," most chose conversion to
expulsion. Over ninety thousand Jews—virtually the entire
Jewish population in Spain in that century—embraced Christianity.

But Christianity had only a century in which to capture
the minds and hearts of these reluctant converts. The Muslim
conquest of the Iberian peninsula in 711 put an end to the
forcible conversion of the Jews. The conquering Arabs did
not care what religion their subjects professed, so long as all
"nonbelievers" paid a special tax. Under their five-hundred-
year rule there emerged what has been called the "Spain of
three religions and one bedroom"—a Spain where Muslims,
Christians, and Jews shared a brilliant civilization that blended
their cultures, bloodlines, and religions.

Under Muslim rule, Spain became the most civilized country

in the Western world. Jews helped usher in a five-century age of splendor and learning; they soared to the highest posts as diplomats, professionals, and entrepreneurs. In Muslim Spain there dawned a Golden Age of Jewish creativity, an age that spawned not only renowned Talmudists but also brilliant secular poets, philosophers, grammarians, and scientists—an intellectual tour de force not equaled until modern times.

Jews who had been converted forcibly to Christianity by the Visigoths now had five centuries in which to make up their minds about returning to Talmudic Judaism. Though many of these converts and their descendants did return to orthodox Judaism, many did not. Most did not like orthodox Judaism any more than they liked Catholic Christianity. They became the cynics of their age, believing neither in the virgin birth nor in the divine origin of the Talmud. Many became cosmopolitan world citizens, moving with aplomb in the courts of viziers and grandees, marrying into the families of both. It was these converts who were destined to form the nucleus of a most vexing problem in Christian Spain.

By 1250, the *Reconquista*, the two-century Christian reconquest of Spain, was all but complete. At first Jewish life and scholarship continued to flourish under the Cross as they had under the Crescent. As Christians resettled the reconquered territories, however, hostility rose against the entrenched Jewish intellectual and social establishment. In 1350, the Spanish began a series of conversion drives to convert all Jews in Spain to Christianity. In unprecedented numbers, and with little resistance, the Jews converted. This event, unparalleled in Jewish history, is perhaps best summed up by Cecil Roth in *A History of the Marranos:* "In some places the Jews did not wait for the application of compulsion, but anticipated the popular attack by coming forward spontaneously, clamoring for admission to the Church. All told, the number of conversions in the kingdoms of Aragon and Castile were reckoned at the improbable figure of two hundred thousand. It was a phenomenon unique in the whole of Jewish history."

What caused this rush to mass conversion before any real danger confronted the Jews? Centuries of well-being in Spain had made the Jews reluctant to face penury and refugeeism. Expulsions from England, France, and many of the German states had cut off old avenues of escape. But perhaps the most overriding reason is the one stressed by Roth: "It was not difficult for insincere, temporizing Jews to become insincere, temporizing Christians."

Thus, from 1400 on, a new state of Jewish affairs existed in Spain. There were at least some 250,000 unconverted Jews and a like number of converted ones. It is difficult to assess accurately the Jewish population in Spain in the fifteenth century. Estimates have ranged from 250,000 to 1 million Jews, both converted and unconverted. We believe that there were from 500,000 to 600,000 Jews. As time went by, the converted Jews and their descendants were increasingly suspected of not being truly Christian at heart. Ironically, forced baptisms had converted a large proportion of Jews from "infidels" outside the Church to "heretics" inside it.

The usual portrait painted of these converted Jews, or Marranos, is that of pious Jews forcibly converted to Christianity and forcibly kept in the Christian fold. According to this view, the love of these Marranos for Judaism was so great that at the risk of their lives they continued to practice their religion in secret.

But this view of the Marranos runs counter to a puzzling fact—that of the word "Marrano" itself. The Spanish did not call the converted Jews "Marranos." They called them *conversos* (the converted), or *nefiti* (the neophytes), or "New Christians." It was the unconverted Jews who called the converted Jews "Marranos," a Spanish word meaning "swine." The unconverted Jews seemingly had no love, only contempt, for the converted Jews, degrading them with a most derisive epithet. They apparently viewed these Marranos not as fellow Jews in distress but as hypocritical apostates. Had the Marranos been converted under imminent threat of torture, Jewish history would have bestowed upon them the term *anusim,* the "forced ones." This is the Hebrew word used for more than fifteen hundred years to describe such forced converts.

Thus, for the modern historian, the shining image of the Marrano as a beloved Jewish brother in distress has become a bit tarnished. It is difficult for such a historian to visualize the head of a Marrano houshold attending the wedding of his daughter to a Catholic grandee one week and then secretly preparing for his son's bar mitzvah in a dank cellar a week later.

A new historic view of the Marranos is that many did not lead heroic, submerged Jewish lives but wanted to remain Catholic. According to this interpretation, the entire Inquisitorial procedure was a tragic hoax perpetrated by the Spanish bureaucracy in order to proceed against the Marranos, condemn them, and thus enrich itself with the spoils.

The Marrano problem might have been one of class rather than religion. The Marranos, some historians now believe, had perhaps been denounced by the Old Christians not because of suspicion of the sincerity of their religious beliefs but out of envy of their wealth.. The reason the Marranos often confessed to Judaizing was to escape the tortures of the Inquisition.*

Many first-generation converts were sincere; many were not. But both groups, sincere or insincere, lived as Christians, baptized their children, took them to church, and had them married by priests. The havoc was not created by this first generation of converts. The havoc came with the children who were baptized at birth. All doors were open to them— university, army, court, even the Church itself. They were liberated from the legal, cultural, and religious restraints that set the unconverted Jews apart from the rest of society. These

---

* Roth cites this story by Manasseh ben Israel: A Portuguese nobleman, whose personal physician had confessed under torture to "Judaizing," ordered the Inquisitor himself seized, and then extracted from him a similar confession with the aid of the same torture. For more material on this subject, see Roth's bibliography and footnotes to *A History of the Marranos,* which are as fascinating as they are enlightening.

children and grandchildren of the Marranos entered Christian society with enthusiasm. And thus the history of the Jews in Muslim Spain was recapitulated in Christian Spain. By virtue of their learning and sophistication they again rose to positions of great wealth, power, and prestige. They married into the noblest Christian families. Not only did they become grandees, but they also penetrated into the highest Church circles, becoming bishops and archbishops. In fact, according to Roth, "within a few generations there was barely a single aristocratic family in Aragon from the royal house downward which was free from the 'taint' of Jewish blood."

The success of the Marranos proved to be their undoing. Their prominence was galling to the "Old Christians"—the Christians who had no Jewish ancestry—who could not attain the lofty positions held by so many "New Christians." The Old Christians were also incensed by the insincere piety of the New Christians. And many orthodox (that is, unconverted) Jews, were enraged at seeing their Judaism flouted by these worldly, converted Jews. It was at this time in history, in the first half of the fifteenth century, that the epithet "Marrano" was first flung at the New Christians by the unconverted Jews.

As the Marranos grew more powerful, coming to dominate Spanish social and economic life, resentment against these "Jews in Christian clothes" increased and flared into hatred. The Old Christians claimed that the New Christians were not loyal to the Church, that they were in fact "Judaizing" * it, turning it into a "Jewish institution." To stop this trend, the Old Christians held that mere ability should not determine fitness to hold high office. The criterion, they claimed, should be *limpieza de sangre*—"purity of blood." Only those whose ancestry reached back to Visigothic times had "pure" blood. This concept of "purity of blood," first adopted in Toledo in

---

* "In the literature of the Church Fathers, both in the Latin and the Greek, the term 'Judaizing' . . . denotes the policy of imitation of Jewish ideas, practices and customs. . . ."—Louis Israel Newman, *Jewish Influence on Christian Reform Movements*.

1449, was to become, four centuries later, the basis for modern racism.

So persistent was the cry of the Old Christians for a litmus test of *limpieza* before appointment to high office that many New Christians, fearful of this threat, clamored for an Inquisition to examine their beliefs and certify them as loyal Christians. The stage was now set for the Inquisition and Torquemada, the chief inquisitor. The Pope opposed the Inquisition, but so strong was public sentiment in its favor that he was openly defied until he eventually gave his approval.

Torquemada was not a racist bent on extermination of the Jews; he was a bigot concerned with stamping out heresy. Just as Robespierre quoted Rousseau while sending noblemen to the guillotine, so Torquemada quoted the Gospel as he sent heretics to the autos-da-fé. Those brought before the Inquisition and burned at these "acts-of-faith" were Old Christians, New Christians, and converted Muslims condemned for heresy. Jews and Muslims who had kept their own faiths were not brought before the Inquisition, nor were they burned.

But whether the Inquisition was instituted for religious or economic reasons, Torquemada did not demand the extermination of the unconverted Jews. He asked for their conversion or expulsion if they refused conversion, giving the Jews themselves the choice. No charge was brought against them other than that they were not Catholic. The same applied to the Muslims, who were expelled in like manner and in greater numbers than the Jews. In fact, the situation was much the same as that of the Huguenots in seventeenth-century France, when the choice given them by Louis XIV (1685) was either acceptance of Catholicism or expulsion. Like the Jews, the Huguenots for the most part chose expulsion.

Jews who chose conversion could stay in Spain, and some fifty thousand, one fifth of the unconverted Jewish population, chose to convert rather than leave a land that had been their home for fifteen hundred years. The Jews expelled from Spain fled in all directions—to North Africa, to Holland, to

South America, and to the Ottoman Empire. The majority of Spanish Jews, however, fled to Portugal, where new disasters awaited them.

Though the history of the Jews in Portugal recapitulates that of the Jews in Spain, the scenario there lagged a half century behind the Spanish one. After an initial honeymoon of tolerance in the late 1400s, conversion was forced upon the Jews in Portugal just as it had been in Spain. But the edicts, which forbade Jews to leave Portugal and restricted most of their economic activities, were soon rescinded. The Portuguese suddenly found themselves with an empire in Brazil, but with no entrepreneurial class other than the Jews who had the skill to exploit it commercially. Thus the decree of 1507 permitted the Jews what the decree of 1499 had prohibited. It was a Magna Carta for Jews and Marranos. Jews of whatever religious coloration could leave Portugal, trade, and buy property anywhere they wished. They took off, heading mainly for four places: the Ottoman Empire, Holland, the Dutch colonies, and Portuguese Brazil.

These Spanish and Portuguese Jewish refugees—Sephardim and Marranos—had several important characteristics in common. They were not the dregs of society. They were not peasants or an exploited proletariat. In the main they were members of an elite business and intellectual class. They had little or no ghetto heritage, for the ghetto did not exist to any great degree in either Spain or Portugal. They were not refugees searching for religious freedom, but entrepreneurs looking for economic opportunities. When they fled, or emigrated, or moved (according to circumstances), they brought few Torah scrolls and even fewer copies of the Talmud with them.*

These Iberian Jews constituted a unique immigrant group in Jewish history. Piety was not their chief characteristic. True, the Jews of Spain and Portugal had a proud Mosaic

---

* Cecil Roth, when asked what he thought most Marranos knew of Judaism when they arrived in Amsterdam after their flight from Spain and Portugal, answered in one word, "Nothing."

heritage, but this heritage had been enriched by five centuries of Islamic learning, two centuries of Christian thought, adding up to seven centuries of cynicism and worldliness. It was the descendants of these Jews who came to settle in the American Colonies.

By 1500, the race for empire in the New World was on. By 1501 Santo Domingo was Spain's first official New World colony; by 1535 most of the West Indies and Caribbean Islands and most of South America had been claimed by Spain. The conquest of Mexico began in 1518 and was concluded in 1535. Florida had fallen to the Spanish conquistadors by 1574.

Brazil, first discovered by the Spanish, was claimed by Portugal in 1500. Portuguese Jews—Sephardim and Marranos —settled in Brazil as early as 1503, before the decree of 1507 permitting them to emigrate, through one of those improbable turns of Jewish history. A Marrano buccaneer, Fernando de Loronha, agreed to explore three hundred leagues of the Brazilian coast every year, to build forts wherever he landed, and to claim the land for Portugal. In 1501, Loronha set sail for Brazil with five ships, and in 1503 his Marranos built their first fort on Brazilian soil in the name of King Manuel, their persecutor.

Jewish settlements in the New World grew rapidly. Within a century and a half there were Jews in Brazil, Surinam, Barbados, Martinique, Curaçao, Jamaica, and other Caribbean and West Indies islands. They became prosperous settlers, playing for three centuries a commercial role far greater than their small numbers warranted. They developed extensive sugar and tobacco plantations, pioneered in coffee and tea cultivation, engaged in export and import, and created a sizable financier and merchant class.

The villain in this New World paradise for the Jews was a familiar one—the Inquisition, which had set up branch offices in the New World as early as 1511. Here the Inquisition ensnared not only Marranos, but also Indians and English, Dutch and other Protestants, who were burned to chants in

Latin for the greater glory of His name. The Jews became adept island-hoppers, trying, not always successfully, to stay one step ahead of the Inquisition. Denouncing rich Marranos was lucrative. The incentive was high—the accuser shared in the loot.

Though hundreds of burnings took place in the New World, no one was burned on Brazilian soil. Anyone in Brazil found guilty of relapsed faith—Jew or Christian—was shipped back to Portugal for burning.

One of the most important South American settlements was Recife, a prosperous Brazilian center for sugar production, an industry controlled by the Marranos. Here, as in Spain and Portugal, the Marranos married into the most prestigious Christian families. And again they were denounced by Portuguese Old Christians, whose animosity led to the establishment of an Inquisitional office in Recife in 1593. Jewish fortunes again declined. But somehow Jewish life went on in Recife, with death intruding now and then as the Inquisition sent consignments of suspected Marranos to Portugal for further action. Succor for the Jews came in 1630 when the Dutch West India Company captured Recife.

Under Dutch rule the Marranos crawled out of the obscurity of their hiding places back into the limelight. The Jewish population in Recife was increased by new arrivals of Sephardim and Marranos from Amsterdam. By 1645 there was a prosperous Jewish community of perhaps 1,500 in Recife. Again they were mostly merchants, exporters, importers, and plantation owners.

Alas, this Dutch paradise was short-lived. In 1654, after fierce resistance, the Dutch, with the Jews fighting at their side, were forced to surrender Recife to the besieging Portuguese.

Now the same old reel was replayed. The Inquisition was about to move in again, and the Portuguese military governor gave the Dutch and the Jews three months to get out. The Jews embarked for Amsterdam, but a fluke of history took some of them instead to New Amsterdam—the sort of chance event that has catapulted the Jews into the most unlikely places throughout the obstacle course of their four-thousand-year history.

The Transformation of the British Anglicans into Hebraic Puritans

THE FIRST JEWS to arrive in the American Colonies were totally innocent of fulfilling a manifest destiny or founding a new concept of Judaism. They, and those who followed them in the seventeenth century, had only one aim—to find a place of safety and opportunity.

In their long and varied history from Ur in Babylonia to New Amsterdam in America, the Jews had come across some odd and incredible people, but never any so strange as those in the American Colonies. Babylonians, Greeks, Muslims, Catholics, they understood. But nothing in their past had prepared them for Puritans and Quakers.

There had been Babylonians who worshippd a goddess to whom human beings were sacrificed as a token of esteem. There had been Greeks who in the name of religion gave their daughters as whores to strangers. There had been Romans who nailed people to crosses calling it justice. There had been Christians who spent their lives preparing themselves for death in the name of a dead Jew before whose image they knelt in homage.

But these Puritan colonists were something else. They worshipped a Jesus as invisible as Moses. They took the Old Testament as seriously as a Talmudist. They compared their flight from England to the exodus of the Israelites from Egypt. They taught Hebrew as well as Latin at Harvard. They tried to make the Law of Moses the law of the land. They observed a stricter Sabbath than the Jews themselves did, albeit on Sunday. In fact, the American colonists were more Judaic in spirit than the first Jewish settlers.

The Puritan interest in the Old Testament did not stem from a feeling of kinship with the Jews, but rather from a desire to return to the primitive church of the early Christians. The only literature they had on the subject was the Old Testament, and to the Puritan mind early Christian society was an early Israelite society. In establishing a society based on Old Testament guidelines, the Puritans felt they were reviving the spirit of the early Christian church. And thus it came about that Puritan society in the wilderness of Colonial America modeled itself after an Israelite society in the biblical days of Judges and Kings.

But how had these British Anglicans become transformed into Hebraic Puritans? The process began in fourteenth-century England when that country was still Catholic. Several British reformers urged that the Bible be translated from Latin into the vernacular so the common people could understand it. This notion had not occurred to many Christians since the death of Jesus. The Roman Church had forbidden such translations on the assumption (a reasonable one as time was to prove) that a firsthand knowledge of the Old and New Testaments would incite radical thoughts in the minds of readers.

The British theologian John Wycliffe (c. 1320–1384) felt differently. Defying the Church, he reputedly (some scholars aver he did not write the Bible bearing his name) translated into English the entire New Testament and part of the Old. This translation sent a shiver of fright through the Catholic establishment. It almost severed Britain from the Roman Church a century and a half before Henry VIII laid a foundation for the Reformation and paved the way for the "Judaization" of a segment of the British people. Wycliffe, who had died of a stroke, was disinterred at the behest of the Church, his corpse burned and thrown into a river after he had been declared a heretic.

The demand for copies of the Bible in the vernacular was so great that the Wycliffe Bible was often chained to an altar to prevent it from being stolen. This translation became outdated, and a new translation by William Tyndale (c. 1492–1536) appeared. Whereas Wycliffe depended on the Latin Vulgate for his translation, Tyndale used the Greek and Hebrew texts, producing such a beautiful translation that it became the basis for the King James version (1611). Tyndale was arrested, strangled, and burned at the stake for both the crime of translating the Holy Book, and for other heresies imputed to him.

These and other translations of the Bible into vernacular English stimulated a great scholarly interest in Jewish religion and humanism. Jewish religious and philosophical works became widely known among British scholars in the fifteenth and sixteenth centuries. The introduction of Jewish works into the British mainstream of learning, together with the Bible translations, had a profound impact on a segment of the British people in the two centuries from 1500 to 1700. The British became "a people of the book" and that book was the Bible. Although there were few Jews in the realm (they had been expelled in 1290), England became the most Judaized country in the world, "ridden" with Judaizing sects whose members were viewed as "Jewish fellow travellers" by the Anglican Church established under Henry VIII in 1534.

Though England had the good fortune to acquire her Protestant Reformation without a catastrophic civil war, a succession of relatively minor revolts did leave deep wounds in her religious body in the form of "dissidents." Upon her accession to the throne, the Catholic Queen Mary (reign 1553–58) put a temporary stop to their activities by burning at the stake the more ardent dissidents, causing most of the rest to flee to Holland, Frankfort, Basel, and Zurich, the strongholds of the Reformation on the Continent. By the time Queen Mary's five-year bloody reign ended, the Protestantism of the returning British exiles differed greatly from that practiced in England by the Anglicans.

These returning exiles were most angered by the remnants of popery in the Anglican Church. It is a testament to the iron will and vision of Queen Elizabeth, Mary's successor, that the Anglican Church founded by her father and entrenched by her was not shattered by these dissidents. Considering themselves purer than other sects—and therefore called Puritans—they disregarded Anglican Church law, claiming they owed obedience only to the God they had found in the translations of the Old Testament. As long as the Puritans stuck to church matters, the Anglicans tolerated them. But when they began applying Old Testament standards to English social and political life, they invited the persecution that followed. The stage for emigration to the Colonies had been set.

As early as 1597 the Puritans had petitioned for permission to emigrate to the Colonies, where they intended to set up a "Mosaic" state. Though a trickle of Puritan emigration began in 1607, most of it occurred between 1628 and 1640. What eventually stopped the tide of emigration was the final success of the forces of the Reformation to de-Catholicize the Anglican Church. Images, altars, and crucifixes were removed as they had been in Continental Protestant churches. The Puritans were pacified, the persecutions ceased, and the flow of emigration slowed.

The story of the Pilgrim journey to the Colonies gave Colonial history one of its most "American" features. The Pilgrims were English Puritans who had fled to Holland in 1607 instead of Germany and Switzerland. Here they were drawn to the Dutch Protestant Church and came close to adopting Dutch nationality. But in the end they decided to keep their English identity, and they made their historic voyage on the Mayflower from England, reaching Cape Cod in 1620. However, the Pilgrims landed in the wrong place. Since they were outside the jurisdiction of the chartered company that had sponsored them, they were without laws. They drew up their own "constitution," the "Mayflower Compact," a body of laws for the welfare and governance of their settlement. Thus the basis for their government reflected the will of the settlers, not that of the charter company.

Though England lagged a century behind Spain and Portugal in establishing colonies in the New World, she made up for lost time by a novel form of colonial administration. Spain and Portugal annexed land in the name of the crown, with the crown appointing the administrators and writing the laws. Thus their colonies were merely extensions of the mother countries. The Dutch and British hit upon another system of administration. These governments made contracts with businessmen for the commercial exploitation of the Colonies. Thus the "chartered company" was born, marking a revolution in commercial and government theory.

Those granted a charter had an exclusive franchise within a certain territory, with the right to grant licenses to non-members provided they contributed money, services, or their presence to the colony. Charter holders could buy land without limitations. They could enact laws for the territory, provided none clashed with the laws of England, and they could fine and punish individuals. In return for these privileges, those holding the charters had certain obligations—to act as the "English nation" in the territory, to settle the territory, to develop a profitable trade for the mother country, to make payments in gold and silver to England (usually one-tenth of profits), and to take an oath of allegiance to the crown. Though all chartered companies were expected to produce a profit, their main objective was to establish British footholds on American soil, settlements that would be invaluable in the event of a showdown with France or Spain.

But most important was the "people policy," the attitude toward immigration. In the British colonies anyone could settle, whatever one's religion. The Spanish and Portuguese used the criterion of nationality or religion (or both) to exclude "undesirable" settlers from their colonies. They did not realize that in such vast territories it made little difference how people worshipped God, provided they tamed the wilderness and made it productive.

Nobody had planned it that way, but thus four accidental circumstances set the stage for the entry of the Jews into a most important area of their history—the Hebraic element in Puritanism, the concept that government is based on a compact between men, the granting of charters by government to individuals, and a liberal emigration policy not exclusively based on religion. But above all, it was the spirit of the Old Testament which for a century and a half dominated American Colonial life.

The first Jews arriving in the American Colonies did not realize that their Torah had already made the biggest contribution the Jews were to make to the spirit of Americanism. They could not foresee that the Hebraic nature of Puritan society would influence the future course of Judaism, shape Jewish institutions, and reshape Jewish religious thinking—in fact, create an American Judaism, destined to affect the future of world Judaism.

The Transformation of the Colonial Jews into "Puritan" Jews

NOW WE ARE READY to return to our twenty-three Sephardi Jews who, against their will, arrived on that September day in 1654 at a godforsaken place known as New Amsterdam, a "cluster of warehouses" whose seven hundred and fifty inhabitants spoke eighteen languages. But Hebrew was not one of them.

Their journey had begun in the spring of 1654, when the Portuguese recaptured Recife from the Dutch after a long and bloody siege. Instead of a massacre in reprisal for the stiff resistance put up by the defending Dutch and Jews, General Barreto, the Portuguese conqueror, pardoned all the defenders and inhabitants "of whatever quality of religion they may be." He gave the Dutch and the Jews three months in which to sell their homes and prepare to leave for Holland.

In May 1654 sixteen ships carrying the Jews of Recife set out for Holland. Fifteen reached their destination, but the sixteenth, carrying twenty-three Sephardi Jews, was blown off course. It was captured by Spanish pirates and its cargo confiscated; the vessel was sunk, and the passengers held to be sold as slaves. But the pirate ship was sighted by a French bark, the *St. Charles*, and the prisoners were rescued. The penniless Jews were taken to New Amsterdam, the nearest port.

As the Spanish pirates had robbed them of their wealth, the twenty-three Jews of Recife were unable to pay the French captain for transporting them. The Dutch magistrate, in accordance with the law of the time, allowed the captain to hold two of the passengers hostage while the others arranged a public auction of their remaining possessions.

The Dutch, as some accounts have it, taking pity on the refugees, bought their belongings to help raise the money for the fares, then returned their belongings to them. The captain was paid, the two hostages released, and the group reunited. It consisted of six family heads—four men with wives, two women (probably widows), and eleven dependents. Behind them was the Atlantic, in front of them a three-thousand-mile wilderness that stretched to the shores of the Pacific. The scene was set for a new chapter in Jewish history.

These twenty-three Sephardim were not the first Jews to set foot in New Amsterdam. They had been preceded by several weeks by one Jacob Barsimson, who had arrived on a Dutch West India Company boat. History has failed to record whether Barsimson was on hand to greet these refugees.

Peter Stuyvesant, the governor of New Amsterdam, is usually portrayed as an anti-Semite instead of an ordinary bigot because he was not overjoyed at seeing twenty-three Jewish paupers from Recife dumped in his lap. Stuyvesant was a staunch member of the Dutch Reformed Church, the established religion of the Netherlands, and in his New Amsterdam, Catholics were anathema, Quakers and Lutherans banned, and Congregationalists barely tolerated. Among his civic activities at the time the Portuguese Jews arrived were prohibiting the sale of intoxicating liquors on the Sabbath, making church attendance compulsory, flogging a group of Catholics, and getting rid of some Lutherans. Now came the Jews.

Before the arrival of the Jewish settlers, Stuyvesant had complained bitterly to his employers in Amsterdam, the Dutch West India Company, about his Jewish competitors in the British colonies. Jews in New Amsterdam were about as welcome as Reform Jews in Mea Shearim, the Orthodox Jewish enclave in Jerusalem. To allow them to stay ran counter to his better judgment. With sublime confidence he wrote the governors of the Dutch West India Company that he had asked these newcomers to depart, but that the stubborn Jews had refused. Therefore he petitioned their worships for permission to evict these paupers "of this deceitful race" so they would not "infect and trouble this new colony." His request that these "blasphemers of the name of Christ" be denied permission to stay was not exclusively anti-Jewish, for he added that if the Jews were allowed to settle, "we cannot refuse Lutherans and Baptists." A reasonable assumption, which proved to be correct.

Alas, Stuyvesant did not realize that several of the more important stockholders of the Dutch West India Company were Jews, a fact the refugees were well aware of. The Jews sent their own petition to the Company, pointing out their loyalty to the Dutch in Brazil, and the advantages of having them as a business task force in New Amsterdam.

"Your honors," the petition continued, "should also please consider that many of the Jewish nation are principal shareholders of the Dutch West India Company. They have always striven their best for the Company, and many of their Nation have also lost immense and great capital in its shares and obligations. The Company consented that those who wish to populate the Colony shall enjoy certain districts and land grants. Why should certain subjects of this state not be allowed to travel thither and live there?"

And then came an implied threat that if they were not allowed to stay, they would take their experience and business elsewhere—to competitors.

The petition continued: "The French consent that the Portuguese Jews may traffic and live in Martinique, Christopher, and other of their territories. . . . The English also consent at the present time that the Portuguese of the Jewish nation may go from London and settle Barbados, whither also some have gone."

The reply, when it finally came, was a model of corporate diplomacy. It managed to soothe Stuyvesant while denying his petition.

"We would like to effectuate and fulfill your wishes and request," begins the answer, "that the territories should no more be allowed to be infected by people of the Jewish Nation, for we see therefrom the same difficulties which you fear" [i.e., if you let Jews in, Papists and Lutherans will follow].

Having thus soothed Stuyvesant, the governors of the Dutch West India Company gave him the argument the Jews had used in their petition:

"But after having weighed and considered the matter, we observe that this would be somewhat unreasonable because of the considerable loss sustained by this Nation, with others, in the taking of Brazil, as also because of the large amount of capital which they still have invested in the shares of this company. Therefore, after many deliberations we have finally decided to resolve . . . that these people may travel and trade to and in New Netherlands and live there and remain there, provided the poor among them shall not become a burden to the company or to the community, but be supported by their own Nation. You will govern yourself accordingly."

Some historians have viewed this as a mealymouthed, anti-Semitic reply, permitting the Jews to settle in New Amsterdam only because of Jewish pressure within the Company and fear of economic repercussions. We do not believe this to be the case. The Jewish stockholders of the Dutch West India Company were a decided minority. The majority of the board voted for the rights of the Jews to stay. The deciding factor was the fairness of the Dutch. The Dutch had granted freedom to the Jews and shown tolerance for their religion in the Netherlands, and they felt the same policy should be followed in their colonies.

In any event, the Jews were in. Their history in America had begun. To Stuyvesant's discomfort, but not danger, other Jews from both the Dutch colonies and the mother country began trickling in.

Though permitted a cemetery of their own, the newcomers were denied the right to build a synagogue, on the grounds that one never knew where such "anarchy" would end. Lutherans and Catholics might also want to build churches of their own, and such evil could not be tolerated. However, it was decreed that Jews had the same limited rights as Lutherans and Catholics. Like them, the Jews could hold their "superstitious" services privately in their homes but not publicly in synagogues or churches. In this the Dutch West India Company sustained Stuyvesant. The first synagogue in New York had to await the arrival of the British.

But before the British arrived in 1664, the Jews won an important victory. While not insisting on such rights as free assembly, Jews wanted to share the civic duties of the other settlers. A scant year after their arrival, Jacob Barsimson and Asser Levy, one of the passengers on the *St. Charles*, petitioned the New Amsterdam Council to permit Jews to stand guard with the burghers. The council voted "no" and reminded the Jews that they were free to leave whenever they wished. Barsimson and Levy appealed to the directors of the Dutch West India Company, which overruled the council. And thus it came about that Jews stood guard alongside Dutch Christians on the stockade from which Wall Street took its name.

Two years later, the same Asser Levy appeared before the council requesting to be admitted as a burgher because he, like the others, kept watch. There must have been some special circumstances in Asser Levy's case, for in 1657 he became the first Jewish citizen on the American continent. A further testament to the democratic nature of the Dutch is the success the Jews met with when they petitioned for the right to trade and travel, and to own property.

For a short while, after the British had taken over New Amsterdam, the fate of the Jews seemed uncertain. The Dutch people in New York (as the colony had been renamed) were Protestants and thus posed no problem to the British. But the Jews, whom the British viewed as "Portugals," were a puzzle to them. Finally, after vacillating between restrictions and tolerance, they decided to let the Jews shift for themselves in matters of religion. By shutting their eyes, they gave the Jews tacit permission to form their own congregations and build their own synagogues. But this policy in New York applied only to Jews; Catholics and Lutherans were not yet allowed such privileges.

Thus the position of the Jews under the British was essentially what it had been under the Dutch, except that they could now have a synagogue. In 1682, they rented a private house for prayer meetings, a common practice of the Puritan settlers. In 1730, the first official Jewish synagogue, Shearith Israel (The Remnant of Israel), was built on a site now occupied by one of Wall Street's magnificent buildings. Still in existence, this congregation is the oldest in the United States, but now located on Central Park West.

In 1727 the Jews won another victory. The General Assembly voted that they would no longer have to include the words "on the true faith of a Christian" in any oaths they took. This allowed them to become naturalized citizens and was a sign of the gradual separation of church and state.

The Jews in New York prospered and looked upon their first century there as a Golden Age, not of intellect but of liberty and wealth. But although these bounties flowed from the British, the Jews refused to change their cultural ways, still patterned after the Dutch. The Dutch Sephardi Jews regarded the British as barbarians. They continued to speak Dutch and to import mahogany furniture, Oriental rugs, and paintings from the Netherlands. So deep-rooted was this feeling of cultural superiority that they persisted in their rejection of anything British until the upheaval of the Civil War, which smashed their cultural stronghold.

There had been Jews in the Colonies as early as 1621, isolated individuals settling here and there, soon swallowed up by the dominant Christian population. Rather than follow the fortunes of such individuals, let us pursue instead the chronological development of Jewish settlements in the next four Colonies—Rhode Island, South Carolina, Georgia, and Pennsylvania.

RHODE ISLAND

Roger Williams, the man who founded Rhode Island, was a pious, quixotic clergyman, "a twentieth-century man invented in a jest by history in the seventeenth century." Born in England in 1603, he studied law at Cambridge, but abandoned it for the ministry. He started life as an Anglican, but after being a Separatist, Baptist, and Leveler, he evolved into a Freethinker. Arriving in Boston in 1631, he held a pastorate in Salem, but soon became embroiled in a religious conflict with the authorities. Banished from Massachusetts in 1635, he headed for Providence and founded the colony of Rhode Island (chartered in 1644), and with it a commonwealth based on the world's most democratic principles.

Government, said Williams in his charter, should concern itself with law and crime, not with religion and political opinions. The charter proclaimed that none should be "in any wise molested, punished, disquieted, or called in question for a difference in opinion in matters of religion." It offered not only Jews, but also Catholics and Lutherans, freedom, citizenship, and the right to hold office. His political philosophy, said Williams, was founded on the laws of the Old Testament, which to him were the foundation of all justice.

When Williams founded Providence, and later Rhode Island, it became perhaps the first place in the world where there was almost total separation of church and state, with equal opportunity for all, except for slaves. Religious folk predicted it would mean the moral ruin of the Colony and the downfall of religion, but that prediction has not yet come true. In fact, one hundred and fifty years later, the principles behind the Providence experiment were again expressed in the Constitution of the United States.

Word soon got out in the Sephardic world that in a place called Rhode Island, somewhere on the other side of the world, no religious distinctions were made. Those Sephardim with adventure in their souls and a proclivity to believe in the impossible headed for this sanctuary of freedom. The first ones came mostly from the Dutch colonies of Barbados, Surinam, and Curaçao. When the rumors were confirmed, their numbers were augmented by arrivals from Portugal, Spain, and England. Like their brethren in New York, they spoke mostly Portuguese, Castilian, Dutch, and a little English and Hebrew.

There were Jewish settlers in Newport as early as 1658, and they fared better in Rhode Island than Quakers. Roger Williams respected the Jews as the living descendants of the patriarchs and the Prophets, but he viewed the Quakers with distaste and suspicion.

Tombstones in the first Jewish cemetery in Newport are still intact, the earliest dating from 1677. Most of the early tombstones bear Portuguese or Spanish names in both Hebrew and Roman letters. It is difficult to assess how religious these Marrano and Sephardi Jews were. With the exception of the synagogue and the cemetery, they left no signs of Jewish institutional life behind them. They did not get around to building a synagogue until 1763. Touro Synagogue still stands, a beautiful example of Colonial architecture. It was declared a national historic site in 1946.

At the time of the Revolution, the Jewish community in Newport comprised but fifty to seventy-five Jewish families, but their wealth and prestige outstripped that of the Jewish community in New York. They were importers, exporters, and merchants of renown. Wealthy and distinguished they were, but not noted for Jewish learning or piety. Typical of the Newport Jewish community was the Aaron Lopez family, Marranos from Portugal who arrived in 1750. Lopez, an international trader whose thirty merchant vessels plied the seas between the West Indies, Europe, and Newport, was held in high esteem by the Gentile community. He founded the Leicester Academy in Leicester, Massachusetts. There is nothing in the record of these wealthy Marrano and Sephardi Jews of Newport showing contributions to anything Jewish other than the synagogue and the cemetery.

The Revolution put an end to the Newport supremacy. The Jews, most of whom were Whigs, had to flee when the British arrived. Some fled to the Dutch West Indies, others to New York and Philadelphia, but most fled to Massachusetts, founding one of the first Jewish communities in the heart of Puritan country. After the Revolution other cities usurped the trading advantages of Newport, and the city never regained its former eminence.

SOUTH CAROLINA

Winds of chance had taken the Jews to New York, and rumors of democracy had brought the Jews to Rhode Island. But it was the British philosopher John Locke who, in a manner of speaking, invited the Jews to settle in South Carolina, for which he had written the charter. In this charter "Jews, heathens, and dissenters" were granted equality; Indians and Blacks did not come within the scope of his toleration, and were excluded from membership in the colony. Jews, along with Huguenots, were granted the franchise and the right to hold office.

The Anglican board of governors for South Carolina accepted this charter, which allowed the dreaded religious dregs of Europe into their colony, for a most practical reason. South Carolina was "people starved." No one in his right mind wanted to settle in the swamps and wilderness of South Carolina; even those who had nowhere else to go had to be enticed there.

The first official record of Jews in South Carolina is a notation, dated 1695, by its governor, of the capture of Spanish-speaking Indians and of the employment of a Spanish-speaking Jew as an interpreter. Two years later, there is a record of four Jews settling in Charleston. By 1740, there were enough Jews there to found the third congregation in the Colonies. In 1750, on the day of Rosh Hashana, the Jewish New Year, the Jews dedicated their first synagogue in Charleston, destined to become in less than a century the first Reform temple in the United States. By 1800 Charleston was the most important Jewish community in the United States.

GEORGIA

Georgia was founded in 1732 by a group of British altruists, men of wealth and goodwill but no colonial experience. Georgia was meant to fulfill a utopian dream of the rich—a perfect "welfare state" to be the refuge for the unfortunate and unemployed, for paupers and pardoned prisoners. The scheme was doomed to failure. The trustees tried to run their colony in the American wilderness from comfortable chairs in London coffeehouses; none of them had ever seen Georgia, and they made plans to plant crops they thought desirable instead of those that were feasible.

General James Edward Oglethorpe was granted a charter for Georgia in which he inserted the passage "There shall be liberty of conscience in the worship of God in all persons . . . except Papists." The possibility of Jews wanting to settle in his colony had not occurred to the good general, so he had not specifically excluded them as he did the Catholics. He finally ruled them eligible to settle in his welfare paradise. They were not long in arriving.

Oglethorpe himself arrived in Georgia in 1733, leading a band of ne'er-do-wells to settle this new "promised land." A year later, a second ship arrived, carrying forty rather well off Jews of Spanish and Portuguese ancestry from England. They had sensed opportunity and had come to seize it.

The second "consignment" of Jews to Georgia was a sad lot of down-and-out Ashkenazi Jews who had emigrated from Germany to England. The social gulf between the elite English Sephardi Jews and these German Jews was vastly greater than that between the Sephardim and the Gentile nobility. The British Jews were embarrassed by their distant cousins from Germany and looked for ways to be rid of them. General Oglethorpe's need for people to settle his forsaken swampland seemed like a solution sent from heaven. Before the German Jews quite realized what had happened, they were on a slow boat to Georgia, where they arrived in 1734. Whereas the English Sephardim had come to found businesses, the German Jews arrived hoping to find jobs.

By 1752, the London Trustees of Georgia had to admit their experiment was a failure and that the ne'er-do-wells "who had been useless in England were inclined to be useless in Georgia as well." The charter was handed back to the British government. But Savannah, founded by Oglethorpe, was destined to become a cultural center for Colonial and antebellum American Jews.

PENNSYLVANIA

William Penn, born in London, the son of an admiral, and three times imprisoned for religious nonconformity (Quaker variety), had inherited a large financial claim against Charles II. He petitioned the king for a grant of land in the New World in lieu of a cash settlement, and in 1681 was granted Pennsylvania. Trained in law, he drew the charter himself, bidding welcome to all those "who acknowledge One Almighty God as the Ruler of the World." Jews, Papists, and Lutherans and other Protestants qualified under this definition, and all were equally welcome. However, all did not receive the franchise, and the Jews were among those believers in One Almighty God who did not. But they did not cavil. Though they could not vote in Pennsylvania, they were drawn to that colony by its otherwise liberal charter. Pennsylvania's first Jewish congregation was founded in Philadelphia in 1745.

A few decades after the founding of the Philadelphia Jewish congregation, the Jews were forced to join other Christians in biting the Quaker hand that fed them. The Quakers would rather die than fight, but not too many non-Quakers shared that enthusiasm. The Quakers were given the chance to die time and again by the Indians, who were puzzled but not impressed by these crazy white men who would not fight back. However, the Jews and the non-Quaker Christians were not willing to suffer death to prove the Quaker tenet that eventually mankind would live at peace, according to the prediction of Isaiah. The Jews, who were willing to grant that Isaiah knew all about lambs and wolves, did not believe he knew anything about Indians. They joined the non-Quaker Christians in forcing the Quakers to withdraw from government in 1776.

By the time of the Revolution, there were Jewish congregations in these five most tolerant Colonies—New York, Rhode Island, South Carolina, Georgia, and Pennsylvania. All of these congregations were located in seaport towns—New York, Newport, Charleston, Savannah, and Philadelphia. The congregations were still mainly Sephardi, in spite of an already considerable Ashkenazi influx.

There are records of Jewish settlements in the other eight Colonies, though most of these early Jewish settlers eventually converted to Christianity or vanished from Judaism through assimilation in less than two generations. Before assessing the Jews and the Judaism that developed in the century and a half of the Colonial period, however, let us briefly examine the colonies of Maryland, Virginia, and Massachusetts, which had Jewish settlers before, though no congregations until after, the Revolution.

MARYLAND

Maryland was the only Catholic colony among the original thirteen. Its founder, Lord Baltimore, was a liberal Catholic whose toleration extended to Protestants but not to Jews. He excluded them with a deft sentence in his Act of Toleration: "None professing in Jesus Christ shall be molested." Though it did let the dreaded Lutherans in, the Jews were left out in the cold.

There is evidence that there were Jews, mostly Marranos, in Maryland even before the New Amsterdam settlement. Among the varied mix of the early Jewish settlers in that colony was one Dr. Jacob Lumbrozo, who arrived from Portugal in 1656. Referred to as "ye Jew doctor," he was also an innkeeper, Indian trader, and squawman, constantly embroiled with the law. Charged with having "forced himself" upon a woman, he was freed after citing Biblical passages to show that what he had done was not against Scripture. Accused of having performed an abortion, he escaped punishment by marrying the woman so she could not testify against him.

Dr. Lumbrozo was the first and only Jew brought to court in the Colonies on a charge of blasphemy. He was accused of having denied the resurrection of Jesus, explaining it as "necromancy or sorcery." Luck was with Lumbrozo. Held for prosecution, he was released ten days later by a general amnesty in honor of the accession of Richard Cromwell as Lord Protector of England. He died in 1666, no great loss to Judaism, or to Maryland. The first permanent Jewish settlement in this stronghold of Catholicism was not founded until 1773, with the arrival of one Benjamin Levy, who opened a large wholesale and retail establishment on the corner of Market and Calvert Streets in Baltimore.

VIRGINIA

While settlers in the other Colonies were escaping British vices, the Virginians were trying to transplant British virtues. The colony was founded not by oppressed Puritans, zealous Quakers, or muddleheaded philanthropists, but by respected members of the Anglican Church. Many of the early settlers in Virginia were Cavaliers, royalist supporters of Charles I, who fled to that colony after the king's beheading by Cromwell.

The ambition of every rich English merchant in seventeenth-century England was to become a country gentleman. This was difficult to achieve in England, where the aristocracy was skilled in snubbing upstarts. Virginia became their "Little England," with the Anglican Church the official religion. No Jews were allowed to settle in this "gentleman's club." However, the Jews, according to some sources, did trickle in as early as 1621. Those of Sephardi origin married into some of the finest of Virginia's transplanted gentry; those of Ashkenazi roots married Puritans or Quakers of lower social standing. Intermarriage has its social gradations too.

MASSACHUSETTS

It is interesting to note that there were no Jewish congregations in Massachusetts until after the Revolution, for the

Puritans were religious bigots in spite of their democratic politics. Yet Puritanism had a far greater impact on American Judaism than did the spirit of toleration which existed in many of the Colonies.

Puritan New England was a noble experiment in applied theology, where the sermon supplanted ceremony. Massachusetts was intended to be a Biblical commonwealth, a theocracy like Israel in the days of the Jewish kings, with God as the ruler.

The Puritans had a unique concept of the Old Testament. They did not regard it as a historical record of the development of Jewish religion and ethics, but as the Word of God. They made no distinction between the two Testaments except that the New Testament was regarded as the story of the life of Jesus and the Old as the source of laws on how to live. To the Puritan mind the Old Testament was more than a body of laws—it was a set of precedents to emulate. The Old Testament demonstrated the parallels between the history of the ancient Israelites and their own. The Puritans believed that Jehovah was the main lawgiver, that the Old Testament was the main book of Laws, and that they, the Puritans, the Judaized Englishmen, were the stewards of God's will in the same way, perhaps, that the Talmudists saw themselves as the interpreters of God's intentions.

Though there were no Jewish congregations in Massachusetts until after the Revolution, there were individual Jews who, like the Jews in Maryland and Virginia, had little Jewish learning and few Judaic ties. A few converted to Christianity; creeping assimilationism usually took most of them out of Judaism.

Judah Monis, who became an instructor of Hebrew at Harvard, is one example of such individual Marrano or Sephardi Jews who were absorbed into the Christian mainstream before Jewish congregations were established. Arriving in Boston from Amsterdam in 1720, he received a degree from Harvard, the first awarded to a Jew in America; he was also the only Jew to receive a degree from Harvard before 1800.

The famed clergyman Increase Mather converted Monis to Christianity. In 1735, Harvard published his Hebrew grammar, set with imported Hebrew type. Though his life may not be typical, it nevertheless indicates the varieties of Jewish experience in Colonial America.

THE COLLECTIVE COLONIAL EXPERIENCE

As suggested earlier, just as it was not the Jew, but Judaism, that shaped the Christian Colonial framework, so it was not Judaism but the spirit of Puritanism that shaped the larger religious framework for the Colonial Jew. Figuratively, just as the Puritans paid lip service to Jesus and lived a "Mosaic life," so the Colonial Jews paid lip service to the Talmud but lived a "Congregationalist" life.

By stating that the Colonial Jews lived a "Congregationalist life," we do not mean that they were inclined to Christianity but only that they accepted the Congregationalist way of looking at God, synagogue, and state. The Jews during their one-hundred-and-fifty-year-long Colonial experience were affected more profoundly by the Puritan ethic than by the Talmudic code.

There were five main factors that led American Judaism to develop so differently from the Judaism prevailing in Europe.

The first was the Sephardi Jews themselves, the first Jews to arrive in the Colonies. At that time they were already quite different from the Jews in the rest of Europe. The Sephardi Jews had no ghetto tradition or mentality because there had been no ghettos in fifteenth-century Spain or Portugal.*

The Jews were banned from Spain and Portugal before the ghetto was instituted in Europe, and the Sephardim generally did not emigrate to countries where Jews were confined in

* "Ghetto" is used only in its specific meaning—a section of town or city set aside for Jews by the Christians, with the Jews forcibly and by law confined to that section. The first such ghetto was instituted in Venice in the mid-sixteenth century.

such enclaves. They stayed out of Germany, Eastern Europe, and Russia, lands of the ghetto, and headed mainly for Holland, England, the Ottoman Empire, and the Dutch West Indies—ghetto-free countries. Thus the Sephardim (with but few exceptions) wore the same clothes as their fellow Christians and were indistinguishable from them.

The Sephardim and Marranos who arrived in the colonies were not orthodox Jews in the traditional sense—they were not willing to sacrifice their lives for the right to attend synagogue three times a day. As one scholar expressed it: "Many had trouble assimilating into Judaism, and we know of women in the Spanish and Portuguese Synagogues of Colonial New York who continued counting the rosary when reciting Jewish prayers; and crossed themselves when the clock struck twelve." *

Whereas the European feudal Jews clung to the Talmud, these Sephardi and Marrano entrepreneurs did not place so great a stress on it. They brought to America a proud seven-century heritage as free, cosmopolitan citizens. Through conversion or close association they had become conversant with the best and the worst in Christian and Muslim civilizations and had learned to regard all religions with equal skepticism. There are few records of Talmud folios amongst the possessions the Sephardi and Marrano Jews took with them in their flight from countries of oppression. Whereas the scarcity of British law books troubled the Puritans who were seeking precedents in common law, the scarcity of Talmud folios did not bother these Sephardim and Marranos who looked for few Talmudic precedents. Sephardi Jews from England did now and then send questions of religious policy to the chief Sephardi rabbi of England. But in general they adopted the course that suited them, much as the majority of American Jews do today.

The second factor in the development of a uniquely American Judaism was the Hebraic nature of the Puritans. One

* H. P. Salomon, in his introduction to *A History of the Marranos*, by Cecil Roth, revised edition 1974, Schocken Books, page XIV.

historian has observed, "Whereas the Spaniards gave South America the Cross without Christianity, the Puritans gave North America Christianity without the Cross." The Puritans did not come to the Colonies to preach the gospel of the resurrected Jesus; they came with the Old Testament to teach the Decalogue (the Ten Commandments) of Moses. They came not as British Christians but as "Christian Israelites," escaping the oppression of the "Philistines," as they called their Anglican oppressors.

The American frontier psychology was much like the frontier psychology of the Israelites during the Age of Judges in the Old Testament. The problems of the Israelites in settling Canaan were akin to the problems the frontiersmen faced in subjugating the American wilderness. As the frontiersmen never recognized any rights of the Indians to the land, they had no more guilt feelings about displacing the Indians than the Israelites had about displacing the Canaanites. The American continent to the colonists was as much the Promised Land to them as Canaan was to the Israelites.

A Puritan minister did not have to be ordained. He was "called" by a congregation, and when he was no longer needed the "call" was ended. The New England churches were held together not by a central administration but by a shared way of life. Each congregation had its own problems, and each solved them in its own fashion. In fact, in Puritan New England, church and town were more closely linked than church and state in Catholic Europe. Each congregation was autonomous, and each town was a closed religious corporation. The Jewish congregations in the Colonies followed this Puritan model.

The concept of government in most colonies was Judaic. "It is a historic fact," Lecky has remarked, "that in the great majority of instances the early Protestant defenders of civil liberty derived their political principles chiefly from the Old Testament and the defenders of despots from the New." We can see this illustrated in two famous mottoes of the Revolution. The design for a seal of the United States, proposed by

Jefferson, showing the Jews crossing the Red Sea with Pharaoh in pursuit, has the motto "Rebellion to tyrants is obedience to God." The Liberty Bell bears a verse from Leviticus (25:10): "Proclaim liberty throughout the land, unto all the inhabitants thereof."

Though the American Constitution is derived from concepts in British common law, the idea of a balance of power among the executive, legislative, and judicial branches of government also closely resembles the Biblical political structure—the king being equivalent to the chief executive, the Sanhedrin to the judiciary, and the "congregation of Israel" (the popular assembly) to the legislature. The founding fathers themselves pointed out this parallel between the Old Testament and the Constitution, thinking this a good argument for its acceptance.

For an American Jew, it is exhilarating to contemplate that the great principles upon which this nation was founded were based upon a book the Christian world knows as the Old Testament, the product of Jewish genius. Thus, the greatest contribution to the spirit and founding of America was made not by American Jews, but by a book by their forefathers, written over two millennia before the existence of the American continent was known.

A third element in the formation of the Colonial Jew was the fact that the American colonists never developed a feudal state in America. The colonists had not come to America with the idea of doing away with European feudal institutions. It was just that feudalism had a difficult time taking root in American soil. The noblemen and the intellectuals who founded the Colonies often looked upon the frontier as a curse—it made it difficult to keep the servants on the manor and the yeoman in his place. The frontier was an escape route from servitude. Slowly, as the frontier receded, it drew people farther and farther west into the wilderness; they found not "milk and honey," but riches in land and furs. The frontier, the need for people to settle the country, the nature of the charters, the competition for business—all were antithetical to a feudal system of noble, priest, and serf. The influence of the lord vanished. The colonists became a powerful middle class of farmers, tradesmen, artisans, and entrepreneurs.

The Colonial Jews—Sephardim, Marranos, Ashkenazim— had been members of the trading class in Europe; they were small merchants, artisans, exporters, importers, and bankers. The first arrivals were not in quest of opportunities to stay "orthodox" but in quest for economic opportunities. And they found them. When they arrived, they did not have to be integrated. They fit right into the American system, part of the warp and weft of the Colonial fabric.

The Jewish families in Colonial America prospered and became a commercial elite in a largely agrarian society. The first Sephardi immigrants were middle class from the beginning. There were almost no farmers or laborers in this group. However, they were not noted for intellectual achievement, political acumen, or professional skills. Medicine, law, engineering, and architecture were rarely Jewish professions in Colonial America.

At the time of the Revolution, 50 percent of the American people were slaves or indentured servants. But the Jews were neither. They were all free. Though most were shopkeepers and craftsmen, many were manufacturers, importers, exporters, wholesalers, and slave traders. They dealt in coffee, sugar, tobacco, and molasses. They paid the same taxes non-Jews paid, and, by and large, suffered no more disabilities than other minorities did. And these disabilities, such as the lack of franchise in some of the colonies, did not affect their other freedoms. Anti-Semitism was almost nonexistent in Colonial America.

The fourth factor was that the Jews in Colonial America did not need to develop Jewish political institutions. Because they could get justice in American courts, they did not need Jewish courts or judges. They could get redress for grievances through regular channels of administration because there were no special laws either against or for the Jews. Because, like their Gentile neighbors, they paid taxes directly to the state, they did not need a hierarchy of Jewish tax collectors. Since there were no ghettos, there were no ghetto administrators. Most of the Old World Jewish institutions either disappeared or never took root in American soil. The superstructure of a European Jewish hierarchy became obsolete, and most of the institutions needed to maintain the Jews as a nation within a nation in Europe withered in America. About all that remained was the irreducible minimum—the synagogue and the cemetery. New "Puritan-inspired" institutions took their place.

The fifth and last major reason why American Judaism took a different direction from its European counterpart is the rather startling fact that until 1840 there were no ordained rabbis serving permanently in America. The first rabbi to visit the Colonies was Raphael Hayyim Isaac Carigal, who arrived in Philadelphia in 1772, preached briefly in the Newport synagogue, and left in 1773 for Surinam. The rabbis viewed Colonial and antebellum America as unholy, a land where their brand of Judaism had no chance to survive, and they preferred not to come to the "American Babylon."

Thus, the rabbinic system of Europe never got a chance to establish itself in America. When rabbis did arrive, things had drifted so far that any real basis for them to develop religious or political power was gone. The early Jewish settlers in America did not recreate the religious society of European Jewry; they created a secular Jewish-American society, one in which the Old World rabbi would have few functions. The Jewish spiritual leaders in Colonial America were lay people, and a congregation was lucky if its lay leader knew a little Hebrew, and even luckier if he had more than a smattering of knowledge of the Jewish tradition. Colonial Judaism was more or less "made up" by the settlers, who drew on remembrance of things past.

Influenced by these five factors, the Colonial Jews did not have the piety of the European Jews. They were not ardent followers but lukewarm observers. Though there was no formal revolt against the Talmud, there was no great devotion to it either. When confronted with new problems, they did not search for a Talmudic precedent but improvised. When the reality of the frontier clashed with a Talmudic pronouncement of the Babylonian era, or that of a sage from a European ghetto, the traditional teaching was ignored.

To experience the tenor of Jewish life in Colonial America, one can read no more enlightening literature on the subject than Jacob Rader Marcus' *American Jewry: Documents, Eighteenth Century*. As one reads the several hundred letters to Jews from Jews, who never intended them for publication, one is struck by how "un-Jewish" they are. Only a few are written in Yiddish; most are in excellent English. Unless a letter specifically pertains to a synagogue matter, there are hardly any references to Jewish subjects, objects, rituals, holidays, customs. The authors could be any son writing home about his new business; any mother writing to her daughter in another city; any friend sending a chatty letter. Few Jewish signposts are to be found.*

Of special interest is a letter by one Rebecca Samuel, dated 1791, a recent immigrant writing from her new home in Richmond, Virginia, to her family in Hamburg, Germany. Though she is an Ashkenazi Jew, she enthusiastically accepts the Jewish way of life in America. But let her letter speak:

"One can make a good living here, and all live in peace. Anyone can do what he wants. There is no rabbi in all America to excommunicate anyone. This is a blessing here: Jew and Gentile are one. There is no *galut* [separation] here."

Rebecca Samuel rejoiced because there were no rabbis in America to force her to do things she did not want to do. She was willing to dispense with rabbinic and Talmudic Judaism, but not Judaism itself.

The portraits of prominent Colonial Jews depict people of respectable countenance, indistinguishable from other

---

* This is also true of the letters in the three-volume *The Jews of the United States 1790–1840: A Documentary History* by Joseph E. Blau and Salo W. Baron.

well-to-do Americans of the period. None is dressed in the garb of a ghetto Jew; if not for their names, they could be Christians. And their biographies match their faces.

Moses Levy, for example, an Ashkenazi from London who settled in New York around 1695, became a shipowner and slave trader. A leader of the New York Jewish community, he was elected and served as constable of New York, but paid a fine rather than serve as president of the Jewish congregation when elected to that post.

Benjamin Nones was a French Jew from Bordeaux. Joining the Continental Army as a private, he became a major, served on Washington's staff, and distinguished himself for bravery in the siege of Savannah.

The Nathan family came from England to the Colonies in 1773, and had many illustrious descendants. Legend had it that since the days of Solomon the Nathans had been born rich. And it is said that when Mendes Seixas Nathan, who drew up the constitution for the New York Stock Exchange, was asked if this was true, he replied, "At the time of the Crucifixion it was said to be so."

Jacob Franks, one of the wealthiest Jews of Colonial New York, was an Ashkenazi Jew from England, serving as a fiscal agent for the British in the Colonies. A worldly aristocrat, he built an elegant mansion in New York City and entertained lavishly. His son David converted to Christianity and his daughter Rebecca married a British general. A relative, Colonel David Salisbury Franks, was a Whig who served on the staff of General Benedict Arnold. When Arnold was convicted of treason, Colonel Franks was cleared by General Washington, who sent him on a diplomatic mission to France.

The Franks family was typical of the 30 percent of Jewish families in the Colonial period who vanished from Judaism through intermarriage. This high percentage of intermarriage shows both a Jewish and Christian acceptance of one another as marriage partners. Often these intermarriages were in the higher social classes, among some of the most elite Colonial families. However, such intermarriages also took place in the lower social ranks; Jewish peddlers, cowboys, and adventurers who often married Indian women or servant girls. Others lived with slave women in common law marriages.

Had there been Jewish sociologists in the Colonial period, they would have warned that at the rate the Jews were intermarrying there would be no Jews in the United States by 1850. When the American Revolution broke out, a new era dawned for the Jews. Instead of declining, their numbers increased.

The American Revolution was more a rebellion than a revolution. The revolutionary ideals were accomplished facts before the war was fought. To paraphrase John Adams: The Revolution was achieved before the war commenced.

Viewing the Revolution with hindsight, one finds little to quarrel about with the English. The cost of the French and Indian Wars had severely strained the British economy, and Britain asked the colonists to share this burden. They refused. The British imposed taxes. The colonists resisted. After the French had been defeated and the Indians contained, England was no longer needed to defend the Colonies. She had done her duty, and she could now go. Actually, the Colonies had borne no more than a third of the cost of the French and Indian Wars, and England two thirds. In 1775, the per capita tax on the British was fifty times that paid by the Americans. The Sugar and Stamp Acts imposed on the Americans were mild compared to those levied on the British. The cry "No taxation without representation" disguised the issues. The colonists were objecting to a potential tyranny rather than an actual one. They were looking for a reason to rebel, rather than being pushed into rebellion. In fact, after the war, the Americans had to tax themselves more severely than the British had.

George Washington was not a military genius like Lafayette, or an intellectual like Jefferson, or a diplomat like Franklin. Yet he was perhaps more indispensable to the Revolution than the other three combined. He was a general who held the Continental Congress supreme and never imposed by force his military needs on the colonists. He won the trust and loyalty of the people, and with that unity he won the war, in spite of the odds against him.

Most Jews in Colonial America flocked to Washington's banners. However, like most other American colonists, they were not happy at the thought of a war. Even after the Battle of Bunker Hill, the Continental Congress tried to avoid a full-scale struggle, and the Jews joined their Christian neighbors in praying for a peaceful solution.

There is no way of determining exactly how many Jews were Tories, or loyalists, and how many were Whigs, or separatists. In a sense, the Revolution was also a civil war, which set family against family, friend against friend. The loyalist Jews, many from England, were grateful to England for the security it had offered them and found it difficult to take up arms against the mother country. The Jews from the Dutch Colonies and from Spain, who owed no such loyalty, found it easier to side with those in favor of separation. The majority of the Jews were, however, Whigs.

Unlike many Jewish historians, we will not enumerate the Jews who sacrificed their lives and/or fortunes for the Revolution, or who performed patriotic deeds above and beyond the call of duty. Jewish sacrifices differed in no way from sacrifices made by Gentiles. Suffice it to say that Jews did partake heroically. Most started as common soldiers and finished as common soldiers, though many did achieve office rank, some as high as major.

We must discount the many tales of superpatriotic Jews who, through some single contribution, "saved" the Revolution. One of the most exaggerated of such tales is that of Haym Solomon. The scant historical evidence available indicates that Haym Solomon was a "bill-broker" who sold "war bonds." Perhaps he was a most enthusiastic and successful one, but throughout the years his contribution has been successively enlarged until he has become a Rothschild-like financier who single-handedly underwrote the Revolution. We feel that the Haym Solomons, no matter what their financial contribution to the Revolution, did not play as important a part in Jewish or American history as did the Judaic ideals that went into the founding of the Republic.

The unified nation that was formed was not the product of one man's genius but of compromise and horse-trading. Such was the nature of the men who did the horse-trading, however, that the plan of government that they drafted has survived two centuries of civil war, world war, and social upheaval. History has confirmed that the founding fathers were touched with greatness.

The inspiration for the greatness of the future America came from the steadfast belief of the American people in the Old Testament to which the founding fathers gave their constant affirmation. The Constitution reflects that profound belief. One article, and one amendment in it, shaped American Judaism more profoundly than any other document with the exception to the Torah. Article VI, paragraph 3 states:

> . . . no religious test shall ever be required as a qualification to any office or public trust under the United States.

And the First Amendment states:

> Congress shall make no law respecting an establishment of religion, or prohibiting the exercise thereof.

This article and amendment were to have a tremendous effect on the American Jews. The article opened a path for Jews in government—administrative, judicial, and legislative. The amendment opened new horizons for Judaism. In Biblical times the Jewish state had imposed its state religion. In the Diaspora, the conqueror usually permitted Jewish leaders to enforce their own religion upon their own people. But in the First Amendment the American state had spoken unequivocally. Religion is the individual's own business. The Constitution created "voluntary Judaism" for the Jews.

But could Judaism survive unless there was power to enforce it? Could the grandeur of Judaism assert itself without force, or would it evaporate in an atmosphere of freedom? It was not just the Colonial Jew who was to reject the Talmud as the final arbiter in American Jewish life; other Jews in subsequent immigration waves, including those from the Russian ghettos, would also reject such authority. But they did not reject Judaism itself. Though there was no way to keep them forcibly within its fold, they nevertheless clung to Judaism.

In the second phase of Jewish experience in America, the Ashkenazi Jews will wrest the center stage from the Sephardim. Because most of the Ashkenazi Jews came from the ghetto, they had a totally different ethnic background from that of the Marrano-Sephardi Jews. We must examine the ideas in the Ashkenazi cultural mix before we can evaluate what happened when the ghetto-acculturated Ashkenazi Jew clashed with the Americanized Sephardi Jew.

II

THE ANTEBELLUM INTERLUDE (1776–1840)
The Americanization of the Ashkenazi Jews

From Moses Mendelssohn to
Napoleon Bonaparte

ONE OF THE MOST incredible chapters in Jewish history—so full of incredible chapters—is the three-century (1500–1800) imprisonment of the Jews in the dank ghettos of Europe and their subsequent emancipation from them by a Jewish hunchback from Germany and a conquering emperor from France.

When the eighteenth century dawned on the European Continent, the Jews, whose ideas had roamed the universe, were looked upon with contempt by the outside world. Voltaire viewed them as "a greedy and selfish race." Goethe considered them "an inferior and degraded people." And Fichte's idea of saving Western civilization from the Jewish pariah was to have Europe conquer Palestine and send the Jews there, just to be rid of them, a solution that hardly made him a Zionist.

The real tragedy is that if one were to view the ghetto Jew as objectively as an anthropologist views an aboriginal tribe, one would perhaps have to agree with the view that the ghetto Jew gave every appearance of a degraded people. An anthropologist studying eighteenth-century ghetto Jews would find them closer to the concept of an obscurantist, backward, superstitious people than to the proud Man of War of Biblical days or to the people of learning in the Islamic Age.

Ironically, the ghetto, established by the Christians to humiliate the Jews, is now claimed by some Jews to be the source of Jewish strength and the only setting for authentic Judaism. The ghetto Jew, extolled by them as the authentic Jew, was actually the end result of a deliberate policy by Church and State to degrade the Jews. The lingering remnants of ghetto Jewry still wearing earlocks and caftan are historically the most unauthentic Jews in their four-thousand-year history.

Jews in Biblical days dressed like their Assyrian, Babylonian, or Persian contemporaries. Jews in Greco-Roman days dressed in the fashion of Greeks and Romans in chiton and toga. Jews in the Islamic world were indistinguishable in outer apparel from their Muslim brethren. Jews in Renaissance times dressed in the same silks as their Gentile neighbors. The aristocratic Judah Hanasi and the elitist Maimonides would have looked with disbelief and sadness at the state of the ghetto Jew.

Our intent has not been to denigrate the Jew for what he became in the ghetto; he could not help it because he was forced into the life style he led. But we must beware against romanticizing him as noble and ghetto life as beautiful. It was ignominious and ugly. But the customs and rituals that created this sad Jew represented, nevertheless, in a cruel way, the correct response to the horrible challenge that confronted him for three centuries. The use of excessive ritual was part of an attempt to give spiritual meaning to this drab, everyday life. History has shown that it was the correct response because it helped the Jews preserve their sanity during the centuries this ghetto hell was their abode. The accretions of ghetto customs, traditions, and rituals served as a morale builder, as a fence against the enemy; his dedication to his religion lent a nobility and holiness to his life. In spite of ugly, crowded, sordid surroundings, in spite of grinding poverty, in spite of the stultifying atmosphere, a dignity did pervade the ghetto during the Sabbath and festival days. High moral standards prevailed. Though murder, robbery, and rape were rampant outside ghetto walls, such crimes were practically nonexistent inside. But ghetto life itself was demeaning.

But when the walls of the ghetto crumbled, there was no longer a need for ghetto garb, no longer a need for the old responses. History hurled new challenges at the Jews, and Jewish survival demanded new responses. Those who saved Judaism from extinction in the modern age were Jews with programs for reform, generating new responses to these new challenges. The purist orthodox were bystanders hitching a historical free ride while vilifying their saviors.

But how had the Jews—who had fathered Moses, Isaiah, and Maimonides—ended up in the cul-de-sac of the ghetto? How indeed had this Chosen People become a joke of history, a travesty of their former grandeur?

The answer is simple: the Protestant Reformation.

The voice of heresy—that is, the voice questioning the supremacy of the Pope—began to be heard in the wake of the Crusades. As long as heretical sects remained small, the Church was tolerant. But as heresies multiplied, as the voices of dissent grew louder, the Church took alarm. And as one heretic sect after another arose in those areas where the Jews were most numerous, the Church began to associate Christian heresy with Jewish influences. As the voices of heresy crescendoed into a thunder of revolt, the Church also began to wonder if the time had not come to remove the Jews from the mainstream of Christian life and thus eliminate the competition of Judaism.*

At first, as the fortunes and battles between Catholics and Protestants seesawed back and forth, the Jews became of increasing importance to both sides. Each side felt that the tide of victory would run in its favor if the Jews could be convinced to join its forces. The Jews were still regarded by the Church as the "living testament to Jesus," and how could one lose with support like that? In 1523, Luther himself made a bid for the "Jewish vote," because he was sincerely convinced that his Protestantism was a return to authentic Judaism. Similar bids had been made by the Church. The Jews, not recog-

* For an interesting development of this thesis see *Jewish Influences on Christian Reform Movements* by Louis Israel Newman.

nizing the perilousness of their position, in essence answered, "A plague on both your houses," and rejected both sides.

The result was catastrophic. Luther turned against them with a paranoid hatred. The Church washed its hands of the consequences of the actions it was about to take. The first step was the segregation of the Jews in the ghettos, the first such enclaves in Europe. Within twenty years, the Jews were expelled from most papal states. By 1600, Western Europe, which for five hundred years had been the center of European Jewry, was practically empty of Jews, except for those locked away and forgotten in these ghettos.

It was also in the sixteenth century—the century of the gathering Protestant-Catholic storm—that most of the laws aimed at isolating the Jews from the Christians and making them objects of derision were enacted. Within one century Jews lost their status as human beings, and became dehumanized symbols in the eyes of Christian society. A new generation of Christians, who did not know of the proud, learned, dignified Jews of former days, thought of the ghetto Jew as the real and only historic Jew, an object of scorn and pity. Thus, without a master plan, within one century the isolation of the Jews was achieved. The ghetto was the end of the line. The Jew became Europe's forgotten people.

To the credit of the Catholic and Protestant hierarchies, however, neither thought of murdering defenseless Jews as a "final solution," as did the Nazis. Banishment into ghettos, yes. But planned murder, no. The pogroms were a product of the modern age.

Then, after three hundred years of ghetto imprisonment, there was a timid knock on the inside of the massive ghetto portals and a timid voice pleading, "Let my people out."

History must have smiled when it selected Moses Mendelssohn (1729–1786) as the prince to kiss the slumbering Jewish ghetto maid back to life. He was a most unlikely hero for the task—an ugly hunchback from the ghetto of Dessau, Germany, a Jewish Uncle Tom who loved his role as a *Salon Jude* (Salon Jew). But his timid voice penetrated throughout the ghettos of Europe, and eventually reached the ears of the French Revolutionaries.

If not for an accident, Moses Mendelssohn would have ended up a poor Torah scribe like his father. At age fourteen, Moses Mendelssohn came upon two forbidden fruits of knowledge—one Jewish, one Gentile—in the ghetto garden of worldly ignorance. One was Maimonides' *Guide for the Perplexed*,* in Hebrew; the other was Locke's *An Essay Concerning Human Understanding*, in Latin. Maimonides opened new vistas of Jewish humanism to Mendelssohn; Locke, after Mendelssohn had taught himself forbidden Latin, revealed Western civilization to him. Ghetto and Talmud no longer could hold him; he journeyed to Berlin where he acquired an education in philosophy, language, and science. He was swept into the current of the *Aufklärung* (Enlightenment) and became Berlin's leading *Salon Jude*. At thirty he married Fromet Gugenheim, "neither beautiful nor learned," in his words, to whom he taught French literature. Their three children converted to Christianity, and their grandson, the composer Felix Mendelssohn, was born a Christian.

Mendelssohn's *Aufklärung* trail might have taken him straight into the arms of the Church, as it did his children, if not for one of those surprises history always has up its sleeve. Challenged by a Swiss theologian to convert to Christianity or declare himself a Jew, Mendelssohn stopped running, assessed himself, and chose Judaism. But as he could not accept ghetto orthodoxy, he fashioned a philosophy for a modern orthodoxy that would permit Judaism to coexist with Western civilization. This was the beginning of German "Reform" Judaism.

Mendelssohn clearly saw the dilemma of the German Jews. If they stayed in the ghetto, they would become fossils; but if history forced them out of the ghettos too precipitously,

---

* This work, which introduced the "heretical" thought that Judaism was a rational religion, was banned by the Orthodox to anyone under twenty-five, and the Jews of France denounced it to the Church. All available copies were burned in Paris in 1238, an act which prefaced a subsequent three-century wave of public burnings of the Talmud by the Church.

they might vanish out of Judaism, because ghetto Judaism, not Judaism itself, was patently inferior to Western civilization. There was no doubt that Jewish youth, if given the choice, would by and large choose Plato over the Talmud.

Mendelssohn appointed himself the savior of the Jews. He would emancipate them according to a plan that would free them first mentally and then physically from the ghetto. For this the Jews would need a language other than Yiddish, a language such as German, which contained the world's most important literature, science, and philosophy. To accomplish this he decided to translate the Torah into German. But as the ghetto dwellers did not know the German alphabet, he transliterated German words with Hebrew letters. He had calculated correctly. The book was an instant success.

Now, understanding German, Jewish ghetto youth taught themselves the Roman alphabet, and as the world of literature opened up for them, the ghetto could no longer contain them. They forced an opening in that gate and squeezed into the sun outside, carrying with them Mendelssohn's concept of Judaism as a philosophy of revealed religion, not as an obscurantist crown of *pilpul* (the science of Talmudic hairsplitting).

The Jews, said Mendelssohn, should differentiate between the temporary injunctions formulated for ghetto survival and the divine commandments given by God for all times. Whereas it was desirable to slough off those Talmudic dogmas that had no present relevance, Jews should retain those elements of their religion that bound them to their divine past. This mild "Jewish Luther" declared that the breaking of a religious law was an individual offense, not a state offense, and that excommunication to enforce a religious conformity should be banned. Mendelssohn became the first Jew in Jewish history to advocate the separation of church and state, the separation of Talmud and rabbi from education. In no way, however, did he reject the basic principles of Judaism.

Mendelssohn foresaw the coming struggle between the feudal and the modern state, warning that there would be no room for the ghetto in the modern democratic state. He wanted the Jews to dissolve their bonds with the Jewish ghetto establishment, which ruled like a state within a state, and to "sign a contract" with the new secular states in the same way that Christians were dissolving their bonds with the feudal princes in order to become citizens of the modern state.

Orthodox Jews portray Mendelssohn as a Jewish Faust striking a bargain with the devil—willing to give up Yiddish for German, Talmud for the worldly philosophers, and *pilpul* for science—a Faust willing to eat the fruits of Western civilization at the price of losing his Jewish soul. A howl of rage went forth from the reigning rabbis when Mendelssohn's translation of the Torah appeared. They were as alarmed as the popes and bishops had been when the Bible was translated into the vernacular. The invective that the orthodox hurled at Mendelssohn sounded much like the invective that popes had hurled at Wycliffe and Tyndale.

"This translation could prove a danger to Judaism," cried Rabbi Ezekiel of Prague.

"Unclean," thundered a Vilna scholar. "Not fit to be put into Jewish hands. We forbid Jews everywhere to own a copy or read it."

And from the chief rabbi of Frankfort came this obiter dictum: "A work of unprecedented wickedness in Israel and will surely undermine the Jewish religion." He had forgotten that pious and great scholars in previous days had translated the Torah into Aramaic and Arabic.

Had the Orthodox rabbinate had the power, would they have resorted to force and violence to silence Mendelssohn? To judge by the precedents of ancient Jewish history, when the Jews had a state of their own, the answer is yes. But as the rabbis did not have such power, they went to their local princes or bishops, begging them to suppress the wicked writings of Mendelssohn.

Thus, when a glimmer of hope finally penetrated the wall of secular ignorance surrounding the ghetto—when Jewish and Christian emancipators opened ghetto doors, bidding its

pale, culturally starved denizens to step into the light of Western civilization, the Jewish ghetto establishment shredded the
emancipators with invective and excommunicated those who
dared listen to the siren song of freedom. It won the first
round between orthodoxy and reform. The ghetto gates were
closed again, guarded by Christians on the outside and Jewish
zealots on the inside to make sure no Jew would slip out. Only
a tenacious few made it.

Moses Mendelssohn was not a profound philosopher. Few
people today read his pretentious works. Nor was he a militant defender of Jewish rights; he always had his ear cocked
to what the non-Jews might say. Yet this Milquetoast revolutionary proved to be a prophet before his time. His distinction between temporary injunctions and eternal truths in the
Torah and Talmud was an issue the Reform Jews were to
take up again a few decades after his death. His questions
about the relationship of the Jew to the coming modern state
were the same as those Napoleon was to raise.

We must now examine the role of Napoleon as a Jewish
emancipator and his effect on the coming reform movement in
Europe, for it was Napoleon who brought the Jews back into
the mainstream of Western civilization. As philosopher Morris
Raphael Cohen observed, "Suddenly the walls of the ghetto
were removed and we found that the Jews had not been the
only conservators of wisdom and civilization."

When the French Revolution arrived, there were some fifty
thousand Jews in France. Of these, some ten thousand were
in southern France, most of them Spanish Jews, descendants
of the Marranos who fled Spain during the Expulsion of 1492.
They constituted an elite business and professional class. The
rest, mostly Ashkenazim, were concentrated in the province
of Alsace. Although a few were wealthy businessmen, most
were money lenders and peddlers. But, whether rich or poor,
the Ashkenazim were despised by the Christians and looked
down upon by the Sephardi Jews.

The first to receive full freedom under the Revolution were
the Sephardim, because they were considered the most civi-

lized Jews, those whom the French could accept as equals. It took two years of bitter fighting by the more liberal of the French revolutionaries to have the Ashkenazim accepted as citizens. Thus France was the first modern European state to grant citizenship to the Jews.

Events now moved swiftly in France. Louis XVI, who had signed the Declaration of Rights of Man (modeled on the American Declaration of Independence), was guillotined. The revolutionaries were drowned by their bloody massacres and a vapid Directoire took over. It soon asked a Corsican general named Napoleon Bonaparte to break up a royalist counter-revolution. This he did, and nine years later he was Emperor of France, confronted with the Jewish question, which again had become a burning issue. Most of the Jewish gains made during the Revolution had been nullified. The reactionaries and some moderates wanted the Ashkenazi Jews expelled, as did almost all the Alsatians.

Jewish history may yet have to recognize Napoleon as one of the greatest emancipators of the Jews since Cyrus the Great. Napoleon had as acute an insight into the Jewish situation as Moses Mendelssohn had had. He wanted the Jews out of the ghettos, not out of any particular love for them but because he did not want ghetto enclaves in a modern France or in his empire, where they could become islands of political indigestion. He bluntly informed the Jews of his attitude: To the Jews as French, everything; to the Jews as Jews, nothing.

"Paris is worth a Mass," Henry of Navarre had said as he traded his Protestant faith for the Catholic crown of France. "If I would rule a nation of Jews, I would rebuild the Temple," Napoleon said when asked why he had signed a concordat with the Vatican. As it was, he did the next best thing.

To make his Jewish policy public, Napoleon summoned an Assembly of Jewish Notables, consisting of one hundred and twelve outstanding Jewish scholars, financiers, businessmen, and rabbis from France and Italy to affirm their ties to France as Frenchmen of the Mosaic persuasion. An impressive state reception awaited them. The proceedings were held at the

Hôtel de Ville in Paris; an honor guard beat a drum tattoo in welcome.

At the opening session on July 29, 1806, twelve artfully framed questions were posed to the Assembly of Jewish Notables. Their initial rage was supplanted, first by a deep respect for Napoleon's cleverness, then by exhilaration as they realized that the Emperor was enabling them to emancipate themselves from ghetto rule. They were quick to note that but seventeen of their one hundred and twelve delegates were rabbis and that the laymen could outvote the rabbis on any question.

The first three questions concerned marriage, divorce, and Jewish attitudes toward their Christian neighbors. Was it lawful to have more than one wife? Was a divorce granted by a French court valid in Jewish eyes? Did Jewish law permit marriage only to Jews? The assembly affirmed monogamy over polygamy; affirmed that a divorce granted by the state was valid and took precedence over that of a rabbi; and affirmed that Jewish law did not prohibit marriage to Christians.* By their answers, the Assembly transferred control of marriage and divorce from the rabbinate to the individual and the state.

The next three questions were concerned with the attitudes of the Jews toward non-Jews and toward France. Do the Jews consider the French as brothers or strangers? Does Jewish law discriminate against Christians? Are Jews born in France bound to defend their country? The Assembly affirmed that Jews considered the French their "brothers," that Jewish law recognized no difference between Christians and Jews except in mode of worship, and that every French Jew had a sacred obligation to fight for France.

The remaining questions dealt with political and economic issues. Who names the rabbis? Do they have any "police powers"? Is their power derived from Jewish law or custom?

* Nowhere in the Torah is there a direct injunction against marrying a non-Jew. In fact, the Torah cites several instances where prominent Jews, like Moses, for instance, married a Gentile. The phrase in Deuteronomy (7:3) "Neither shalt thou make marriages with them" refers to the seven nations the Israelites had been ordered to destroy.

To the astonishment of Jews in ghettos throughout Europe, the Assembly affirmed that the rabbis held their posts only by custom, that Jewish law guaranteed them no governing powers, and that the sole function of the rabbi, according to Jewish law, was to preach morality, bless marriages, pronounce divorce, and teach Judaism. To the Jews of Europe, this recognition of their own inherent power over rabbis came as a shock. In the United States, this inherent power had already been taken for granted for over a century and a half.

The answers to the last three questions—Does Jewish law forbid Jews from entering professions? Does it permit the taking of usury from Jews? From Christians?—were a marvel in diplomacy. No, replied the Notables, there was no law prohibiting Jews from entering the professions. Usury, they said, whether to Jews or Christians, was forbidden by Jewish law. With these answers, a path was blazed for Jewish children to enter the professions; no longer could the ghetto hierarchy forbid the study of medicine and law. And usury, the chief occupation of the Jews of Alsace, fell into disrepute as a vocation and died out.

Napoleon declared himself satisfied with the answers, but he wanted them endowed with religious prestige. He now played his trump card—he convoked the first Great Sanhedrin in eighteen hundred years, the first in Jewish history since the fall of Jerusalem in the war with Rome. His move not only stunned the Jews but moved them to tears of pride.

The Great Sanhedrin, the "Supreme Court" of the Jewish Commonwealth before its destruction by the Romans, had been one of the most revered institutions in Jewish life. And now it was to be revived. The news swept throughout the Jewish world. Paeans of praise for the great Emperor rose from the ghettos of Europe. With great solemnity, eighty delegates from France and Italy, constituting this Napoleonic Sanhedrin, gathered in Paris in February 1807. This time there was a preponderance of rabbis (forty-six out of eighty delegates) to give religious sanction to the answers of the Assembly of Notables.

The Sanhedrin endorsed what the Assembly had approved. It again affirmed that all Jewish laws were religious in nature and that French civil courts had precedence over Jewish tribunals except in matters of religious ritual. It affirmed the love of the Jews for their Christian fellow citizens and swore loyalty to the French state in peace and war. Usury was publicly condemned, and the right of Jews to enter any profession was reaffirmed.

Having received a "spiritual" approval to all the answers and knowing that the power of the ghetto rabbinate had been broken, Napoleon adjourned his special Sanhedrin. Jews in his empire had ceased being considered a nation, and became merely practitioners of a religion. For West European Jews, the affirmation of the Sanhedrin was a blast of the shofar that toppled the walls of their ghettos. Moses Mendelssohn's thesis had been affirmed.

Napoleon himself was quick to recognize the greatness of his actions, and in recognition of it authorized the striking of a silver commemorative coin in his honor. One side shows the bust of Napoleon, the other portrays him as an imperial Moses in regal robes handing the tablets of the Law to a kneeling Jew, dressed as in Biblical days.

The Sanhedrin also fully realized the implications of its affirmations. The president of the Sanhedrin, Abraham Furtado, a suave Sephardi financier, in praising Napoleon with an effusiveness eclipsing Isaiah's praise of Cyrus, stated it this way: "The function of this body . . . is to bring us back to the practices of our ancient virtues . . . to restore to society a people commendable for private virtues, to awake in men a sense of their dignity by insuring them the enjoyment of their rights. . . . Such are the favors for which we are indebted to Napoleon the Great." In these words of Furtado, we hear the coming revolt against the Talmudists.

The Jews in America watched these Napoleonic antics with puzzlement. The questions seemed superfluous and the answers self-evident, for all the freedoms the Napoleonic Sanhedrin affirmed had been theirs since the arrival of the first Jews in the Colonies. As we shall see, the Jewish reformation was completed in America before it commenced in Europe.

The Napoleonic proceedings and reforms did not affect the Jews in Eastern Europe and Russia, since these Jews were only briefly under Napoleonic influence. There is a Jewish legend that sums up the dilemma in which Napoleon placed nineteenth-century European Jews. As Napoleon's armies advanced into Eastern Europe, a Jew ran jubilantly to his rabbi. "Master, master," he shouted, "the liberators are coming. At long last we shall be free and secure, treated like human beings, given dignity, and . . ." But the rabbi shook his head. "Yes, we shall be rich and safe. And we shall forget all about God and His Law, break His commandments, run after worthless goals. I'd rather have us poor and oppressed as we are now, but faithful to our Judaism." Or, as Jesus put it in an earlier age: "What profiteth it a man to gain a world and lose his soul."

Perhaps both Jesus and the legendary rabbi are wrong in viewing faith and secular learning as antithetical. History has shown it was ignorant, poverty-stricken Christians who brought forth the dull stupor of the early Feudal Age, whereas it was enlightened, wealthy Christians who brought forth the splendor of the subsequent Renaissance. History has also shown that every golden age of Jewish creativity was brought about by men of learning, not by ignoramuses, and that poverty is not a necessary ingredient either in Jewish or non-Jewish genius.

But for the Western European Jews, in the aftermath of the Napoleonic Age, the paramount question was: Would this new freedom produce a new Judaism, or would the Jews abandon Judaism now that there was no pressure from state and rabbi to enforce it? The orthodox predicted Judaism would not survive. The reform Jews set out to prove otherwise.

But what should the reformers do? What should they reform, and how should these reform measures be legitimized? They were traveling through an uncharted terrain and were faced with unlimited possibilities. Lay reformers fortuitously rushed into the void with ideas before the professionals could invade with programs. Against all odds, it was these amateurs who, by and large, formulated the basic outlines of Reform which the professionals later sanctified with philosophy, "beatified" with scholarship, and institutionalized with synods. The Talmud as a vehicle for change was bypassed for the fourth time since the fall of the Temple. The first three revolts against the Talmud will be discussed later.

The first bold step toward Reform was taken not by the Ashkenazi but by a Sephardi community in Holland. In 1796 the Sephardi congregation Adath Jeshurun in Amsterdam abolished all redundant and obsolete portions of ritual and prayer books, modernized the demeaning ghetto burial customs, and introduced sermons in Dutch instead of Hebrew so people could understand what was said. The walls of Adath Jeshurun did not fall, nor did a bolt from heaven destroy its members. In fact, these Sephardi reforms became the foundation for subsequent Ashkenazi ones.

The Reform congregation in Amsterdam was only an isolated early success. In the rest of Europe, Reform was not as successful. The first attempts by two German laymen—David Friedländer (1750–1834) and Israel Jacobson (1768–1828)—ended in failure, but they did establish an environment that allowed a professional Reform rabbinate to move in and take charge.

Why could German Jews not have both Judaism and Western civilization? asked both Friedländer and Jacobson. Was it dangerous for Jews to appreciate Holbein, read Goethe, or listen to Bach? Not at all, they answered, and set out to prove it.

Regretfully, David Friedländer, described as a Reform Jew, was actually an unconscious assimilationist. Settling in Berlin in 1771, where he became a successful silk merchant, he was a member of the Moses Mendelssohn coterie of Salon Jews. Imbued with the teachings of Mendelssohn, Friedländer founded the Jewish Free School in Berlin. Here Jewish children were taught geography, German, French, drawing, mathematics, and science, in addition to Talmudics. In his eagerness to please the Gentiles, however, Friedländer was ready to throw the baby out with the bathwater. Thus he was willing to abolish not only the Talmud but all Jewish observances, and even to embrace Christianity if the Church would not ask rational Jews to believe in "such foolish things" as virgin birth and the trinity. When he suggested that Polish Jews could be saved through assimilation, even the Reform Jews rejected him. However, his own children followed their father's advice to the Polish Jews and vanished into Christianity.

Israel Jacobson was more modest in his solution to the Jewish predicament. He did not want the Jews to assimilate, but he did want to win Christian respect for the Jews and their traditions. His father, a rich Orthodox Jew, urged his son to become a rabbi, but as the French philosophers interested Jacobson more than the Talmudists, he decided on a career in banking.

Brooding on the condition of the Jews in the ghettos, Jacobson structured his own Reformation, based not so much on what was Jewish as on what he thought would make a better impression on the Christians. In 1801 he founded the Jacobson School for Jewish and Christian pupils in Seesen, Brunswick. In 1810, he opened a Reform temple in this school with an organ, choir, and sermons delivered in German as well as Hebrew. A reversal had taken place. In the third century A.D. the Church had modeled itself after the Jewish synagogue; now the synagogue modeled itself after the Protestant Church. To the horror of the Orthodox, Jews flocked to this *goyeshe* synagogue where not only God but the congregation understood what was said. What shook the Orthodox was not only that confirmation was substituted for the bar mitzvah, but that girls were also confirmed. To add insult to injury, women were allowed to participate in the synagogue ritual—today considered proper even in Conservative synagogues.

In 1813, Jacobson had to flee to Berlin, where he held "Jewish-Protestant" services in his palatial home. And in Berlin, the sanctuary of the respectable, rich Jewish Orthodox, all hell broke loose. "Subversive," cried the Orthodox, and went to the King of Prussia to request a ban on this sinful worship. In 1823, the King decreed that Jewish services could be held only in accordance with Orthodox ritual, with no innovations in "language, prayer, and song." The latest expert on Judaism had spoken. Reform Judaism was banned in Berlin, and the Orthodox Jews exulted.

With the Friedländer and Jacobson innovations, amateur reform came to an end. Theirs was a "public relations" Judaism, designed not so much to emancipate the Jews from ghetto ways as to give them a more dignified image in Christian eyes. Though their programs were aimed in the right direction, their emphasis was ultimately self-destructive.

During this same period, how did Judaism fare in America without a Moses Mendelssohn, without a Napoleon, and without "public relations" Jews? There were many parallels, but more important were the differences that transformed European Reform prototypes into new American concepts of Judaism.

The Transformation of the Ashkenazi Jews
into Congregational Jews

IF THERE HAD BEEN a Jewish Tocqueville in early antebellum America, would he have seen Jews forsaking the ways of Orthodox Judaism, intermarrying at a dizzying rate and rapidly taking themselves out of American history as Jews? Would he have seen an ever greater influx of Ashkenazi Jews, overwhelming and diluting the older aristocratic Sephardi lines with their ghetto traditions and becoming American versions of European ghetto Jews?

Or would he have seen the beginning of a Jewish renaissance in America—Jews shedding their ghetto traditions, garbing themselves in hues of American congregationalism, hurrying to a rendezvous with destiny as future leaders of a New World Judaism?

Whatever such a Jewish Tocqueville might have seen, in 1800 the Jews in America had no insight into their past or any inkling of their future. Even legend and pious fraud would have had a difficult time dredging up a few Jews of national distinction in the years after the Revolution. In fact, hardly a single Jewish intellectual, writer, theologian, statesman, or artist of note had graced the American-Jewish scene in the whole of the eighteenth century. And, at the end of the Revolution, the Jews were about to lose the only distinction they had—that of being a business elite in an agrarian society. The war, which had saved them politically, was about to bankrupt them financially.

There was a price to pay for the successful Revolution. Many a Whig, Jewish as well as Gentile, had the time now to reflect on whether he should have been a Tory. The Revolution had played havoc with the American economy. No longer a colony of England, with all the trading privileges that status entailed, the United States had lost most of its overseas markets. Export-import trade had rapidly diminished, sweeping into bankruptcy most Jewish traders. The Embargo Act of 1807 and the War of 1812 did not help matters. By 1814 exports had dropped from $61 million a year to $7 million. Money and credit were scarce.

The Jews as a group were hardest hit because they were concentrated in export and import, and to a lesser extent in small-scale banking and finance. However, there were three avenues of opportunity. One was government service. We now find Jews working as customs inspectors, Treasury agents, Indian agents, auditors, and consuls in foreign ports. The second was a greater concentration in the booming fur trade and in land speculation. The third economic outlet was the lowly field of retailing. Though agriculture flourished during these lean industrial years, few Jews went into farming.

But there was an ever-growing group within the Jewish community that was most affected by the economic hardships, and that was the influx of Ashkenazi Jews. These immigrants were mostly Jews escaping from the ghettos whose gates Mendelssohn and Napoleon had opened. They were not the *Salon Juden*, but the lower and middle-class Jews who, though not intellectually emancipated from the ghetto, had had enough of its "blessings" to want a new life. These Jews were to play a decisive role in the shaping of antebellum American Jewish history.

Though the Ashkenazi Jews who came after the Revolution were greeted with contempt by the Sephardim, they were quickly absorbed into Sephardi institutions. The new arrivals did not dare change these institutions, even though they were different from those they had been accustomed to in Europe. They stood in awe of the Sephardim, whom they viewed as their social and intellectual superiors. But when this immobilizing sense of inferiority finally vanished, so had the desire to remodel the Sephardi institutions. The Ashkenazi immigrants found that these American-Jewish institutions perfectly suited their new way of life.

Fortuitously, the post-Revolutionary wave of Jewish immigration coincided with America's vast territorial expansion. With victory, in 1783 the United States had acquired from the British vast territories, including the Northwest Territory, which more than doubled the original size of the Thirteen Colonies. And in 1803 the Louisiana Purchase extended the United States from the Mississippi to the Rockies. This expansion opened new paths of opportunity, not only for Christians but for Jews too, especially the Ashkenazim. Whereas the more established Sephardim tended to remain in East Coast cities, the Ashkenazi immigrants were attracted into this vast hinterland.

America was on the move. The pull to the West was power-ful. The freedom of movement released dynamic forces of un-rest and challenge. To the Jews, especially, it was a heady feeling. It pulled them from the vortex of their ghetto *Yid-dishkeit* into a frontier territory that was to transform them. The orthodox customs of the Jew heading west vanished in direct proportion to the distance from previous Jewish anchor points.

During the eighteenth century most American retailing was done by "Connecticut Yankees," as the pack peddlers were called. After the Revolution, many impoverished Jews joined these Connecticut Yankees with pack on back, or on mule, funneling through the Cumberland Gap into Kentucky, Ohio, and points south and west. The Jews became so numerous in this profession that peddlers became known as "Jew peddlers." Within a few decades, as they followed the wheels of the Conestoga wagon elite through the wilderness, the Jewish ped-dlers were to become leading retailers, and would help settle, and sometimes found, towns like Nashville, Montgomery, Lex-ington, Detroit, Cincinnati, and St. Louis.

Most of these backpacking Jews led obscure lives and little record remains of them. A few are remembered for their flam-boyance and initiative. Abraham Mordecai, reputed founder of Montgomery, Alabama, was one such adventurous Jewish trader. He fought in the Continental Army, helped develop the fur trade, introduced the cotton gin in Alabama, and was a "squawman" who spent most of his time with the Indians.

If Abraham Mordecai typified the untypical Jew in ante-bellum America, Joseph Philipson and Joseph Jonas typified the Ashkenazi Jew who, with retailing in mind, helped settle the West.

There may have been Jews in the Louisiana Territory when it was purchased, but Joseph Philipson, who opened a general store in the village of St. Louis in 1807, is the first Jewish set-tler to be mentioned in records of that region. Philipson had arrived in Philadelphia from England in 1800, where he had engaged in the fur and lead business. It was natural for him to have come to Missouri, where both these products were found in abundance.

Joseph Jonas had also come to the United States from England, but he headed for Cincinnati, reaching that city in 1817 after a two-month trek through the wilderness. He was the only Jew among a few settlers, mostly Virginians, who had made their way through the Cumberland Gap to Cincinnati.

The news of a Jew in the wilderness of Ohio reached the ears of an incredulous Quaker woman, who could not contain her curiosity. She made her way to the Jonas house, looked him over, and asked, "Art thou a Jew, one of God's Chosen People?" When Jonas acknowledged that such indeed was the case, she asked, "May I examine thee?" The Quaker woman walked around him several times, then pinched his arm and exclaimed with a snort, "Hmpf! Thou art no different from us."

Jonas persuaded two of his brothers and two friends to join him in the Cincinnati wilderness, and in 1819 these five Jews formed their own *minyan*,* oblivious or indifferent to the fact that it took ten Jews to form a *minyan*. The vanguard of the Chosen People was setting its own "Wilderness *Minhag*," † declaring itself a quorum and holding a Friday evening service composed of whatever snatches of prayer its members remembered. But Jews they were because they wanted to be Jews. And that was the essence of American antebellum frontier Judaism—the wanting to be Jewish.

By 1824 there were enough Jews in Cincinnati to form a congregation, Bene Israel. But these Jews could no more go back to ghetto Judaism after having tasted the freedom of the frontier than today's Orthodox rabbis could go back to the cult of sacrifice of Temple days. In Cincinnati, Orthodox Judaism evolved a receptiveness to Reform. The reformation of Bene Israel was to commence twenty years before the arrival

---

* Hebrew word for "number" but standing for a quorum of ten adult male Jews, minimum required for communal prayer.
† *Minhag:* Hebrew word for custom or observance.

of the German Reform rabbis would formally "found" it.

The settling of Cincinnati repeated itself over and over again—New Orleans in 1828, Louisville in 1832, Chicago in 1837, Cleveland in 1839, and then, with the Gold Rush, headlong on to San Francisco in 1849. By the time of the Civil War, Reform had polarized itself west of the Alleghenies, while the eastern seacoast remained the stronghold of the Orthodox.

It is false to imagine that isolated Jewish families in Christian communities surrounded by wilderness and Indians kept kosher homes. The hard-core *kashrut* (dietary law) prevailing on the frontier consisted of abstaining from eating ham and horsemeat. If one was holier than one's neighbor, meat and dairy meals were not mixed, even if served in the same set of dishes. While they did not forget their Creator on the Sabbath, God was not prayed to thrice daily. Most of the religious customs the frontier Jews had brought with them from the ghettos of Europe vanished soon after they crossed the frontier. With no Talmudic authorities to consult, they interpreted the will of the Lord as they thought the Lord would want it under the circumstances.

The Jewish experience in antebellum New Orleans offers a good example of how such improvisations worked. When the first New Orleans congregation was established in 1828, so many Jewish men had married Christian partners that the pragmatic New Orleans Jews discarded the doctrine that Jewish identity could be passed only through the maternal line. They made their own *halakah:* "No Israelite child shall be excluded either from schools or the temple or from burial grounds on account of the religion of the mother."

There was also the problem of miscegenation. From wills by Jews leaving sizable bequests to Blacks, we know of many instances of children sired by Jewish fathers with Black women, creating a problem for the synagogues. Thus Congregation Beth Elohim in Charleston stipulated in its charter that proselytes could be accepted provided they "are not people of color." In some other synagogues, however, Black proselytes were accepted, but children having Jewish fathers and Black mothers were excluded. There are no records of children by Jewish mothers and Black fathers.

In the six decades or so of the antebellum period, the Jewish experience in America produced many colorful characters. Already their life styles resembled those of the twentieth-century Jews more than those of the eighteenth century. Three antebellum Jews highlight that variety. They are Uriah P. Levy (1792–1862), a bold, blustering adventurer who became a commodore in the U.S. Navy; Mordecai Noah (1785–1851), an editor and politician who was a Zionist well before Zionism existed; and Penina Moise (1797–1880), the first woman hymnal writer in Jewish history.

Born in Philadelphia of a distinguished family of patriots, Uriah P. Levy set out to sea at the age of ten as a cabin boy, and by twenty-one was master of a sailing vessel. During the War of 1812 he was captured by the British and imprisoned until the end of the war. In the Navy, as a Jew and an officer who had risen from the ranks, he faced both anti-Jewishness and the snobbery any upstart from the ranks encounters. The overly sensitive Levy detected anti-Semitism in every snub. He fought a duel, was court-martialed six times, and finally was demoted from his rank of captain. He succeeded in having a special commission of inquiry appointed by Congress, proved his loyalty, and was reinstated as captain. He died a commodore.

Much of Levy's trouble stemmed from his opposition to corporal punishment. His tomb states that he was the "father of the law for the abolition of the barbarous practice of corporal punishment in the United States Navy." His epitaph, however, does not mention his great admiration for Thomas Jefferson. It was Levy who donated to the United States the figure of Jefferson that now stands in the statuary hall of the Capitol in Washington. At one time Levy also owned Monticello, the home of Jefferson, which he turned into a memorial for his hero.

Mordecai Noah, born in Philadelphia and the son of a Revolutionary soldier, anticipated Zionist ideology before Zionism was born. He was editor of several New York papers and the author of several successful but undistinguished plays; at various times he was sheriff of New York County, surveyor of the Port of New York, United States consul to Tunis, and a member of Tammany Hall. He also helped found New York University in 1831.

In 1825 Noah conceived the idea of resettling Diaspora Jews on Grand Island (which he owned), in the Niagara River near Buffalo, New York. The Jews of the world were invited to come to the inauguration of this resettlement. Noah also invited the American Indians because he believed that they were the descendants of one of the ten lost tribes of Israel. Many dignitaries, including the Governor of New York, came to the opening. But there were no Jews and no Indians. The project was dropped.

Thirteen years later Noah presented another proposal. In his speech, "Discourse on the Restoration of the Jews," he anticipated Theodor Herzl by five decades. Noah proposed that the Jews of the world purchase Palestine from the Turks and populate it with Jews who wished to emigrate from lands of oppression. The cost of the resettlement would be borne voluntarily by Jews and Christians, with some American grants-in-aid. Noah's call went unheeded. His ideas reflected the Christian millenarian sentiment more than Jewish Zionist aspirations in America.

Born of French-Jewish parents in Charleston, South Carolina, Penina Moise left school at the age of twelve to help support the large family that was left destitute by the death of her father. She showed literary talent at an early age, becoming a prolific writer of verse, which was published in journals and newspapers throughout the United States. Very devout, she was superintendent of the Beth Elohim Sunday School in Charleston. When that congregation installed an organ in 1841, Penina Moise became the first woman to compose hymns. A book of her hymns was published by Beth Elohim and was used by most Reform temples of the day. Many of her hymns still live in the Reform Union Hymnal. In 1854, when yellow fever broke out in South Carolina, she devoted herself to nursing its victims, irrespective of their color or creed. She was reduced to poverty by the Civil War and fell victim to misfortune after misfortune, the final blow being complete blindness.

Neither Uriah P. Levy nor Mordecai Noah nor a host of other such free-spirited Jews were synagogue Jews. Organized religious life was already encountering resistance in this continent of freedom, expansion, and adventure.

The synagogues of these frontier Jews bore a superficial resemblance to the European Orthodox synagogue, but closer examination reveals their Protestant Congregationalist underpinnings. No rabbi ruled over these synagogues. The congregations had the power, but the elected officers of these congregations did not have any power of excommunication. It was a voluntaristic organization, where conformity could not be enforced beyond a threat of not burying a maverick in the synagogue cemetery—a threat of little effect. The westward expansion absorbed the restless, the adventurous, the sinners.

By and large, the westward movement was an Ashkenazi undertaking; by and large, the Sephardi families did not participate. Thus it was the Ashkenazim who established their dominance in the West, before challenging the dominance of the Sephardim concentrated mainly in the East.

Three factors brought about the eventual end of the Sephardi cultural dominance. First, there was the high rate of Sephardi intermarriages which diminished their ranks. Second, because of the flow of Ashkenazi immigrants, they soon outnumbered the Sephardim in America. Finally, the Ashkenazim overcame their feeling of cultural inferiority in relation to the Sephardi elite.

In the first half of the nineteenth century, the position of the Sephardim in America was similar to that of the Marranos in fifteenth-century Spain, who had married into the highest social strata of Spanish society, abandoning their Jewish heritage. Thus their descendants, some of whom were statesmen, financiers, and social leaders, often were unaware of their Jewish ancestry. The Sephardim in the United States underwent a similar experience. Malcolm H. Stern, in his book on the genealogy of Americans of Jewish descent, traces some of the progeny of these aristocratic Sephardi families into the most socially prominent Christian families in the American social register today—the Rockefellers, the Ingersolls, the Lodges, the Ten Eycks, the Van Rensselaers, the Tiffanys, the Vanderbilts.

Stephen Birmingham, in his book *The Grandees*, tells the story of a socially prominent San Francisco gentleman who found his name listed in Stern's genealogy as being of Sephardi descent. Showing this to his mother, she commented, "At least we were good Jews."

Though they were astonishingly prolific—a Sephardi family usually ranged from six to fifteen children—their rate of intermarriage, though not as high as during Colonial times, was around 15 percent. In these marriages, only some 8 percent of the non-Jewish partners converted to Judaism. However, though the vast majority of the Jewish partners in these intermarriages vanished into Christianity, hardly any did so through the positive act of conversion. They disappeared into Christianity passively through assimilation, which eventually took, not them, but their children or grandchildren, out of Judaism. These intermarrying Jews did not line up at baptismal fonts—they simply did not attend synagogue, or perform a *brith* (circumcision), or attend Jewish social events.

The second reason for the loss of Sephardi influence was the steady increase in Ashkenazi immigration, which gave the Ashkenazim growing numerical superiority. It has been estimated that as early as 1820 the Ashkenazim outnumbered the Sephardim. By 1840, of an estimated fifteen thousand Jews in America, only some three thousand were Sephardim. But in spite of the minority status of the Sephardim, their synagogues still dominated Jewish life in America. The Ashkenazim went to Sephardi synagogues and followed the Sephardi ritual, but the Sephardim continued to hold the positions of power. The situation was akin to the present one in Israel. Though the

Oriental Jews in Israel outnumber the Ashkenazi Jews, the latter hold the important administrative, judicial, and legislative posts.

The third factor was the most irritating. In the early nineteenth century the Sephardim still set the standards for Jewish manners, morals, and education. The Ashkenazim felt culturally inferior and uneasy in the presence of the haughty Sephardim, who looked down on these "uncouth" immigrants much the way the Boston Brahmins would later look down on the "shanty Irish," or in the way German Jews would look down on Russian Jews.

Language, too, was a barrier between the Sephardim and Ashkenazim. At home, cultured Sephardi families spoke either Spanish, Portuguese, or English. On lower social levels, the Sephardim spoke Ladino, a Spanish dialect based on medieval Castilian and intermixed with Hebrew words and expressions. The Ashkenazi Jews, especially the new immigrants, spoke Yiddish, a German dialect intermixed with words and expressions from many East European languages as well as Hebrew.

These three factors combined to cause a permanent rift between the Sephardi and the Ashkenazi Jews. The controversy that precipitated this rift began in 1825 over a most trivial matter in Shearith Israel, New York's most prestigious Sephardi synagogue. It centered itself over a *mikvah*, a ritual bath used mainly by post-menstrual women and by brides before their wedding.

When Shearith Israel was founded in 1726, it had no *mikvah*. The worldly Sephardim then in power regarded the institution as archaic. The congregation's few orthodox members were advised to use a natural spring near the synagogue for purification ablutions. The ladies were not advised what to do during inclement weather.

In 1759 there were enough Ashkenazi congregants to force a vote for a *mikvah*. A generation later, however, when Shearith Israel moved to a new location, the Ashkenazim had become Americanized and no *mikvah* was built in the new structure. Members either disregarded the laws concerning ritual purification or used the ritual pool of a neighboring synagogue. Out of an estimated population of four thousand Jewish families in New York in 1851, only some two hundred women used a *mikvah*, and such services could be had in but two synagogues that maintained rigorous Orthodoxy. One could almost state the phenomenon of the *mikvah* as a law: As the *mikvah* appears, Orthodoxy is in ascendance; as the *mikvah* vanishes, Orthodoxy is in decline.

By 1825 Shearith Israel was again torn by a dispute over the *mikvah*. A vociferous Ashkenazi minority wanted it restored, but the majority voted against it. In a fury, the protestors walked out to found their own synagogue with a *mikvah*. The first formal break between the Sephardim and Ashkenazim had been made, and the process of this alienation was to be accelerated. In another three decades the cultural dominance of the Sephardim would be over.

While professing themselves Orthodox, however, both the Sephardim and the Ashkenazim transgressed most of the tenets of ghetto orthodoxy outside the home, while retaining a few customs within it—like lighting the Sabbath candles and abstaining from eating ham. Since they knew little theology and since there were no rabbis to direct them, their practice passed for Orthodoxy. Nineteenth-century American Judaism became more and more voluntaristic—a kind of religious smorgasbord. Jews could help themselves to whatever religious practices they liked and ignore those they did not.

Before 1840 there were few ordained rabbis in the United States; all were European born, and none were permanent residents. Thus, the approximately forty congregations were under the spiritual leadership of cantors, whose qualifications were not impressive: they could chant hymns, slaughter chickens, perform weddings, circumcise male infants, and bury congregants. The less ignorant led the more ignorant.

By 1820 it became apparent that the synagogues could not meet the inchoate demands of its unruly, free-spirited members. There was a revolution in the air, a receptiveness to reform, a need to fashion a new, dedicated Judaism out of this chaos of memories and rituals. Five Jews shaped that need into a reformation and a counterreformation, both of which were to give American Judaism a new direction.

The American quintet of reformers was far less imposing than the august European quartet of Mendelssohn, Napoleon, Friedländer, and Jacobson. There was Gershom Mendes Seixas (1746–1816), an underpaid New York cantor, honored by the Christians more than by the Jews; Isaac Harby (1788–1828), a Gentile-descended Sephardi Jew of Charleston, South Carolina, buried in a New York "Jewish potter's field"; Gustav Poznanski (1804–1879), a descendant of four thousand years of obscure Jews, who succeeded where Harby had failed; Isaac Leeser (1806–1868), a lonely Jew who was accorded after death the honors he deserved in life; and Rebecca Gratz (1781–1868), a beautiful Philadelphian who died a spinster because she loved a Christian her faith did not allow her to marry.

In Gershom Mendes Seixas, history has provided us with a symbolic Jew who embodies the Colonial past and the emergent antebellum Judaism. Born in Colonial New York of a Sephardi father and an Ashkenazi mother, Seixas became the best-known Jewish preacher of his time, who set the standards for the future American rabbi as a Jewish congregationalist minister.

Though he is often pictured as an ardent patriot, there is reason to suspect that Seixas was torn between loyalty to England, where his parents had been born, and dedication to the Revolutionary cause, before he finally threw in his lot with the Whigs. After six years of schooling, he was apprenticed to a mechanic. He married early and fathered sixteen children. By pure chance Seixas was offered the position of cantor at Congregation Shearith Israel in New York City because he knew a smattering of Hebrew.

Seixas was looked down upon by his congregants as a menial who chanted hymns, taught children, and was at everyone's beck and call for weddings, circumcisions, and funerals. But the Gentiles regarded him as a "handsome young priest" and paid him the same respect they paid their learned clergymen. Though not a scholar, Seixas was intelligent and ambitious enough to acquire diplomacy, dignity, and enough learning to give him respectability.

Seixas was the forerunner of a new type of Jewish spiritual leader, hitherto unknown in Jewish history, modeled after the Puritan lay minister. He was the first Jew in history to deliver Thanksgiving sermons and speak in churches, colleges, and universities. He was one of fourteen ministers invited to President Washington's inauguration. As a trustee and board member of Columbia College, and one of its incorporators, Seixas often found himself in the most august Gentile company, which did impress his congregants and add stature to his office.

As his prestige increased, he was accorded the role of mediator between the Sephardi and Ashkenazi members of Shearith Israel. He was also to become powerful enough to introduce some decorum in the synagogue by curtailing the practices of praying interminably at breakneck speed, carrying on loud conversations, and coming and going at will during services. Seixas was a teacher, pastor, orator, and community servant, and his reforms indicated the course American Reform Judaism was to take.

The next step toward reform came in a Sephardi congregation, Beth Elohim, in Charleston, South Carolina, and was initiated by a layman, Isaac Harby, a Sephardi Jew partly of Christian origin.

Historians have tended to overlook Harby. Yet from this man's mind sprang forth a Jewish "Reform Pallas Athena" fully clothed with thirty-one articles of organization so modern they could be used as a basis for a constitution for a Reform temple today.

The origins of Isaac Harby can be traced to late fifteenth-century England, where one Nicholas Harby, a faithful son of the Church, lived in Cambridge. With his great-great-grandson, Clement, a respected member of the Anglican Church, Jewish blood enters the Harby genealogy. In 1681,

Clement married a Sephardi woman in Greece and shortly thereafter settled in Morocco, where he became lapidary to the king. Here he gained immense wealth and was knighted in 1699 in Whitehall.

Clement's son also married a Jewish woman, a member of the Frangipani family of Rome, that city's noblest and richest Jewish family and its leading bankers. Their grandson Solomon, in 1778, at the age of twenty-one, lost the family fortune. He fled to Jamaica for reasons unknown, and in 1781 arrived in Charleston, South Carolina, again for unknown reasons. Here he married Rebecca Moses, the daughter of Myer Moses, "a rich and patriotic Israelite, who assisted his country during the Revolutionary struggle." They had seven children, among them Isaac, who was destined to become America's first native-born Reform Jew.

Great Jewish scholars, according to their biographers, were usually early bloomers, mastering the Torah at eight, the Mishna at ten, the Gemara at twelve. Isaac Harby was also an early bloomer, but not in the established Jewish tradition. He was a voracious reader of the French, Greek, and Latin classics, but not of Talmudic or Hebrew literature. At seventeen, he started studying law, but abandoned that study and turned to journalism and teaching. He subsequently became in turn a novelist, critic, and essayist. A dilettante in all, he seldom rose above mediocrity. His only fame was to come from his brilliant insights into the American-Jewish condition, when nothing in his background should have prepared him for it.

In 1810, Harby married Rachel Mordecai, the daughter of Samuel Mordecai, in Savannah. She died in 1828 after a long illness. Harby, whose health had declined with his finances, left Charleston the year his wife died. Within six months, at the age of forty, Harby died a miserable death, in abject poverty. He was buried in the cemetery of the Eleventh Street Synagogue in New York City.

And so ended the life of Isaac Harby, a religious reformer without depth. Admittedly it is difficult to take him seriously, but it is a serious mistake not to do so, for Harby was the real father of American Jewish Reform, which received its bar mitzvah in Charleston, not in New York or Philadelphia.

There was logic in history's selection. In the first quarter of the nineteenth century Charleston had the most important and populous Jewish community in the United States. It set the tone for manners and mannerisms for the rich to emulate and for the poor to ape. But in the area of synagogue practice, Gresham's Law was in effect—the bad had driven out the good.

Though the Sephardi ritual was still in force in Beth Elohim, the manners had slowly become those of the Ashkenazim. Little by little, Old World customs had crept in as Ashkenazi membership increased. Many of the Sephardi elite found the synagogue proceedings vulgar and intolerable.

As in most synagogues at this time, Sabbath services in Beth Elohim was three hours long and consisted in large part of endless repetition of prayers, shouted or mumbled at top speed. The congregation was noisy and irreverent; they chattered and came and went as they pleased during the service. The elite minority witnessed with distaste the selling of the honor of reading a Torah blessing.

These were some of the conditions that prompted Isaac Harby to draw up the petition to the vestry of Beth Elohim. In it, Harby and the forty-six cosigners proposed to abridge the Sabbath service, to repeat in English the most solemn part of the service "so its beauty and meaning would be understood," to install an organ to solemnify services with music, and to provide an English sermon on the Sabbath to acquaint the congregants with the ideas of their forefathers.

When the vestry rejected the petition, twelve of the original forty-seven dissenters, again led by Harby, seceded from Beth Elohim and established their own congregation, The Reformed Society of Israelites. Within two years, they had fifty members and had instituted some amazing changes. Forty years of subsequent platform writing by German Reform rabbis who had come to America did not substantially change the framework of Reform constructed by Harby and his fellow dissenters.

The founders of The Reformed Society of Israelites adopted a resolution stating that they no longer would be bound by blind observance of ceremonial law. They drew up a charter of thirty-one articles, modern, lucid, and all-embracing. Harby sent a copy of these to Thomas Jefferson and received this reply:

> I am little acquainted with the liturgy of the Jews or their mode of worship but the reformation proposed and explained appears entirely reasonable. Nothing is wiser than that all our institutions should keep pace with the advance of time and be improved of human mind . . . I pray you to accept assurance of respect and esteem.
>
> TH. JEFFERSON

The Reformed Society published a new prayer book, introduced organ music, shortened the ritual, banned head covering, and did not pray for the messiah to arrive. They urged that Jewish youth be educated in English, Latin, and Hebrew.

Harby was quick to see the similarity between his reform movement and that of Luther. "The pen of Luther," he wrote, "was a great intellectual lever which shook the papal supremacy to its foundation. Why may not the virtuous example of a few Israelites, then shake off the bigotry of the ages from their countrymen? Our principles are rapidly pervading the whole mass of Hebrews throughout the United States." As Harby envisaged it, the Jewish Reform movement would do for Judaism what the Protestant Reformation had done for Christianity.

Scholars still debate whether Harby was aware of the Friedländer and Jacobson reforms. The weight of evidence is that he was not. French, Latin, and Greek writings were his sources, and thus far nothing has linked him to Friedländer and Jacobson. The great Reform movements in Germany had yet to take place. And there is nothing in Harby's thirty-one articles to indicate German influence.

Although The Reformed Society of Israelites lasted only nine years, its ideas excited interest and curiosity throughout America's Jewish communities. The thought of sermons in English, rather than in German or Portuguese, was novel and attractive. But would God understand English? And would He approve of organ music, decorum, and shorter services? It was decided that He would, and congregation after congregation began adopting clusters of Harby's ideas. By 1850 there were dozens of semi-Reform congregations in the United States, which, because they still viewed themselves Orthodox, were classified as Orthodox. There were also three completely Reform congregations which embodied Harby's principles. Congregation Har Sinai in Baltimore was founded as Reform in 1842, and Congregation Emanu-El in New York City instituted Reform in 1845. But the first official one, in 1841, was Beth Elohim in Charleston, the congregation that in 1824 had rejected Harby's proposals.

This turnabout was achieved through the efforts of Gustav Poznanski. He was not a rabbi, or a prodigy, or a scholar, or German. He was a Polish Jew who did manage to establish the first successful Reform congregation in the United States.

Gustav Poznanski (1805–1879) came to New York from Poland in 1832 at the age of twenty-three. Devoutly Orthodox, he was employed as the lay leader of Congregation Shearith Israel. His duties were the usual ones of a *hazan* in those days—chanting the liturgy, shofar blowing, chicken slaughtering—all for the princely salary of two hundred fifty dollars a year. He must have done his job well, for in 1836 he was invited to Beth Elohim in Charleston to perform the same duties at a higher salary with the title of rabbi instead of lay leader. The title was honorary.

At Beth Elohim, Poznanski, who meanwhile had shed his Orthodoxy, succeeded where Harby had failed. One by one he reintroduced Harby's ideas—prayers in English, sermons in English, dignity, decorum. In 1838, a fire destroyed much of Charleston and most of Beth Elohim. When the doors to the rebuilt Beth Elohim were opened, organ music greeted the congregants. An exultant Poznanski intoned, "This synagogue is our Temple, this city our Jerusalem, and this happy land our Palestine." In spirit, Poznanski was not much different from the medieval Rhineland rabbi who exulted, "From Germany shall come forth the law, and from France the word of God"—words that have been enshrined in Talmudic commentary. One by one, the diehards died or resigned. By 1841 Beth Elohim was the first fully Reform congregation in America. Harby's dream had been realized.

While Gershom Mendes Seixas, Isaac Harby, and Gustav Poznanski shaped the structure of American Reform, Isaac Leeser and Rebecca Gratz formed the framework for a modern orthodox counterreformation. Whereas Harby and Poznanski were concerned with the religious aspects of Judaism, Leeser and Gratz were more concerned with its secular needs. Ironically, these two ostensibly Orthodox Jews did more to secularize Judaism than did the reform leaders of the times.

Leeser and Gratz are thought of as Orthodox because there is no other label for their brand of Judaism, a Judaism that centered itself mainly on the concepts of a "Torah from Sinai" and less on the binding nature of Talmudic *halakah*. Though most of their secular reforms were not enacted until after 1840, they are included here because they were not inspired by the coming German Reform rabbis but grew out of the antebellum environment. The ideas of Leeser and Gratz were adopted by the coming German reformers, rather than other way around.

Isaac Leeser looked like a sedate Baptist minister, with his unrimmed glasses, pale, clean-shaven face, long white hair, wing collar, and black cravat. Born in Westphalia, Germany, his Gymnasium studies in Latin and German were supplemented by instruction in Hebrew and the Talmud. He was not ordained. He arrived in Richmond, Virginia, in 1824, at the age of eighteen, to work for an uncle in an accounting house. Six years later, he wrote an article responding to an anti-Semitic attack in a magazine that changed the course of his life. The article came to the attention of the Portuguese congregation Mikveh Israel in Philadelphia, which offered him its "rabbinic" post—that is, the post of cantor—which Leeser accepted. The next thirty-eight years, from 1830 until his death, were remarkably busy ones, during which, unsung and unheralded, he hammered out a new orthodoxy more akin to Conservative Judaism than to *shtetl* Orthodoxy.

Though insisting that prayers be in Hebrew, Leeser delivered his sermons in English and translated the prayer book into English so his congregants could understand the Hebrew text. He founded the first Hebrew day school, the first Jewish publication society, and the first Hebrew college. All three failed, but they served as prototypes for future ventures. He founded and edited a newspaper, *The Occident and Jewish Advocate*, which carried articles on Jewish faith, life, and history. This paper had a great impact on American Jews, rousing them from their intellectual torpor. He wrote textbooks for Jewish education and translated such works from German. Though he was a dull and pedantic writer, his books were far superior to the drivel published at the time. His greatest and most enduring work was his translation of the Torah from Hebrew to English. It was a pedestrian translation, far inferior stylistically to the King James version, but more faithful to the original Hebrew text. For fifty years, until a more modern translation was published, it was the standard English version of the Bible in Jewish homes.

Leeser was a bachelor who led a lonely life, living frugally on a meager salary. His greatest joy was that he lived long enough to be appointed head of Maimonides College, which he helped found. He died in the firm belief that the split of American Jews into the Orthodox and Reform camps would be healed, and a new American Judaism would emerge. He was a lesser Jewish Erasmus who tried to moderate between the extremes of Orthodoxy and Reform much as Erasmus tried to moderate the extremes in Catholicism and the Reformation. History, having thus far denied victory to either side, may yet prove Leeser right.

History may also prove that Rebecca Gratz, the first woman of importance in American Jewish history, may have had an even greater impact on American Judaism than Leeser.

The Gratz family was of Ashkenazi stock. The American branch of the family, founded by two brothers, Barnard and Michael, arrived from Germany just in time to be swept into the Revolution. Both brothers became shippers and financiers in the cause of the Revolution. After the war, both made fortunes in land speculation. Four of Michael's twelve children rose to distinction in vocations unknown in European ghetto society. Hyman became a captain of commerce; a philanthropist, he founded Gratz College in Philadelphia. Benjamin became a lawyer and soldier. Jacob served in the Philadelphia legislature. Rebecca, who became the founder of the Jewish Sunday-school movement, was a woman of extraordinary organizational ability, drive, and tenacity.

Two stories surround her life, both probably true. Though rich and beautiful, she never married, because, as persistent rumor had it, she was in love with a Gentile whom she refused to marry because of her faith. The other story is that she served as a model for Rebecca in Sir Walter Scott's *Ivanhoe*. Washington Irving, a friend of both Rebecca Gratz and Sir Walter Scott, told the latter of Rebecca's love for a Christian, of her beauty, pride, and religious devotion, the traits of the character Rebecca in *Ivanhoe*.

Rebecca Gratz blazed a trail through the cultural-poverty jungle that comprised Jewish education of the day. The interest of the Colonial Jews in Jewish education had been sporadic. In 1731, the Jews in New York City established a Hebrew school, but it failed. In Colonial times, wherever the Sephardim predominated, instruction was in English. Only enough Hebrew was taught to enable the students to read prayers in that language. But whatever the language, Jewish education was haphazard, abysmal, and unsuccessful. Rebecca

Gratz stepped into this disintegrating educational system with an idea she borrowed unashamedly and without apologies from the Protestants. In 1838 she successfully introduced into the Jewish educational structure the first Jewish Sunday school.

Just as it had never occurred to either Harby or Poznanski that they were imitating the Christians, or that they wanted to be Christians, it never occurred to Rebecca Gratz either. When she borrowed the idea of a Sunday school, which Christian churches had initiated in 1791, it seemed to her a practical way of solving a Jewish problem.

But even greater than her contribution to Jewish education was her role in the decline of the synagogue as a central social institution of American Jewish life. Under her direction, control of Jewish philanthropic and welfare activities became vested in lay organizations, which were independent of synagogue and rabbi.* She served as secretary for the Female Association for Women and Children in Reduced Circumstances. She founded the Philadelphia Orphan Asylum.

Thus this quintet of early reformers—Seixas, Harby, Poznanski, Leeser, and Gratz—rather than the German Reform rabbis who arrived with the next wave of immigration, set the foundations for American Reform Judaism.

To understand the nature of the great transformation that took place in the next phase of American Judaism, we must journey to Germany and examine the Jewish religious upheaval that was taking place there.

---

* A group of Jews in Charleston had formed a social welfare and orphan society in 1784, but it was disbanded in 1801.

III

THE MANIFEST DESTINY
(1840–1890)
The Conquering German Jews

The Rise and Fall of German
Scientific Judaism

AFTER ITS INITIAL SUCCESS, the Reform movement in Germany suffered a series of telling defeats. Salvos of abuse from the Orthodox had shaken the Reform leaders, and a succession of Orthodox bans had sown seeds of fear among their followers. But the most serious setbacks resulted from the alliance between the Orthodox rabbinate and Christian rulers. The Orthodox hated reform more than they feared Church or Prince.

Having no armies to crush the Reform forces, the Orthodox tried to destroy them with invective. Orthodox leaders of the past had denounced the great Gaon Hai to the Caliph of Baghdad as a traitor; they had denounced the famed Talmudic codifier Alfasi to the Sultan of Fez as a spy; and they had denounced the renowned Maimonides to the Church as a blasphemer. But the true crimes of those accused was the introduction of new ideas into Judaism. The charges resulted in the imprisonment of Hai, the banishment of Alfasi, and the public burning of a work by Maimonides. And now, in nineteenth-century Germany, the Orthodox denounced the Reform leaders to the civil German authorities. At their behest, Jacobson's temple in Seesen was forced to close, and

Friedländer's temple in Berlin was closed by order of the King of Prussia.

In Eastern Europe, Reform fared even worse than it did in Germany. Hungary's leading Reform rabbi, Aaron Chorin, was stoned by Orthodox rabbis in the courtyard of his synagogue. Like Galileo, he was forced to recant his Reform beliefs, and like Galileo, he later recanted his recantation. In Austria the Orthodox, opposed to the Reform views of Rabbi Abraham Kohn, were suspected of murder. The Kohn family's food was poisoned. The rabbi and one child died; the rest of the family recovered. The trial of some Orthodox fanatics was eventually suppressed by the Austrian government, and the poisoners went unpunished.* All "true believers"—whether followers of Moses, Jesus, or Mohammed—are fanatics under the skin.†

Reform did score one small but significant victory. That was the precarious survival of the Hamburg Temple, founded in 1818, and its sister temple in Leipzig which had opened in 1820. Seeing the Hamburg Temple leaders survive such epithets: as "slanderers and liars," the Orthodox turned to the Hamburg authorities, hoping they would close that temple as Frederick William III had closed the Berlin Temple. But the Hamburg senate turned them down, advising them that Jewish services were of no concern to the senate.

The Orthodox had special reason to fear the Hamburg experiment. The Seesen and Berlin temples had been private undertakings, but the Hamburg Temple was led by an ordained rabbi. Although hats were still worn and women still

---

* The Jewish Encyclopedia states: "On September 6, 1848, a man, hired by the fanatical clique [the Orthodox] entered Kohn's kitchen and poisoned the dinner. While other members of the family recovered, Kohn and his youngest son died the following day. A wearisome trial ensued; but for some unknown reason was suppressed." The Encyclopedia Judaica states: "After Kohn and his son died from food poisoning, murder was suspected. An investigation was ordered by the authorities, and the leaders of the Orthodox sector . . . were arrested. After a time, both were released for lack of evidence."

† For a fascinating account of the mind of the fanatic—whether for good or for evil—see Eric Hoffer's *The True Believer*.

segregated from men, two changes in its liturgy especially angered the Orthodox. These were the elimination of the chanting of the Torah and the prayers beseeching the messiah to arrive.

The rage of the Orthodox against the Reform resembled the early fury of the Church at the first Protestants. The existence of the Hamburg Temple was as much an affront to the Orthodox Jews as Luther's ninety-five theses tacked on the door of the Cathedral of Wittenberg had been to the Church. The rage of the Orthodox became so extreme that they openly quoted an unfortunate passage from Maimonides which stated that anyone who does not believe in the Talmud "belongs to the class of infidels whom it is permitted to slay."

The main conflict centered around the authority of the Talmud. An analogy can be made between the function of the Church in the Middle Ages and the function of the Talmud prior to the Modern Age. The Church, vilified by the Protestants, and the Talmud, disparaged by the Reform, had both served vital functions in their times.

For a thousand years, from 300 to 1300, the Catholic Church, in spite of all that can be said against her, was also a vital instrument that protected the spirit of humanism in an age of barbarism that threatened to obliterate the last vestiges of learning in Europe. The Church stemmed the tide of invasions in Italy, Spain, France, Germany. Her monks held back the flood of illiteracy and preserved the manuscripts of past knowledge. For a millennium, the Church inspired the art of Europe—its painting, sculpture, music. And paradoxically, even as she built magnificent Gothic cathedrals for the adoration of "idols" (as the statues of Catholic saints were called by the Protestants), she fostered the first universities for secular learning.

Alas, what the Church so painstakingly built in one millennium, she quickly lost in two centuries. Having begun as a shrine for international morality, she degenerated into vested interest. The sale of indulgences (certificates of absolution for sins past, present, and furture), simony (the selling of church posts to the highest bidder), and the monopoly of property (the Church owned as much as one-third of the land and wealth in the countries where she was supreme) finally precipitated that revolt known as the Reformation, resulting in half the Christian world calling the other half "heretic."

Similarly, for fifteen hundred years, from the first century A.D. to the sixteenth, the Talmud was a vital instrument that preserved the Jews from extinction as an ethnic entity. In the bleak centuries following the devastation of Jerusalem, the Talmud stemmed a Jewish flight into paganism and Christianity and preserved the Jews as Jews while history hurled them from civilization to civilization. Just as the Church had extended its power through a series of reinterpretations of dogma, so the Talmudists extended their power through a series of reinterpretations of the Torah. The Talmudists were mindful that the interpretation of one generation might be reinterpreted by the next. In the way the Church had served to unify the Christians, so the Talmud served to unify the Jews. And paradoxically, even as the Talmud kept the Jewish religion intact, it became a liberal instrument of law and learning.

Alas, what the Talmudists had so painstakingly constructed over fifteen hundred years was shattered by three centuries of ghetto imprisonment. Having begun as a repository of Jewish learning, Talmudists now confused their former interpretations with the eternal will of God. For the first time in its history, the Talmud, hemmed in by ghetto walls, began to atrophy. No new vital views were permitted to invade its pages. In the ghetto it became a dead creed, or as Mordecai Kaplan expressed it, "theological deadwood." And thus, when "sixteenth-century" ghetto Jews spilled out into the nineteenth century, the Talmudists, who refused to modernize the Talmud, were challenged by Reform Judaism, and one segment of the Jewish world was now calling the other segment "heretic."

The course of the "Jewish Reformation" of the nineteenth

century was in many instances similar to that of the earlier Protestant Reformation but without open warfare. Just as the Protestant reformers set up their churches and ministers in defiance of the Catholic establishment, so the Jewish reformers set up their own temples and rabbis in defiance of the Orthodox. The Protestant Reformation inveighed against images and the sale of indulgences; the Jewish Reformation inveighed against phylacteries and the practice of selling *aliyahs.** The Protestants did away with Latin as the language of worship and eliminated what they considered pagan ceremonies; the Jewish reformers did away with Hebrew as the only language of worship and abolished what they thought of as obsolete customs. And just as the Protestant Reformation questioned the infallibility of popes, so the Jewish Reformation quetsioned the judgment of the Talmudists. Both Reformations, the Christian and the Jewish, were kindred in spirit, though one was resolved with blood and the other with invective.

Having achieved their reforms thus far without resort to force, the Jewish reformers were nevertheless faced with a troubling question. Did what they had done constitute a "reformation" or a "heresy?" What was the distinction between the two? A cynic might observe that a heresy is a reformation that fails, and a reformation is a heresy that succeeds. The Vatican considered Protestantism a heresy until the popes realized it could not be overthrown; only then did Protestantism become a permissible sect of Christianity. And the Protestants had to accept Catholicism as a branch of Christianity when they discovered they could not defeat the Church.

The Jewish Reform leadership realized that it needed some certification for the changes it advocated, proof that its actions were neither heretic nor arbitrary, as claimed by the Orthodox, but consonant with the evolution of the Jewish

* An "ascent" or "calling up" to read the Scroll of the Law in the synagogue during worship.

religion. For confirmation of their beliefs, the intellectual elite of Reform turned, not to the Talmud, but to the Bible and secular scholarship.

In 1819, fifty prominent Jewish intellectuals met in Berlin to discuss how to divert Judaism into the mainstream of western civilization. They wanted to "de-ghettoize" the Jews and restore the intellectual and secular vitality of Judaism that had been lost in the ghetto. They wanted to imbue the Jewish consciousness with a sense of the grandeur of the Jewish past, and to demonstrate to non-Jews the great Jewish contributions to world civilization. To achieve their ends, these intellectuals formed the Association for Jewish Culture and Knowledge, which laid the foundation for the movement Science of Judaism (*Wissenschaft des Judentums*).

Chief founder of the Science of Judaism movement was Leopold Zunz (1794–1886), whose works were to shock Orthodox Jews by showing that the historical community of Israel and its literature had interacted with the world community. Among its members were the poet Heinrich Heine (1797–1856), who was to give up the struggle against orthodoxy and convert to Christianity, his "passport to civilization," and the theologian Abraham Geiger (1810–1874), who was to play a stellar role in formalizing German Reform. Among its last stars was Heinrich Graetz (1817–1891), the Jewish Macaulay who wrote an epoch-making eleven-volume history of the Jews.

It proved difficult to convince the Jews that the ghetto Judaism of their parents was not the eternal form of Judaism. To show that the changes advocated by the Reform were part of the Jewish tradition, Zunz undertook the task of reconstructing historic Judaism. As no systematic record had been kept, his monumental *The Sermons of the Jews* (1832) was a tour de force of original research. In it he proved that many of the ghetto practices had no historic sanction, and that most of the changes advocated by the Reform movement were actually intrinsic to ancient Judaism. Zunz demonstrated that the Talmud, for instance, sanctioned praying in languages other than Hebrew; that the prayers in the Jewish liturgy had not been handed down by Patriarchs and Prophets but had been compiled by Jews through the centuries, and that the Torah had been translated by Jews into both Aramaic and Arabic centuries previously.

The proof that Judaism had always experienced change—that it was not a dead creed but a living deed—shocked the Orthodox but did not silence them. They shouted "Heresy" louder than ever. This forced the Reform scholars into an inquiry of the role heresy had played in past Jewish history.

It is almost a heresy in itself to point out that neither Torah nor Talmud had created Judaism. Both were products of Jews who preexisted these two documents. The Torah was revealed (or was written) eight hundred years after Abraham, and the Mishna came about one thousand years after Moses. Thus the Patriarchs of Judaism—Abraham, Isaac, and Jacob—got along without the Torah until the arrival of Moses. All the kings of Judah and Israel and all the Prophets had lived without the Talmud, yet they were authentic Jews.

This fact had troubled the Pharisee theologians of the past. But, as one can always count on an explanation to fill an empty space, they came up with an ingenious answer. The Torah, they explained, predated Abraham and the Patriarchs, who had divined its contents before it was given to Moses. As for the Talmud, these specialists averred that God had given both the Torah and the Talmud to Moses at Sinai. But whereas the Torah was given openly, they said, the Talmud was handed covertly to Moses, to be revealed in later stages to the people. Thus, the Torah became known as the "written Torah," and the Talmud as the "oral Torah." Christian theologians, troubled by the fact that God was so late in sending the Holy Ghost to bring forth Jesus, found this Jewish explanation useful. They announced that Jesus was actually born at the time the world was created, but was not introduced physically until the proper time came for revelation.

Since Mosaic times there have been six major revolts against the established Jewish religion. The first revolt was against

Moses himself; the second a defiance by the Pharisees against the priesthood; the third, the Karaite "heresy"; the fourth the Sabbatean "heresy"; the fifth, the Hasidic protest; and the sixth, the nineteenth-century Jewish Reformation. Let us briefly review the first five rebellions as a background for the sixth religious revolt.

The first rebellion in Jewish history was against the supreme authority of Moses. But it also had elements of a religious revolt, for the rebels, led by Korah and two hundred and fifty "princes of the Assembly," also opposed the priesthood of Aaron. The punishment Moses meted out to them was drastic. Korah and the princes were buried alive or burned to death, an action attributed to God. The magnitude of this revolt is indicated by the statement in Numbers (16:49) that 14,700 people "died about the matter of Korah." After the rebels were subdued, the priesthood of Aaron was entrenched in the new Jewish faith, which had not had a priesthood previously.*

With time, the priests became the "orthodox" who held that the essence of Judaism was expressed in the cult of sacrifice. A "reform" revolt against them was first led by the Prophets. Just as the Protestant reformers would thunder that the worship of images was an abomination unto God, so also, many of the Prophets of the eighth to the sixth centuries B.C. thundered that the ritual sacrifice of cows, bullocks, rams, and goats was an abomination unto God.

Though the Prophets did not succeed, their cry for reform was taken up around the second century B.C. by a new party known as Pharisees, who worshipped in synagogues where they offered prayers to God under the leadership of rabbis. Their opponents were known as the Sadducees, the "orthodox" of those days. The Sadducees went to the Temple, where they offered animal sacrifices to God under the leadership of priests.

After the fall of Jerusalem in the war with Rome (66–

* For interesting accounts of this Korah–Moses conflict, see *Korah* in The Jewish Encyclopedia and Encyclopedia Judaica.

70 A.D.), the Pharisees saw their chance to wrest power from the Sadducees, toppling the supremacy of the priests with a machiavellian gambit.* They substituted their synagogues for the Temple and prayer for sacrifice, and they eliminated the priesthood, naming themselves the teachers—the rabbis—of the new Judaism. With time, "Phariseeism" became "rabbinic Judaism." †

The third religious revolt, the Karaite heresy, originating in and around Persia, then known as the Abbasid Caliphate, came in the eighth century, almost tearing Judaism apart in the Islamic Age. Led by Anan ben David, a descendant of the House of David, the Karaites felt that the only Jewish truths were those embodied in the Torah. They rejected the authority of the Talmud and abandoned the use of phylacteries. Within two hundred years Karaism had invaded every stratum of Jewish society, and its rapid spread sent a shiver of fright throughout the rabbinic world. Excommunications did not stop the spread of Karaism. The heresy was finally contained in the tenth century by Saadia Gaon, the famed head of the Academy of Sura, who used scholarship, not the ban, to defeat the Karaites. His most effective move was to translate the Torah into Arabic so that Arabic-speaking Jews, who no longer knew Hebrew, would not have to depend upon Karaite preachers to learn what was in it. Slowly the tide turned against the Karaites, and they faded out of history.

The fourth massive religious revolt was the Sabbatean heresy in the seventeenth century. Within a decade, the founder of the movement, Sabbatai Zevi (1626–1676), swept almost half of Europe's Jews into a revolt against the Talmudists. The fantastic aspect of this rebellion was that so many of Sabbatai's adherents were wealthy and educated. Gershom Scholem has remarked that "Sabbateanism . . . was"

* There are two brilliant monographs by Ellis Rivkin of Hebrew Union College on the subject of this takeover. One is *Defining the Pharisees: The Tannaitic Sources;* the other, *Pharisaism and the Crisis of the Individual in the Greco-Roman World.*

† There is a great controversy as to just when "Pharisee Judaism" became known as "rabbinic Judaism" but the usual date is set around 200 A.D.

the first case of mystical ideas, "leading directly to the disintegration of orthodox Judaism of the believers." *

The rabbis were incapable of stopping the spread of this heresy that threatened to take the Jews out of Talmudic Judaism. The Jews flocked like lemmings to Sabbatai's banners, and, like the Karaites, they too were heedless of bans. A fluke saved the Talmudists. After Sabbatai returned to Turkey from a successful messianic mission in Palestine, where he had been hailed as a messiah, he announced that he would assemble an army, march against the Sultan at Constantinople, and depose him. The sultan clapped the "messiah" into irons and gave him the choice of conversion to Islam or death. The "messiah" chose conversion and that was the end of his "messiahship."

The Talmudists rejoiced, regarding their deliverance as a miracle from heaven. But within a century came the fifth revolt, another heresy that almost became more "Jewish" than Talmudism itself. It was the passive revolt of the Hasidim, followers of Israel ben Eliazer (1700–1760), known by all as Baal Shem Tov, "Master of the Good Name." Like Sabbateanism, Hasidism was, in Scholem's words, "a rebellion of religious energy against petrified religious values." †

Culturally starved in ghetto and *shtetl*, the eighteenth-century Jews found in Hasidism an emotional and mystical outlet for their pent-up frustrations and smashed egos. In the doctrines of Baal Shem Tov they found an affirmation of the Jewish spirit without recourse to the Talmudic tradition. It gave them strength through joy, an ecstasy of knowing God through emotion. Baal Shem Tov turned weakness into strength, defeat into triumph. Had not Napoleon's armies breached the walls of the ghetto and had not the Haskala (Jewish Enlightenment) found its way into Eastern Europe, Hasidism might well have swept most European Jewry out

* Gershom G. Scholem, *Major Trends in Jewish Mysticism*. Schocken Books, 1941, page 299.
† Ibid, page 338.

of Talmudic Judaism into religious mysticism. Instead, in the light of freedom, it withered into a few insignificant sects.*

The Sabbatean and Hasidic experiences had not been empty of meaning. They had made those Jews not rigidly Orthodox wary of mystic escapes from reality, and readied them for the Age of Reason around the corner of the next century, where the Jewish Reformation, the sixth major religious revolt in Jewish history would be waiting for them.

The orthodox establishment, mindful of the five previous revolts against formalized Judaism, fought fiercely against the Reformers. The keepers of the Talmud were also aware, however dimly, that four of the six revolts—the Karaite, the Sabbatean, the Hasidic, and now the Reform—were not against the Torah but against the Talmud. Karaism had been contained; Sabbateanism had been "smitten by God"; Hasidism had made its peace with Talmudism. The Orthodox prayed for some similar solution to this new Reform revolt.

The Orthodox viewed the Reform leaders as new Karaites who were challenging the essence of Judaism. The reformers saw themselves as new Pharisees, challenging the Orthodox abuse of Judaism. By the mid-1830s, it became apparent that Reform was losing ground to the concentrated onslaughts of the Orthodox. For all its brilliance, scientific Judaism accomplished little. Its scholars had a dazzling knowledge of facts but little understanding of the spirit. Its learning neither convinced the Orthodox nor stirred the masses. Rationalistic moralizing had made *Wissenschaft* Judaism as dry as the unscientific legalisms of the Orthodox.

And thus it came about that in 1837, thirteen troubled Reform rabbis met in Wiesbaden, Germany, to assess the spiritual sources of their beliefs. Their task was not to find scientific explanations for Jewish religious existence but to

---

* Today's revival of Hasidism bears little actual resemblance to the Hasidism of the eighteenth century. The Hasid in that century was not the romantic figure portrayed by Martin Buber. A more sober and historic view is presented in Solomon Schechter's essay *The Chassidim*, in his *Studies in Judaism*, and in Solomon Maimon's *An Autobiography*.

establish a spiritual relation to the Jewish past. The meeting
had been called by Abraham Geiger, the rabbi of Wiesbaden,
the *enfant terrible* of Reform Judaism, who enjoyed being the
center of the storms he created.

Vexing questions faced Geiger and his colleagues. What
precedents gave them the right to make changes? What were
the permanent features of Judaism, and what were the temporary? Were the reforms they advocated really necessary, or
were they merely expressions of personal preference? Could
circumcision be discarded? Should the Torah be dismissed as
well as the Talmud? Should messianism be abandoned? Did
resistance to Reform spring from the sanctity of Orthodoxy or
from ignorance? The Reform rabbis resolved to meet again
within a year to discuss these and other questions in depth.

None of these questions had troubled the native American
reformers because they did not structure their Reform—they
"lived" themselves into it. They could do so because, as we
have seen, there was no established religion to interpose itself
and no hierarchy to account to.

The resolve at Wiesbaden to meet again within a year
evaporated until two controversies—one over a prayer book,
the other over circumcision—again put Reform and Orthodox
at each other's throats.

All had been relatively peaceful in the Hamburg Temple
after the initial onslaughts by the Orthodox had failed to
close it. But in 1841, it published a prayer book which aroused
Orthodox ire because it opened from the left, like Christian
prayer books, instead of from the right, like Hebrew ones.
And the Hamburg Temple had taken Mendelssohn's innovation but reversed it—the prayers were in Hebrew, printed in
Roman letters. The prayers were also translated into German
so the worshippers could not only read them in Hebrew but
understand them as well. The sight of Hebrew words in
Roman letters threw the Orthodox into a frenzy. "A mutila-
tion of the sacred text," they cried. The Reform were faced
with the question Was this a heresy or a needed reform?

The second incident showed that the Reform could still

inspire the Orthodox to exceed their previous peaks of invective. Close upon the prayer-book embroglio followed the circumcision controversy, caused by accident but fanned by design into hatred by a new radical wing of the Jewish Reformation—the Reform Society of Frankfort. It was founded by Samuel Holdheim (1806–1860), whose tenets of reform have been characterized as a "confession of unbelief." Though born of rigidly Orthodox parents and weaned on the Talmud, he nevertheless leaned toward the humanistic sciences of the Gentiles, adding a doctorate to his rabbinic title. He became an apostle of radical reform, throwing out the vestry door practically all the tenets of Judaism—the Hebrew language, the Sabbath, the messiah, the bar mitzvah, and all holidays except Rosh Hashana. At the same time, he continued to declare his adherence to and admiration of Judaism. One is reminded of Freud's retort to Jung when the latter professed admiration for Freud's theories: If he does not accept my dream interpretations, denies the primacy of infantile sexuality, and rejects the death instinct, what's left to admire?

The great circumcision controversy arose when several Jewish infants in Frankfort died from improper circumcision by unskilled Jewish practitioners. The city placed the rite of circumcision under its jurisdiction and set minimum standards of health and skill for its practitioners. It is difficult to assess who was more stupid in the ensuing fracas—the radical reformers, who insisted the circumcision was an outmoded, meaningless gesture, or the Orthodox, who claimed the circumciser needed no training, merely divine guidance. In any event, the dispute ended in a draw. The reformers backed down from their radical position that circumcision was unnecessary, and the Orthodox accepted minimum health standards for the rite. Judaism did not die with the acceptance of these standards, as had been predicted.

Although the Reform Society of Frankfort mercifully expired in 1845, its radicalism had frightened not only the Orthodox but also the Reform, who realized that the Jewish faith could not long exist without religious observances and tradition. The circumcision furor of 1842 gave the moderates courage to break with the Frankfort group and to call for a uniform creed of reform. Geiger seized the initiative and issued a call for a conference in Brunswick that same year.

Now German Reform Judaism began its dreary journeys to conferences and synods—Brunswick, Frankfort, Breslau, Leipzig, Augsburg—where the official tenets of Reform were hammered out in tired, uninspiring prose. The writers of Scripture had not feared to portray God as a Man of War; Jesus cursed the Pharisees in language that would make a sinner blush; and Luther denounced priests in prose that made popes shiver. But the apostles of Jewish Reform wrote sentences that would not offend a bigot. The wonder is that the Orthodox, who expressed their dissent in colorful vituperation, became enraged at these tepid sentences. History, however, has rendered its verdict—Reform Judaism was mightier than its prose.

The Brunswick Conference opened on a note of high expectations. "The issue before us concerns the entire content of our religion," was the heroic opening statement. Few hopes were realized, but many committees were appointed to give reports on a new concept of the messiah, modification of marriage and divorce laws, a program for reasonable Sabbath observance, and other subjects. The conference adjourned with the resolve to meet the following year at Frankfort, where new committees were appointed to report on more problems.

Again a phenomenon in Christian history recapitulated itself in Jewish history. The Church, while reeling from the onslaught of Protestant attacks and fearful it would lose the fight, began to reform itself, creating a counterreformation. So too with the Jews. The more thoughtful among the Orthodox and among those opposed to the radical drift Reform was taking, began to realize that invective was not a remedy. Two segments of the opposition—one led by Zacharias Frankel (1801–1875), and the other by Samson Raphael Hirsch (1808–1888)—began two Jewish counterreformations.

Zacharias Frankel, ill at ease in the Reform camp, seceded to form his school of Positive Historical Judaism. He felt there was too much reason and too little heart in the reform movement. He believed that Judaism expressed the will of the Jewish people and thus did not have to conform to any "spirit of the times"—Judaism created its own spirit. His thoughts became the foundation of American Conservative Judaism.

Samson Raphael Hirsch was a university graduate who, in spite of secular learning, loved Talmudism, and retained Orthodoxy, humanism, and his sanity. The Jewish spirit, not Judaism, needed reform, he claimed. Religious reform, he contended, leads to the degeneration of Judaism and empties it of content. His school of neo-Orthodoxy—new Orthodoxy— was the basis of the American neo-Orthodoxy that arose as a response to the American Reform challenge.

The Breslau Conference in 1846 followed the Frankfort meeting. The committees gave their recommendations: equal rights for women in religious matters, reform of mourning customs, and modernization of marriage and divorce laws. The committees held that it was not essential to Judaism for married women to shave their heads and wear wigs, or to visit the *mikvah*, and that one did not have to go unwashed and unkempt for seven days in order to show grief. The Torah commanded only one day for most holidays, but the Orthodox had trumped the Torah by instituting two. The committee, however, upheld the Torah. A resolution to transfer the Sabbath to Sunday was defeated.

But for all its brilliant reports, the Breslau Conference left a trail of dissatisfaction. A fourth conference, to resolve the failures of the third, was set for the following year. But it was postponed for twenty-four years by the Revolution of 1848 and its bloody aftermath.

As a smoldering quiet eventually settled over Germany, the Reformers called a synod in Leipzig, where the old was affirmed and new committees were appointed to reconsider the reconsiderations. They resolved to meet in Augsburg in

1871, the last synod in this dreary tale of the life and death of German committee Judaism.

Though eleven problems were resolved and only one new committee appointed, the Augsburg synod signaled the decline of the German Reform movement. The patient had been operated on by so many committees that, though it did not die, it became a permanent invalid.

What had happened? The causes were complex, but out of the welter of explanations three valid ones emerge. One was the Jewish counterreformation. Neo-Orthodoxy was a passport back to Torah Judaism. At the price of weakening itself, Reform had achieved a reformation of the Orthodox, a victory in itself. Orthodoxy was also victorious—it had shown it still had the resources for change within the Talmudic tradition.

The second was the phenomenon of modern anti-Semitism and its counterreaction—Jewish nationalism and socialism. A considerable segment of the Jewish intelligentsia was siphoned from religion into political movements.

The third reason for the sudden collapse of German Reform at the height of achievement is perhaps the most important. German Reform was a monster—all mind and no heart. Never a mass movement, it was smothered by too much science, too much reason, too many committees. The German reformers were public relations-minded gentlemen, afraid to sully their doctorates with a good fight. Moses did not debate, he commanded; the Prophets did not confer, they exhorted. Timidity, not lack of ideas, killed German Reform. Because they could not take a stand and fight, they drifted from platform to platform until they fell from sheer exhaustion.

The German Reform leaders did not see themselves in a larger perspective. Because they were afraid to enlarge their revolt against abuses into a firm stand against the Orthodox establishment, the Reform movement died out in Germany in less than four decades. It would have become extinct if American reformers had not adopted its ideas and changed those ideas into a genuine social and religious program. In fact, American Reform Judaism achieved what Mendelssohn had not dared to envision—a new Judaism for the Diaspora Jews.

The scene now shifts to the United States, where we shall hear the American pragmatic counterpoint to the German intellectual orchestration in this Jewish Reformation symphony.

The Age of the American Reform Jews

THE YEAR IS 1850; the day is Rosh Hashana. Congregation Beth El in Albany, New York, is filled with worshippers and ominous silence. The Holy Ark is open. The Torahs gleam with purple and gold. In front of the open Ark stand two men. One is Louis Spanier, president of the congregation, a successful businessman, as American as corned beef on rye. Next to him stands the spiritual leader of Beth El, Rabbi Isaac M. Wise, who, for the past four years, has been preaching the doctrine of Reform in a German accent to a divided congregation. There is tension in the silence and hostility in the air. Everyone expects something to happen, and it does.

The rage within Louis Spanier has been contained for a long time. There had been controversies about seating men and women together, about a mixed choir, about equal rights for women, about higher education for girls—unheard of deviations from "authentic" Judaism as Louis Spanier knew it. But now this rabbi from Bohemia had transgressed all bounds of decency. In a speech in Charleston, South Carolina, Rabbi Wise had stated that he believed neither in a messiah nor in a bodily resurrection after death. Spanier had fired him, and the Orthodox community had "excommunicated" him. But Wise had heeded neither. And there he stood, the arrogant "blasphemer." As Rabbi Wise reached into the Ark to pick up a Torah, Louis Spanier clenched his hand into a fist and punched Wise in the nose. All hell broke loose.

"The people acted like furies," Wise wrote later. "The Poles and Hungarians struck out like wild men. The young people jumped down from the choir galleries to protect me. Within two minutes the whole assembly was a fighting mass. The sheriff and posse who were summoned were belabored and forced out." Finally, the whole assembly surged out of the sanctuary and continued the fight on Herkimer Street. Here Wise and Spanier confronted each other.

"Louis Spanier," cried Wise, "there is a law to which I can appeal."

"I do not fear the law," Spanier shouted. "I have a hundred thousand dollars more than you. I will ruin you."

That punch in the nose in 1850 was a turning point in American Jewish history. It not only set tongues wagging but also set historic forces in motion. Rabbi Isaac M. Wise (1819–1900), though not the father of American Reform, made it into a force that affected the entire body of American Judaism.

Who was Isaac M. Wise? No distinguished Talmudists, wealthy court Jews, or bankers of renown studded his ancestry. His father was an impoverished teacher in a small Bohemian town in Germany. Isaac, one of thirteen children, was saved from becoming a Talmud-chanting ghetto dweller by Emperor Joseph II and his "anti-Semitic" (according to the Orthodox) Patent of Toleration, which permitted Jews to attend Christian secular schools for higher education. Exactly what Wise's ghetto peers had predicted happened: Let a Jewish boy attend one of those ungodly secular universities and he will forsake ghetto traditions.

However, Wise did not walk directly from the University

of Prague into Reform. He was first ordained rabbi at the age of twenty-three in Prague by an Orthodox rabbinic court. In 1843 he held his first pulpit in a small Jewish community in Bohemia, where he got into a dispute, not with the Orthodox, but with the Imperial Council of Prague. He refused to uphold a law limiting the number of Jewish marriages, and had the courage to denounce it to the council members as inhuman. At twenty-seven, Wise had had enough of Europe, and in 1846 he came to the United States with his young wife and infant son. True to the immigrant tradition, he is said to have arrived penniless.

The foregoing is the biographical gospel of Wise according to Wise, but other biographers dispute it. They point out that there is no record of his attendance at the University of Prague, or of his ordination. His account of his dispute with the Imperial Council of Prague has also been challenged. If this counterbiography is correct, it may help explain why Wise could perceive the true nature of American "frontier reform" better than his peers. He was not confined by the rigid framework of German Reform.

Wise's new American friends advised him to abandon the rabbinate, a profession held in low esteem in the United States at that time, and take up a profitable trade like peddling. He ignored their counsel and opened a night school in a one-room basement to teach English to Jewish immigrants. Wise, however, soon became the rabbi of Beth El in Albany, a post he was offered after delivering a trial sermon. One congregant told him, "Our people like and admire you so much because they don't understand you." We have seen what happened when they finally did.

The civil authorities fined Spanier after the riot, and the Beth El board members dismissed Rabbi Wise. He promptly organized a competing rump temple in the downtown Albany business district, which became the fourth Reform temple in the United States. The five years he subsequently spent in Albany marked Wise's Americanization years. The positive aspect of the Beth El incident was that with that punch in the nose, Spanier seemed to have "Americanized" him. From a flowery German preacher, Wise became a pragmatic Yankee organizer.

While still holding his pulpit at Beth El in Albany, Wise received an offer, at a considerable increase in salary, of a rabbinic post in Charleston's Beth Elohim. Jubilantly he first accepted this offer, then reneged on his contract. Wise does not explain why. He manipulated his wife into changing his mind for him by so alarming her with tales of yellow fever in Charleston that she begged him not to go. Wise allowed himself to be persuaded not to accept the post.

We can only speculate about the reasons for his sudden reversal. Perhaps he envisioned himself as a future leader of Reform. At Beth Elohim, in Charleston, many reform practices had already been instituted. If he took the Charleston post, all his innovations would be regarded as mere extensions of the Harby-Poznanski ideas. He would be an imitator, not an innovator.

Wise was restless in his small synagogue in downtown Albany. Though his congregation accepted his innovations, he felt isolated from the Reform movement. Reform rabbis from Germany were beginning to arrive in the United States in the aftermath of the revolutions of 1848. It seemed as if each German Reform rabbi was introducing his own brand of Judaism as soon as he stepped off the gangplank. If Wise wanted to become a force in the Reform movement he would have to bestir himself. Thus, when a call came in 1854 from Temple B'nai Jeshurun in Cincinnati to fill its rabbinic post, he accepted it with alacrity.

The settlement of Cincinnati was begun in 1788 by Anglo-Saxons from the Eastern seaboard. By 1820 the town had a population of about 45,000, of whom a third were Germans from Bavaria. The Presbyterian clergy was at the helm. By mid-century it was a city of brick buildings and wide, unpaved streets. The city fathers subscribed to the prevailing theory of sanitation—throw the refuse into the streets, then turn the pigs loose. Charles Dickens visited Cincinnati and called it "cheerful, thriving, animated."

The first Jew settled in Cincinnati in 1817. A year later there were enough Jews to form a *minyan* of five (American wilderness style) and by 1824 enough to form Congregation Bene Israel, known as the English Congregation because most members had come from England. They were at first as rigidly orthodox as the Presbyterians were unbending. Twenty years later the English Jews were outnumbered by German Jews, and by 1840 animosity between them ripened into secession. The German Jews founded their own congregation, B'nai Jeshurun, and were willing to experiment with Reform. This was the congregation that invited Wise to its pulpit, and here, he sensed, a new era was dawning for American Judaism.

Wise was now to make history, not as a German rabbi serving in America but as an American rabbi serving American Jewry. With this move, the spotlight of American Jewish history focuses on Cincinnati, where it will remain for the rest of Rabbi Wise's life. In the subsequent four decades, American Jewish history was largely that of the Reform movement. During this period, whenever Reform sneezed, Orthodoxy caught a cold and the Conservatives took preventive medication. Wise became a force, an institution, a legend, the single most influential individual in the shaping of modern American Judaism.

If there was one word to describe American Judaism in the decade before the Civil War, that word was "chaotic." The social and economic changes during the years from 1840 to 1880 were to affect profoundly both America and American Jews. The Jewish population swelled from fifty thousand to two hundred and fifty thousand as German Jews fled to America (in company with 7 million Christians) to escape the economic and social havoc that convulsed the European Continent. Fortunately these events in Europe coincided with the needs of the United States. People were needed for the coming transformation of America from an agricultural into an industrial society. The Christian immigrants, mostly peasants, became farmers and laborers. The Jewish immigrants, mostly lower middle class, became small-scale entrepreneurs.

In the years following the American Revolution, Jewish settlers had poured through the Cumberland Gap and scattered throughout the Northwest Territory. By 1840 they stood on the western border of the Louisiana Territory, ready to be swept in 1842 by the "Oregon fever" into Oregon country; to be drawn in 1845 into Texas in time to hail its annexation; to be enticed in 1848 by the Gold Rush to settle California as part of the Forty-niner elite. The first Jews in San Francisco held their Yom Kippur service in a tent. By the end of 1849, enough Jews had arrived to form two congregations. Because the Jews were a part of the founding elite of that city, they became prominent in civic affairs, banking, and industry.

The German Jews quickly sensed the opportunities offered by the American frontier. They worked hard, lived frugally, and saved their money to invest in businesses of their own, their first investments often being peddler's carts. As they trekked across the continent, they left ever larger retail establishments as milestones of their enterprise.

They improved the prevailing standards and enlarged the scope of the department store. They extended the mail-order business, pioneered in installment buying, and introduced a stream of retail products—innovations and inventions that immediately became necessities when introduced—like Levi's, the product of an enterprising Jewish peddler, Levi Straus. Having exhausted his supply of normal yarn in making coveralls for farmers, he experimented with copper-colored yarn and metal rivets for denim pants—and the Levi "denims" were born—still one of the most wanted clothing items by farmers, workers, and youth.

Vast empires in steel, oil, railroads, shipping, coal, and chemicals were created after the Civil War, founded by the WASP (White Anglo-Saxon Protestant) elite, who tended to hire other WASPs for management posts. As a consequence, most Jewish fortunes were not made in these fields, but in banking and retailing. In the process, this German-Jewish elite became wealthy beyond the dreaming in the ghettos of Europe. They became a merchant-prince class.

But what a vast difference there was between this Jewish merchant prince and the medieval prince. The medieval prince thought of wealth only as a means of self-aggrandizement. He built resplendent castles, filling them with works of art to be viewed by only a favored few. His wealth was squandered on war and vanity, while multitudes of his people went in hunger and ignorance.

Unlike this medieval prince, the Jewish merchant prince thought of wealth also as a responsibility, a means of improving public welfare. He spent a large part of his riches on charitable works. He may not have followed Maimonides' dictum that the most noble charitable act is that done anonymously, but the millions he gave publicly did far more good. The merchant princes, called "Our Crowd" by Stephen Birmingham, "invented" modern philanthropy. Families like the Guggenheims, the Warburgs, the Rosenwalds, the Strauses, the Schiffs, the Kahns, the Altmans—and there were many, many more—became patrons of art and education; they donated imposing art collections to museums, funded symphony orchestras, supported the opera and theater, established trust funds for universities, and endowed chairs in the humanities and sciences. Through their largesse, eleemosynary Jewish institutions were established across the land—the Montefiore homes for the aged, the Jewish hospitals, the first Jewish colleges for education in Jewish humanities.

Brief word portraits of a few of these German-American Jews will bring into sharp relief the difference between their life styles and those of the Colonial and early nineteenth-century Jews.

Meyer Guggenheim emigrated from Switzerland at the age of nineteen and became an "upper-class" peddler (he had a horse and buggy to haul his goods). He peddled in the coal-mining regions of Pennsylvania, where he found out that lye and stove polish were needed, and catered to that need. He accumulated his savings and eventually became the world's foremost producer and smelter of copper and silver. He used his money to patronize art, help artists, and endow foundations. His sons, as the cliché goes, followed in their father's footsteps.

Jacob H. Schiff, born in Frankfort, emigrated to the United States at an early age and worked his way up in Horatio Alger fashion, becoming a powerful financier. Among his many financial negotiations was the reorganization of the Union Pacific Railroad. Schiff viewed capitalism as an ideology that rewarded you with profit for doing the right things well—the Puritan ethic at work. His all-embracing love was his hate for Czarist Russia, and in this spirit he floated a $200 million bond issue for Japan to help that country defeat Russia in the War of 1904–05. His philanthropies were numerous, liberal, and nonsectarian. His son-in-law, Felix M. Warburg, as wealthy as Schiff, became known for his contributions to Jewish charities.

Lazarus Straus, founder of the Straus clan—Isidor, Oscar, and Nathan, all businessmen and philanthropists in the grand manner—arrived in the United States from Bavaria and peddled his way to success through Georgia. He opened his first store in the hinterland of that state, in Talbotton. Out of the profits from that store and from other enterprises grew R. H. Macy of New York. His son Nathan introduced a new concept of charity with dignity when, in the panic of 1893–94, he established depots where five- and ten-dollar packages of food and coal were sold for five and ten cents. The homeless could also get a night's lodging for five cents. The Straus family also became known for their financial support of museums, symphonies, and universities.

Unlike Guggenheim, Schiff, and Straus, Julius Rosenwald was born in the United States. His career began as an errand boy in a clothing store in New York. Within nine years of that first job, he was part owner and vice-president of a firm called Sears, Roebuck and Co., which he developed into a world-famous mail-order house. He was among the first to recognize needs of Blacks in America; he gave large sums for educational aid to help Blacks become self-sustaining in agriculture and the professions.

"Our Crowd" of German Jews constituted not only a Jewish but an American elite. They were, as a group, cultured and well-to-do. They lived comfortably, kept servants, entered the professions in numbers unmatched by any other social group, and encountered little discrimination, with most social doors open to them.

A statistical survey of 10,000 German Jews who arrived in the United States between 1850 and 1880 shows that by 1890, 1,000 of the 10,000 had three or more servants, 2,000 had two, and 4,000 had one, leaving but 3,000 without a servant. Of the 10,000, half were businessmen. One out of every 20 was in a profession, including banking. One fifth were accountants, bookkeepers, clerks, agents. One out of every eight was engaged in such occupations as tailor, jeweler, cigar maker, butcher, or the like. Less than 1 percent were farmers, common laborers, or servants. The German-Jewish peddlers had done well by 1890. Only one out of every hundred was still a peddler. On the average, there were five children per family.

During these decades, vast political, social, and economic changes took place. The Civil War divided the Jews the way it did the rest of the country. Though some Jews dealt in slaves, most were antislavery. Southern Jews fought for the Confederacy because they loved the South, not because of a strong belief in the legitimacy of slavery. Like Southern Christian ministers exhorting their coreligionists to volunteer for the Confederate Gray, and Northern Christian ministers exhorting their brethren to join the Union Blue, so most rabbis in the South exhorted Jews to fight for the Confederacy, and rabbis in the North urged Jews to give their all for the Union. When the war was over, there were nine Jewish generals in the Union Army and several in the Confederate ranks. Many were but honorary, brevetted generals, that is, holding higher ranks than they got paid for. But while the war was on, the North gave the Jews their first American anti-Semitic *cause célèbre*, "l'affaire Grant" and the South gave the Jews their first American statesman of note, Judah Philip Benjamin.

The Grant affair grew out of General Grant's victories in Tennessee (1862), which forced the surrender of Memphis. The area became the scene of a boom in cotton trade—some of it legal, most of it illegal. The North needed cotton, and Grant's "opening of the South" created a path for profits. Along with the cotton buyers came smugglers, speculators, and profiteers, many of them high-ranking Union soldiers. And among these buyers and speculators, legal and illegal, were Jews.

It is not clear why Grant, a brilliant general, though not a great intellect, singled out the Jews as the main perpetrators. It may be that he was influenced by Christian speculators who needed a scapegoat. At any rate, in December 1862, Grant issued his General Order No. 11, summarily expelling all Jews from the entire "Tennessee Department" within twenty-four hours, with the stipulation that any Jews returning to that area would be arrested.

The life of Order No. 11 was short, less than a month. When he learned of it, President Lincoln had it rescinded immediately. The incident became an issue in Grant's 1868 Presidential campaign, but it had little effect, since Grant publicly regretted his action and Jewish Republicans endorsed him.

The Grant bagatelle has been blown up by some historians from its blunder-origin into an anti-Semitic plot. Anti-Semitism played no role in nineteenth-century Jewish-American history. Nor has anti-Semitism ever been officially elevated into a philosophy of hatred in the United States or become an expression of ideology by the state.

The Southern statesman Judah Philip Benjamin (1811–1884) was the last of the old grand style Sephardi notables in

American-Jewish history. He typified the dashing, romantic Colonial Jew more than he did the stodgy post-Reconstruction Jew. Born to a Sephardi family in the British West Indies, he was brought to Charleston, South Carolina, at age eleven. Expelled from Yale, he studied law privately and was admitted to the bar in New Orleans, where he married a Catholic girl of great beauty. After making a fortune in law, he was elected to the Senate. He declined an appointment to the Supreme Court, preferring the turmoil of political life. When the South seceded, Benjamin seceded with it, and his former Senate colleague Jefferson Davis, now President of the Confederacy, appointed him attorney general. He served briefly as Secretary of War, and in 1862 he was named Secretary of State, a post he held until the end of the war. Though dubbed the "brains of the Confederacy," he was highly unpopular for advocating the arming of slaves in the Confederate cause. The South preferred to lose the war without the aid of Blacks rather than win it with their support.

When the Confederacy collapsed, Benjamin fled to England, where he carved out a new legal career; he became wealthy, was named Queen's Counsel, and won fame as the author of a book on sale of personal property, a work still consulted in England. He retired to Paris, where he rejoined his wife. His Judaism expired with his life in 1884, when his wife buried him in a Catholic grave with the blessing of the Church. Though never denying his Jewishness, he had never supported a Jewish cause.

For all its wealth and power, the German-Jewish elite in America was intellectually sterile. Four decades of German-Jewish dominance produced few scholars, statesmen, or scientists of national note. The picture was equally dismal in the field of Jewish scholarship. There was no native Haskala to stimulate an American Jewish intellectual awakening. The Jews of this era were generally unaware of any Jewish mission to fulfill. They would have had little idea of what was meant had someone preached to them of Judaism as a manifestation of God's continuous revelation. They just wanted to be Jewish and were searching for values that would permit them to be Jewish—the American way.

The religious orthodoxy brought to America by the German immigrants tended to evaporate within a generation. As the generation of Orthodox died out, their children wished neither to live by the Orthodoxy of their parents nor to abandon their Judaism. They tried to solve this dilemma in the same pragmatic way their predecessors had. They were very much like many American Jews today, and the Colonial Jews of the past. Away from home, in the business world, they were "Gentiles" among the Gentiles, but at home and in the synagogue they were semi-Orthodox among the semi-Orthodox. As the years slipped by, more and more children of American-born parents completely rejected Orthodoxy. They did not, however, line up at baptismal fonts as did their counterparts in Europe; in America they simply disaffiliated themselves from Judaism and were eventually phased out of Judaism through passive assimilation. The synagogue, by and large, was shunned by the young.

There were four Reform congregations in America in 1850. The rest professed themselves to be Orthodox. But many religious stances hid behind this label of "orthodoxy." At one end of the Jewish spectrum was a small, unorganized, amorphous "orthodoxy," which insisted on observing remembrances of things past from ghetto days. At the other end was an equally small cluster of unorganized "Reform" Jews who instituted unauthorized changes based on what they thought of as common sense. In between was a diffused mass of American Jews who paid lip service to "Orthodoxy" while practicing unstructured "Reform."

However, there was a vitality in this amorphous mass. In 1850, it represented fifty thousand Jews in search of a viable Judaism—fifty thousand Jews who wanted to be Jewish. American-Jewish history began to recapitulate itself. In the same way that Colonial Sephardi Jews bequeathed their congregationalist religious structure to the arriving Jews in the early nineteenth century, so these antebellum Jews now bequeathed this congregationalism to the arriving German Jews.

With the two hundred thousand German Jews who settled in America between 1840 and 1880 there arrived German rabbis, both Orthodox and Reform. The Orthodox German rabbis made little impact on American-Jewish history during this period. But the Reform rabbis, who split into two groups, played a most important role in shaping American Judaism. One group, the radical wing, thought that the best Judaism for the American Jews was the scientific Judaism which had been conceived at Brunswick and had died at Augsburg. This "Radical Reform" Judaism also died in the United States. The other group, the moderate wing, was more perceptive. Instead of shaping American Judaism in its own image, it furthered the growth of Reform by grafting its ideas on the prevailing American-Jewish congregationalism.

Three leading German-born rabbis—Max Lilienthal, David Einhorn, and Samuel Hirsch—are representative of the German Reform rabbinate that dominated the American scene from 1845 to 1885. Their collective biographies (as well as a dozen others one could select with equal justice) present a picture of unrelenting virtue—a covey of saints with nary a sin amongst them. All were born in Germany; all had been precocious, mastering the Talmud before puberty and exchanging it for Hegel before earning doctorates from prestigious universities. All became rabbis at an early age. All came to the United States after having been hounded from home, hearth, and pulpit by either the Jewish Orthodox hierarchy or reactionary Christian rulers.

Max Lilienthal (1815–1882), was born in Germany of wealthy but Orthodox parents. At twenty-four, he became principal of a Jewish school in Riga, Latvia, and subsequently was invited by the Russian government to help educate its vast mass of illiterate Jews. Lilienthal discovered, to his horror, that the Hasidic life, so romanticized at a safe distance, was actually one of ignorance and intolerance. Denounced by Orthodox Jews as a traitor to his faith because he urged Jewish emancipation through secular learning, and disillusioned by suspicions that the Russians were manipulating him, Lilienthal immigrated to the United States in 1844, becoming the second ordained rabbi to reside permanently in America.* He became Rabbi Isaac Wise's closest friend and at Wise's recommendation took the second rabbinic pulpit in Cincinnati.

David Einhorn (1809–1879), leader of the Radical Reform wing, was ordained rabbi at seventeen, and then went to a Bavarian university for an education in the humanities. He held a succession of pulpits in Germany, but was dismissed from each post because of his commitment to reform. He immigrated to America in 1855, holding successive rabbinic posts in Baltimore, Philadelphia, and New York.

Einhorn's oratorical ability soon made him the leader of Radical Reform in America. A gaunt, embittered man, he was intractable, brooked no compromise with the Orthodox, and opposed Wise in all his conciliatory gestures. To Einhorn, Reform was not a mode of worship but a principle. Though an ardent reformer who contributed much to the Reform cause, he was nevertheless an anachronistic carry-over of the waning influence of German scientific Judaism, which he could not, or would not, realize had no place in America.

Samuel Hirsch (1815–1889), rabbi in Dessau at twenty-three, published a book on the religious philosophy of Judaism at twenty-five. Though the Reform acclaimed him as a genius, the Orthodox denounced him as a heretic and forced his resignation. In 1841 he became chief rabbi of Luxemburg, a post he held until 1866, when he accepted a pulpit in Philadelphia. He, too, was a firm advocate of Radical Reform, and a leading critic of Wise.

These three intellectuals—and dozens like them, equally

---

* The first was the Bavarian-born Abraham Joseph Rice (Reiss), who came to America in 1840. Named rabbi of the Baltimore Hebrew Congregation that same year, he was a bitter foe of Reform, and it was he who "excommunicated" Rabbi Isaac Mayer Wise.

•

important—vied with one another to become the "Jewish Luther." Each tried to outdo his equally brilliant colleagues in Reform innovation so he would be remembered as the "Great Reformer." Max Lilienthal introduced confirmation into American Jewish life. Samuel Hirsch proposed that Sunday be "Judaized" into the new Sabbath. Einhorn wrote a prayer book, tossing out old hymns to make room for his own compositions. The abundance of brilliant Reform rabbis threatened to break Judaism into a number of competing sects.

This radical drift culminated in the founding of the New York Society for Ethical Culture, which took this brand of "Judaism" out of Judaism. It dethroned God, making Him a dues-paying member. Ethical Culture attracted both Jews and non-Jews who had become disenchanted with the conventional concept of God, faith, and ritual. As its central core of "revelation," it substituted manmade ethics for God-inspired tenets of faith. Instead of reciting Kaddish for a departed member of the family, the mourners read a poem by Browning.

The villain in this nineteenth-century revolt against religion was science. The period was one of constant assault on Bible and God by scientists. Darwin's *On the Origin of Species* (1859) dealt a death blow to the concept of special creation. The new science of higher Biblical criticism demonstrated that the Gospels did not contain gospel truth and that the Old Testament had not been written by Moses. The entire account of Creation was falling apart, and only the "True Believers" remained religious fundamentalists.

Such was the economic, social, and religious milieu into which history had catapulted Rabbi Isaac M. Wise. He clearly perceived the Radical Reform movement as a serious threat to Judaism. If not halted, it might cause Judaism to disintegrate into a multitude of bickering sects. He perceived that no reform except one rooted deeply in the American soil could survive. It would have to be grafted in the existing

American spirit and nourished by its American roots. Wise decided to make Americanism, not *Wissenschaft*, the keystone of his reforms.

Wise began cautiously in his new Cincinnati rabbinic post. First he introduced the mixed choir, then the organ, and then the family pew, where husbands, wives, and other family members could sit together; finally he eliminated the practice of wearing hats during services. His sermons were intended to enlighten his congregation, not to impress other rabbis. People came to listen and learn. Whereas Radical Reform rabbis like Einhorn insisted on preaching in German, Wise not only preached in English but also called for all rabbis to do likewise.

Wise observed that Jews who worked late on Fridays or lived too far from the synagogue to walk there on Saturday, would go to the nearest church, not to venerate Jesus but to be in a place of worship. They closed their eyes to the Christian architecture, and, whenever appropriate, substituted words from the Jewish liturgy, remaining silent during other prayers. If Reform could not do something about this situation, Wise contended "there would be Episcopalian Jews in New York, Quaker Jews in Pennsylvania, Huguenot Jews in Charleston . . . and so on, everywhere according to the prevailing sect."

A realist, Wise instituted the practice of holding Friday services late in the evening instead of right after sunset. Attendance soared, and the practice was quickly adopted by practically all Jewish synagogues and temples except for a few diehard Orthodox outposts.

Wise also ruled that riding a wagon to the synagogue on the Sabbath was not a sin but a virtue. Attendance in Reform temples again jumped, and Jewish attendance in churches dropped. Many ostensibly Orthodox congregations have unofficially accepted this view as well.

Wise's ideas gained recognition through his indefatigable travels as a speaker and his prolific writings. For fifty years he wrote, edited, and published the *American Israelite* (an

English-language weekly), as well as a German-language monthly. Though stilted in style by today's standards, these publications contained forthright articles that dealt with current problems, Jewish dilemmas, and theological questions. He also wrote seven novels in English, and three novels and two plays in German. These last works met a quick and deserved death.

Wise was also formulating a plan for making Reform supreme by uniting all shades of Judaism into one American congregationalist house. The first step was to impose liturgical uniformity. In 1857, Wise published his *Minhag America*, an American prayer book for American Jews. Published in English and German editions, it had enough Hebrew to give it authenticity, and enough English (or German) to make it comprehensible.

In 1873, the second of Wise's dreams came true. In that year, delegates from thirty-four Reform congregations voted to establish the Union of American Hebrew Congregations, with one of its main objectives being the unification of all Reform programs. It was the first cohesive Jewish religious body in American history.

Indefatigably Wise now pushed for his third objective, a rabbinic college. "Let us educate our ministers here, in our own colleges," he said, "and soon we will have American ministers, American congregations." In 1855 he opened Zion College with fourteen students, but it failed. The indifference was still too great.

Luck succeeded where diligence had not. In 1874, Henry Adler of Lawrenceburg, Indiana, contributed ten thousand dollars to found a rabbinic college. And so, in 1875, Hebrew Union College in Cincinnati, the first rabbinic college to succeed in the United States, formally opened with thirteen noisy students, including an eleven-year-old girl. As the rabbinate was still not a reputable profession in America, most of the students were recruited from orphanages and slums. The girl was allowed to enroll to increase the size of the student body. She was among the nine dropouts, but the four who did graduate became the school's most distinguished alumni. The female student, however, had set a precedent, and Hebrew Union College was to be beset with the "problem" of women students, who were kept from graduating by alert College administrators who arranged a marriage to prevent an ordination. The College, however, no longer arranges marriages, only education. In 1972, the first woman graduated and was ordained.

The fourth of Wise's dreams, that of uniting all rabbis into one house of Judaism, was finally realized in 1889, when the Central Conference of American Rabbis was founded. Its goal was to effect a degree of unity, if not amity, between the Orthodox and the Reform.

By 1880, American Reform Judaism reigned supreme in the land. It had subdued the Orthodox, organized its own rambunctious congregations, established the first successful rabbinic college, and ringed the continent with a string of magnificent Reform temples. Of the two hundred largest congregations, only eight were Orthodox, and Reform did not even aspire to "convert" them, for, in their eyes, they were insignificant, lacking in money and manners. Like the Sephardi Jews in Colonial America, the German Jews regarded themselves as social leaders and the arbiters of culture. They had it made. And then, confident of total victory, they almost blew it. At the height of their glory, sheer folly, in the form of the *trefah* * banquet, delivered a blow below the belt, and intellectual arrogance, at a happening now known as the Pittsburgh Platform, dealt them a punch that almost took Reform Judaism out of its leadership role.

The fateful banquet was held in 1883 in Cincinnati, in celebration of the tenth anniversary of the founding of the Union of American Hebrew Congregations and in honor of the graduates of the first rabbinic class of Hebrew Union

---

* *Trefah* (from Hebrew, meaning torn) referred originally to an animal unfit to eat, presumably because it had died in pain. Through the centuries, the word came to be used for anything "not kosher,"—that is, foods not permitted to be eaten by Jews.

College. The banquet was also planned as a gesture of amity toward rabbis of every hue of observance, and a large contingent of Orthodox rabbis attended as a gesture of goodwill. To ensure that all dietary laws were observed, the banquet committee engaged a Jewish caterer. Alas, the caterer had a limited knowledge of *kashrut* laws. He managed to serve the assembled notables three sins in one elegant meal.

The great banquet hall was brightly lit as two hundred guests were seated around the glittering, festive tables. But the Orthodox who glanced at the menus could hardly believe their eyes. The appetizer was littleneck clams (on the prohibited list of foods since the days of Moses) to be washed down with Amontillado Sherry. Soft-shell crabs and a "Salade of Shrimps" (both also on the list of foods banned by Moses) followed the clams. For entrée there was a choice of "Sweetbreads à la Monglas" and "Grenouilles à la Crème"—creamed bullfrog (the latter on the top of the forbidden list). The dessert, an assortment of cheeses, was served with "Café Noir," black coffee, presumably out of deference to the Orthodox, who are not permitted to drink milk with a meal that includes meat.

When the elegantly dressed waiters brought the clams, the Orthodox took one horrified look at this *goyeshe* delicacy and stomped from this *trefah* banquet in a rage. Those who remained had all the clams, crabs, shrimp, and liquor they desired, for no less than seven "Spiritous Liquors" were listed on the menu. According to one graduating student attending the dinner, the rabbis of the graduating class got "comfortably obnubliated."

The *trefah* banquet unified the unorganized Orthodox forces and gave them the ammunition they needed to launch a counterattack. The Orthodox press fired salvo after salvo at Wise, the Union, the College, at anything Reform. Wise tried to placate the Orthodox by explaining that the caterer had been at fault, but this did not stem the onslaught. The opposition was driving for solidification of conservative and orthodox forces. After a year or so, however, the controversy simmered down. But the Reform rabbis thoughtfully provided new fuel for the fires of Orthodox outrage.

No one at this point had planned the Pittsburgh Platform. It was the surprise outcome of a Reform testimonial dinner where one of the speakers took the opportunity to blast away at the Orthodox as a regressive element in Judaism. The Orthodox answered with a counterblast at the Reform as "destroyers of Judaism."

Par for the course! Except that a new ingredient was added this time. As long as the American Orthodox rabbinate, schooled mostly in *pilpul* and dogma, had attacked the giants of Reform, it had been a farce, like parish priests attacking Isaiah. But now it was different. The Orthodox had imported an intellectual giant of their own, Hungarian-born Alexander Kohut (1842–1894), a leading European rabbi armed with Talmudic honors and a secular doctorate. With him, American Orthodoxy leaped from the oratorical bleachers to a box seat.

Though Kohut's father was a famed linguist, he nevertheless lived in such abject poverty in a small Hungarian village that Alexander was illiterate until the age of eight. But when, because of his extraordinary good looks, he was kidnapped by gypsies, and then recovered, the family decided to move to a town where young Alexander could be educated. By the time Alexander received his doctorate from the University of Leipzig, he was a noted orientalist and Talmudist. His rabbinic sermons were so renowned that Hungarian dignitaries and churchmen came to listen. He wrote prolifically on many subjects, but his magnum opus was an eight-volume dictionary of the Talmud, still a definitive work. After his appointment as superintendent of Hungary's school system, the prime minister named him to the Hungarian parliament as representative of the Jews. In 1885, Kohut was elected chief rabbi of the prestigious Ahavath Chesed in New York City; and he arrived just in time to throw himself into the Reform-Orthodox fight, armed with scholarship and chiseled phrases that maimed.

In a series of six lectures, imperiously entitled "The Ethics of Our Fathers" (the title a steal from the Talmud's *Pirke Avoth*), Kohut thundered out his thesis that a Reform movement outside the Mosaic tradition was a deformity. Boldly he called for the banishment of Reform from the ranks of Judaism. The gauntlet had been flung with force into the face of Reform.

The Reform leadership chose its own newest intellectual giant Kaufmann Kohler (1843–1926)—also an import from Europe, and also a descendant of a family of scholars—to answer the challenge. Educated in a string of the most prestigious German universities—Munich, Berlin, Leipzig, Erlangen—Kohler received his doctorate at the age of twenty-five. His early tendencies to reform eliminated any chance of a pulpit in Germany. However, after some desultory writing for German Reform periodicals, he accepted in 1869 a call to a pulpit in Detroit, Michigan. In 1871, he took the rabbinic post of Sinai Congregation in Chicago, where he introduced Sunday lectures as a supplement to his Saturday sermons. Ten years later, he became rabbi of New York's Beth El, and from 1903 to 1921 he was president of Hebrew Union College.

Alas, Kohler's scholarly counterattack withered under the sustained barrage of Kohut's barbed phrases. The Orthodox were jubilant. In desperation, Kohler hastily called for a meeting of the cognoscenti of Reform, and in late 1885 nineteen delegates, the elite of the American Reform rabbinate, met in Pittsburgh, where they structured their platform of disaster.

Though the hand was the hand of Wise (as chairman), the voice was the voice of Kohler (as leader of the radical wing of Reform). Dramatically, Kohler revealed the new Radical Reform theology—rejection of the Bible as a divine document, rejection of Mosaic legislation, rejection of *kashrut*, rejection of the priesthood, rejection of the concept of bodily resurrection after death, rejection of a hoped-for return to Israel, and a formal dismissal of the messiah.

"It's a declaration of Jewish independence," Kohler cried exultantly.

"Independence from what?" shouted a critic.

"Independence from Judaism," hooted a third.

Kohler made the same mistake at Pittsburgh in 1885 that the German Reform rabbis had made at Augsburg in 1871. Like the "Augsburg confession," the Pittsburgh Platform said nothing about faith, hope, and piety. It stressed the negative— what *not* to believe in, what *not* to do.

The Pittsburgh Platform represented the last victory of the radical wing of the German Reform rabbis, that element which was still German in spirit and disdainful of the American way. After 1885 American Reform began taking over, and inexorably overcame, those who wanted to "scientificate" Judaism. To his credit, after a brief flirtation with these Radical Reform *Wissenschaft Wunderkinder*, Wise returned to his American pragmatism.

The Cincinnati *trefah* banquet and the Pittsburgh Platform were to have great repercussions in American Judaism. They led to a counterreformation by the American Orthodox that changed Orthodoxy more radically in two decades than European Orthodoxy had changed in a millennium. These events also led to the formation of American Conservative Judaism. But these two movements properly belong to a discussion of the arrival of the Russian Jews, from whose ranks came the members of American neo-Orthodoxy and Conservatism. Wise did not live to see these changes. One Saturday afternoon in March 1900, he suffered a stroke and died a few days later.

In paying tribute to Rabbi Wise, one must look beyond his accomplishments, great though they were. His thoughts were shaped more by external realities than by inner convictions. His greatness lies in the perceptiveness that prompted him to shed the mantle of German *Wissenschaft* for the coat of American pragmatism. He was American in his thinking, and respected American traditions, intuitively understanding the nation's spirit. He was not a profound man or an iconoclastic one. He was a teacher, an administrator, an organizer. He perceived the drift of the times, seized it and shaped it, not in his own image but in the image of America. He did not create the American-Jewish tradition. He channeled it. He did create a consciousness of Jewishness, a sense of the Jews as a people with a mission, if not a destiny. He united America's Jews and enabled them to assert that they were Jews, that they were modern, that they were American.

Wise was never afraid to allow two contradictory thoughts to dwell in his mind at the same time. He could believe in science, but did not fear to tell scholars to stop meddling with the sacred books of Moses, at least with those parts he believed in. He rejected the authority of the Talmud, but he also rejected the authority of mere reason. Wise might be compared to the Gaonim of the Islamic Age (800–1100), who accurately assessed the needs of the times and invariably found in the Talmud the interpretations that served those needs best. In most of his major decisions, Wise, like the Gaonim, made the correct choice. He was the right man, in the right place, at the right time.

With his *Minhag America*, Union of American Hebrew Congregations, and Hebrew Union College, with his conferences and platforms, his writings, lectures, and exhortations, Wise structured a viable American Judaism for "Our Crowd" of German-Jewish immigrants. Had no "American Reform" been awaiting them, these German Jews would most probably have vanished out of Judaism, for it is certain that they would not have embraced a European-type ghetto Judaism. They would have done what German-Jewish intellectuals did in eighteenth-century Germany—where their only choice was between ghetto Orthodoxy and Western Enlightenment—line up at the doors of Christianity for passports into Western civilization.

Gracious, wealthy, and influential as the German-Jewish "crowd" was, it was destined to be eclipsed by a new, totally unexpected wave of immigrants—the Russian and East European Jews, who, by the sheer magnitude of their numbers, would threaten to obliterate the framework of the existing American Judaism. But far from shattering this framework, supported by a mere two hundred and fifty thousand American Jews, the 3 million immigrants were to be influenced by it. And this framework would perform the same function for the Russian Jews that the frontier had performed for the Colonial and antebellum Jews. It would strip them of their European past and clothe them in the American spirit. And, even more incredibly, the Russian Jews would become the catalyst in the American melting pot from which would emerge a new Jew—not a Sephardi, not a German, not a Russian, but an American Jew, a Jew who no longer identified himself by his European roots but by his new American bonds.

But, since the antecedents for this migration of Russian Jews lie in Russia and Eastern Europe, we must first examine the Jewish condition there, and then evaluate the impact America had on them and the impact they had on America and American Judaism.

IV

THE TIDAL WAVES OF IMMIGRATION (1880–1940)
The Russian Jews Are Coming

Sad Sacks and Intellectuals

THE HISTORY of the Jews in Russia is one of comedy and tragedy, paradox and folly. It often strains credulity, and sometimes flies in the face of Jewish "folk memory" of the Russian experience.

The first startling fact is that the Jews were in Russia over a thousand years before the "Russians." Another is that for the first two thousand years of their sojourn in that land—from 800 B.C. to 1700 A.D.—they produced little of any historic significance. History bypassed them with the same indifference that it did the Hottentots and the Eskimos. Then, in the last three centuries—from 1700 to the present—they produced a panoply of quixotic personalities who helped shape both Jewish and world history—a Baal Shem Tov and a Weizmann, a Vilna Gaon and a Ben-Gurion, a Trotsky and a Chagall. They also produced a coterie of world-renowned scholars, philosophers, poets, and writers who created a Jewish secular literature, and a host of Hasidic mystics and pietists who created a new religious Jewish literature. Most incredible of all, they produced a Russian-Jewish *Massemensch* (mass man)—five million *Luftmenschen,** of whom 3 million came

---

* Literally, "air men," people surviving with no visible means of support, living on thin but honest air.

to the United States, where they became the catalysts for the first Jewish-American Haskalah, or Enlightenment. Historically they played a greater role in the intellectual history of American Judaism than the Sephardi and German Jews combined.

How did the Jews get to Russia, and when? The truth sounds improbable, but history has a penchant for disregarding the laws of probability. No less a personage than St. Jerome states that Jews had been in "Russia" since the eighth century B.C. "The Assyrians," wrote St. Jerome, "had conducted the Jewish people in exile not only in Media and Persia but also in the Bosphorus."

In the sixth century B.C., in the aftermath of the Babylonian victory over Judea, a second group of Jewish exiles headed for "Russia." And six hundred years later, after the destruction of Jerusalem by the Romans in the first century A.D., came the third band of immigrants. From then on a small but steady stream of Jews trickled into that vast land mass between the Black and Caspian Seas. In the ninth century, when Swedish Vikings known as the "Rus" (Rowers) steered their bird-headed boats of prey down the rivers from the Baltic to Kiev, Jews were there to greet them.

A tenth-century Russian chronicler charmingly relates as gospel truth the story that Vladimir, the pagan Duke of Kiev, called upon three spokesmen of the three competing monotheistic religions in his realm to recite the merits of their respective creeds, so he could choose the best. The Jewish sage, explaining why the Jews were not in Jerusalem, repeated the doctrine so prevalent in Jewish Orthodox quarters today that "the Lord was wroth with our forefathers and scattered us all over the earth for our sins." With indignation, Vladimir thundered, "How dare you teach others when you yourselves are rejected by God?" * Whereupon he promptly embraced

* This is also the theme of Judah Halevi's work, Ha-Kuzari, in which Bulan, King of the Khazars, consults an Aristotelian, a Christian, a Muslim, and a Jew on the merits of their respective religions, but unlike Vladimir, chooses Judaism. Legends speak in many tongues and serve more than one master.

Christianity. With Vladimir, historic Russia was born.

We hear little of the Jews in Russia in the subsequent five centuries (1000 to 1500), as a succession of rulers expanded Russian frontiers and consolidated new conquests. But with the sixteenth century begins a two-hundred-year Russian-Jewish comedy of errors that culminated in a two-century tragedy of blunders. Around 1500, a fantastic episode catapulted the Jews into Russian history. Two Jews, who had been forcibly converted to Christianity, began to preach Judaism to the Russian peasants. To everyone's amazement, the Russians liked this version of their religion without Jesus and converted to Judaism in droves. Frightened, the Russian Orthodox Church embarked on a severe policy of stamping out this Judaizing heresy. Death was the punishment for converts to prevent recidivism; the Jews were expelled to teach them a lesson.

History hauled them back. With its annexation of parts of Lithuania, Russia acquired more Jews in the seventeenth century than she had expelled in the sixteenth, and the work of expulsion began all over again. But the Jews were back in Russia for a third time when Czar Peter the Great wrested the Baltic lands from the Swedes.

From the death of Peter the Great (1725) until the accession of Catherine the Great (1762), Russian-Jewish history was a tragic farce as six "musical chair" successors to Czar Peter expelled, readmitted, and reexpelled the Jews. It must be stressed, however, that most of these expulsions were motivated not solely by anti-Semitism but by xenophobia (fear of foreigners). Empress Elizabeth, daughter of Peter the Great, persecuted Muslims more vigorously than she did Jews. At her orders, for example, 418 of the 436 mosques in Kazan were burned.

With the accession of Catherine the Great begins the real history of the Jews in Russia, a tragic drama in which Russian despotism clashed with Jewish fanaticism, a drama in which good and bad intentions alike were eventually swept away in a tide of fear, hate, and revolution. We must understand this heritage to appreciate the magnitude of the subsequent Russian-Jewish renaissance in America.

Soon after her coronation, Catherine showed her liberal colors. In an edict concerning Jews, she stated, "Religious liberty and inviolability of property are hereby granted to all subjects of Russia, and certainly Jews also." New laws permitted the election of Jews to courts, to merchant guilds, and to city councils.

The "Jewish trouble" in Russia started with the three successive partitions of Poland (1772–1793–1795), which placed nine hundred thousand Polish Jews in her Majesty's lap. These Polish Jews were as different from the "native Russian" Jews as the Oriental Jews in Israel today are from its Western Jewish founders.

Though Jews had been in Poland as early as the ninth century, their period of greatness there dates from 1100, when Jews began fleeing the Rhineland in the wake of marauding Crusaders. Enlightened Polish rulers welcomed them, encouraging them to settle there and help build Poland into a modern feudal state. For three centuries the Jews prospered in Poland. They held most of the business and professional posts; they owned property, built beautiful synagogues, and were recognized as the prime commercial movers in a Poland where aristocrats never worked, priests never stopped praying, and serfs never ceased toiling.

This golden economic age lasted until 1400, when internal dissension and external invasion plunged Poland into chaos. The Jews now were relegated to a ghettolike existence, deprived of their former glory. By the time Poland was partitioned, Jewish learning in Poland had all but vanished. The century between 1700 and 1800 witnessed the nadir of the long slide of the Polish Jews into a dull stupor. These were the Jews Russia inherited.

Catherine, realizing that the Polish Jews were essential to the economy of the conquered territories, did not want to exile them. Neither did she want this illiterate mass of ghetto

Jews on Russian soil. She had enough illiterates in her own muzhiks. The decision was made to permit the "Polish Jews" to live in all the acquired territories west of an invisible line that ran from Riga on the Baltic to about Rostov on the Sea of Azov. This strip of land became known as the Pale of Settlement, or simply the Pale. East of that line, however, on the holy soil of Mother Russia, the Polish Jews could not settle except by special permission. But even within the Pale there were enclaves, like Kiev, Yalta, and Sevastopol, where Jews could not live except by such special permission.

Within a century of Poland's partition, three distinct Jewish societies emerged in the Russian Empire—a small, often rich, intellectual elite of some three hundred thousand favored "Russian Jews," permitted to live outside the Pale in the cities of Russia; a mass of some 1,700,000 urbanized, largely proletarian Jews, living in the cities of Russia-held Poland; and, last, some 3 million Jews doomed to a medieval existence in the Pale. Here these Jews vegetated, according to one viewpoint, or flourished into a rich *Yiddishkeit* (Jewishness) according to another.

The Pale was more stultifying to the Jewish spirit than the ghetto. The ghettos were generaly located in large Western European cities, where rays of secular culture now and then did break through to illuminate bleak streets and captive minds. But in the Pale the Jews were sequestered and isolated, mostly among illiterate Polish and Russian peasants. Here they led a degraded existence.

The Russians used the Pale as the Church had used the ghetto, as a means of isolating the Jews from the Christians. But both ghetto and Pale also inadvertently isolated the Jews from Torah Judaism. Here, in ghetto and Pale, the Jews, separated from the mainstream of secular learning, became fossilized. The once expanding Talmud atrophied in these cramped intellectual confines, and smothered the spirit of universal Judaism. It now concerned itself with hairsplitting *pilpul*, the art of extracting meaningless meaning out of passages in the Torah. In three centuries of ghetto and *shtetl* imprisonment, Talmudic deductions came to be more venerated than the original Torah passage.

And yet, in a cruel sort of way, this perversion of the Talmud by the pilpulists was a proper response to the challenge of isolation. Until the age of the ghetto and Pale, the horizons of the Talmud had always expanded. The ghetto and Pale constituted the first regressions in Jewish history; consequently the Talmud also regressed to accommodate the limited view from ghetto windows. However, it was still the same Talmud of Grecian, Roman, and Islamic times which had sharpened the Jewish intellect for over fifteen centuries. Thus, though its limited application in the Pale did maim the spirit, its study exercised the intellect while the Jews waited for a better day.

For those not familiar with how *pilpul* worked, let us cite but one example, of which there are hundreds if not thousands, to illustrate how Jewish life came to resemble a madhouse of obsessive rituals attributed to Moses and God.

There are 613 commandments in the Five Books of Moses. Of these, 265 are negative (clearly understandable ones like "Thou shalt not murder," or puzzling ritualist ones like "Do not mix wool and linen"). The other 248 are positive (universally meaningful ones like "Honor thy father and mother," or cryptic particularistic ones like the commandment to wear a fringed garment). The Talmud, however, has expanded these 613 commandments into thousands of other commandments, much as the American Supreme Court has deduced a great body of constitutional law from the Constitution. In the Pale, the rules of logic and reason whereby new Talmudic laws were deduced from the Torah were applied so tortuously that all too often the result was trivia and absurdity.

Though Moses says little about how to mourn, the pilpulists inferred innumerable new laws on mourning. For instance, during the first three days of mourning, mourners should neither greet anyone nor respond to a salutation. On the fourth through the seventh days, the mourners should not greet but should acknowledge greetings. From the seventh through the thirteenth day, the mourners may greet others but cannot be greeted. According to the pilpulists, the mourner's hair should not be cut for one year, unless it so alters his appearance that he would be subject to ridicule among people of different belief, in which case it was permitted to cut the hair after thirty days. Mourners are forbidden to bathe for thirty days, or to wash their hands and feet in warm water. Bathing in warm water is permitted after thirty days only if it is not done for pleasure.

None of these commandments can be found in the Torah, yet they were proclaimed to be God's holy words and were to be observed as religiously as the Sabbath itself. By 1700, the teaching of such *pilpul* constituted the essence of Jewish education in one-room classrooms known as *heders*, usually a room or basement in the home of an impoverished teacher. The curriculum was narrow, learning objectives limited, and teaching methods antiquated. This *heder* "transforms healthy children into sickly, nervous ones; and it has been said with much truth that the physical degradation of the Jewish masses is due in part to the baneful influence of this class of schools. . . . The *heder* teachers represent a copy in miniature of the medieval Inquisition applied to children." *

The Talmud Torah schools, the higher institutions of the Pale, present a still sadder picture. "Their programs consist of cold, hunger, and corporal punishment. They are filthy rooms, crowded from nine in the morning to nine at night with starved children, most of them clad in rags, their faces pale and sickly. . . . He who has not listened to the almost absurd commentaries of the ignorant teachers, cannot even imagine how little the children gain from such instruction. . . . They were scarcely less ignorant upon leaving them than when entering." †

The Polish Jews entered the Russian realm fighting among themselves. The Talmudists, in their hatred of the Hasidim,

* The Jewish Encyclopedia, volume 10; subject: Russia (pages 518–575).
† *Ibid.*

denounced them to the Russian police as subversives and traitors, while affirming their own loyalty. It is a sad commentary that under Catherine the Great, Paul I, and Alexander I, the Russian government had to protect the Hasidim not only from fanatic Christians but also from vengeful Talmudists.

But the real tragedy in the relations between Russians and Jews stemmed from the controversy over education. The irony is that while the Russians wanted to introduce a modern school system into the Pale, the Jews of the Pale clung to their antiquated *heders*, resisting every effort to impose any other educational system on them.

The showdown between Jews and Russians came in the nineteenth century, which was dominated by five Romanov czars (Alexander I, Nicholas I, Alexander II and III, and Nicholas II). These five czars are so entrenched in Jewish lore as bloody villains that any attempt to portray any one of them as a part defender or protector of the Jews is met with skepticism and hostility, no matter what the facts. Because what occurs in this century is crucial to our understanding of the twentieth-century Russian-Jewish happening in America, one must deal, if ever so cursorily, with this little-known aspect of Russian-Jewish relations.

The Romanovs had no consistent policy. Whim, not logic, dictated their actions. They gave too little, too late, or took away too much, too soon. Torture was abolished but a police state was instituted. Serfs received freedom but no land. Enlightenment was an avowed aim, but the masses were kept illiterate. A "Russification" program was imposed on all subjugated people, but political freedom was not granted. In fairness to some of these Romanovs, it must be stated that such behavior was dictated by the fact that the desirable was not always possible. No sooner did a czar promulgate a liberal policy than the nobility opposed it. No sooner was a restrictive policy enacted than a people's rebellion brewed. Too shortsighted and weak to have long-range goals, the Romanovs vacillated between liberalism and reaction, and they reaped disaster. In one century of ineptitude they succeeded in snatching Russia from the brink of enlightenment and plunging her into communism.

The Romanov policy toward the Jews was equally paradoxical. Jewish self-government was abolished, but citizenship was not granted to the Jews. They were urged into agriculture, but land for such enterprise was nearly as impossible for a Jew to buy as it was to induce a Jew to take up agriculture. Attempts were made to integrate the Jews into Russian society, but new laws herded them back into an ever-shrinking Pale. Educational institutions were opened for Jews but were rejected by them. Both czars and Jews were villains and victims.

Alexander I (reigned 1801–1825) inherited the "Jewish problem" when he inherited the Pale with over one million Jews who "lived a religious national life, narrowed and marked by ignorance and fanaticism." * Isolated, hostile, and suspicious, they refused to give up any part of their way of life. Alexander I, generally liberal during the early years of his reign, enacted a policy toward the Jews of "a minimum of restrictions and a maximum of liberties." He was also well disposed toward the Jews because they had not joined Napoleon when the French armies invaded Russia but had remained loyal to the czar. Little did his Majesty suspect the real reason for that loyalty. The Russian-Jewish establishment feared Napoleon's policy of emancipation from the ghetto more than they did the Czar's imputed anti-Semitism. They knew what had happened to the Jews of Europe's ghettos in the wake of Napoleon's armies. For political liberty, West European Jews had traded away their ghetto autonomy, an unforgivable sin in the eyes of the Orthodox.

But the Jews in the Pale had not foreseen that the Czar would borrow a chapter from Napoleon's book. Alexander did indeed plan to strip away the remnants of power remaining in the hands of the *kehillas*—the organized Jewish community having autonomous rights—to encourage agriculture,

* The Jewish Encyclopedia: Russia.

to establish a secular school system to supplant the *heders,* and to disperse the Jews throughout Russia after they had been taught new skills. In encouraging a fusion of the Jewish with the Russian population, a task labeled "Russification," Alexander "had in mind civil and cultural fusion rather than religious assimilation." * Seen from the Russian point of view, the policy of Alexander I was a sincere attempt to Westernize the Russian Jews in the same way Czar Peter had Westernized the Russian Christians. Whatever his intentions, however, the Orthodox Jews put up fierce resistance.

The Enactments of 1804, the first systematic attempt by Alexander I to introduce secular education system for the Jews in the Pale, were "marked by a humanitarian and tolerant spirit and provided for the admission of Jewish students to the general educational institutions of the Empire." †

These Enactments also stated that Jews would be granted the same degrees on equal terms in all branches of learning, including law, medicine, physics, and mathematics.

When these Enactments failed because of fierce opposition by Talmudists and Hasidim, a second plan was proposed— separate schools for Jews, where they would be taught not only Hebrew and Bible but also Russian and science. Russian teachers would be used only if Jewish teachers were not available. But this too was fanatically resisted, because it was believed that *heder* and *shtetl* Judaism would disappear if the system were adopted. And thus while 3.5 million Jews in the Pale fiercely resisted any secular education, the three hundred thousand emancipated Russian Jews outside the Pale—in Moscow, St. Petersburg, Minsk, Pinsk, Odessa—fought to get into schools of higher education in larger numbers because restrictions kept all too many out.

The experience of Isaac Bar Levinssohn (1788–1860), who advocated secular education for Russian Jews in the Pale, exemplifies the insuperable difficulties that confronted the czars. Born to wealth, and married into it, Levinssohn was a

* S. M. Dubnow: *History of the Jews in Russia and Poland,* Vol. II.
† The Jewish Encyclopedia: Russia.

renowned Talmudist by the time of his bar mitzvah. Early in life, he fell in with "bad company"—Jewish intellectuals—from whom he learned that there was a world beyond the Talmud. The fruit of this exposure was a satiric work on the Hasidim, in which he urged the Jews to acquire a secular education that would enable them to abandon their *Luftmensch* life for careers in agriculture, commerce, and the professions. For these heretic views, he was forced to flee his home town by the pressure and abuse of the Orthodox.

The Russian minister of Education became interested in Levinssohn's work and wrote him a letter asking thirty-four questions about the Jews. "Is it true," he asked, "that the Talmud forbids the study of foreign languages and science, as well as the pursuit of argicultural occupations? Do the Jews possess schools or learned books? How do the Jewish masses regard schools?"

His puzzlement at the opposition of Talmudists to secular education is evident, as is his puzzlement about the Talmud itself. "What is the object of the numerous rites that consume so much useful time?" he queried. "Can the condition of the Jews be improved, and if so, by what means? How can a Jew be admitted into Christian society and be accorded full civil rights when he keeps himself aloof from the Christians and takes no interest in the welfare of the country where he resides?"

These questions inspired Levinssohn to write another book explaining authentic Judaism and Jewish spiritual values to the Christians, a task that proved less difficult than selling secular education to the Orthodox. In this work, Levinssohn stressed the necessity of Jewish elementary schools for Jewish youth, to resettle them on land outside the Pale. For this he was denounced by the Orthodox as a "destroyer of Judaism." But he was listened to by Baron Edmond de Rothschild in Paris, who took Levinssohn's ideas and established agricultural schools and settlements in Palestine that gave birth to the kibbutz movement. Under the impetus of Zionism, former Jews of the Pale reclaimed that devastated land from two

thousand years of neglect and within two generations transformed it into an important agricultural state. But Levinssohn
died without seeing his hopes realized in Russia.

The oppressive policies that marked the rule of Alexander I's successor, Nicholas I (reigned 1825–1855), were aimed
primarily at the Russian people. The Jews were the secondary
victims of his despotism. His policy toward the Jews was not
anti-Semitic, since he did not wish to exterminate them, but
religious, since he wished to convert them.* His program was
threefold—to diminish the number of religious Jews in Russia
by conversion to Christianity, to educate them so they would
not remain an alien element in the population, and to train
them in agriculture and handicrafts so they would not be
concentrated in such occupations as saloon-keeping, peddling,
and usury.

The Czar's liberalizing and modernizing efforts did not
succeed because they were again vehemently opposed by the
Orthodox leadership, who saw them as a threat to their concept of Judaism. The Russian nobility and clergy sided with
the Orthodox Jews in this opposition, preferring with them
to keep all Jews ignorant of secular learning and in the Pale.
As the Czar was not strong enough to overcome the combined
resistance of nobility, clergy, and Orthodox Jews, all his well-
intentioned programs slid into oblivion.

After half a century of trying, the Russian rulers gave up.
In 1879 they abandoned their plans for an educational system
for the Jews. The victory of the Orthodox opposition to
secular education in the Pale was tragic for the Russian Jews,
for it kept them culturally but one notch above the Oriental
Jews in the Near East, and led the emancipated Jews of the
West to view them as the most backward element of Jewish
society.

* A distinction must be made between anti-Jewishness and anti-Semitism.
The first was concerned with converting the Jew to Christianity; the moment the Jew converted, he became an honored Christian. The latter sought
the extermination of the Jews, whatever he did. Conversion of the Jew is
not the goal of the anti-Semite, but his death is. Thus there is both a psychological and political difference between the two.

But where czars had failed, a totally new breed of Jewish "educator" succeeded. As the Western Enlightenment edged toward the Pale, it was transformed into a Jewish Enlightenment, or Haskala, which aimed at secularizing the unemancipated Jews of Russia. In this effort, the Maskilim, as the supporters of the Haskala were called, received unexpected aid from one of the great Talmudists of note to emerge from the ghetto experience—the Vilna Gaon of Lithuania (1720–1797). He was among the few Talmudists who criticized the pilpulists as narrowminded dogmatists, and though not a rabbi, he excommunicated the Hasidim, labeling them "ignoramuses." Interested in science since childhood, he urged his students to study science to enrich Judaism with its findings. As they began waging war on the Hasidim, the Maskilim found their best recruits among the Vilna Gaon's students.

Like Czar Peter's literally cutting off with a sword the beards and trailing skirts of his boyars to pull them into the orbit of Western civilization, so the Maskilim symbolically used the pen to cut off the earlocks and caftans of the Orthodox to drag them out of their obscurantism. In the end, the pen of the Maskilim proved as effective as Czar Peter's sword. But, while the Western Enlightenment had led the "Western Jews" to religious reform, the Jewish Haskala led many of the "Eastern Jews" to a rejection of religion. They turned either to Zionism or socialism, but not to Reform Judaism. Though affirming their Jewishness, those who came under the influence of the Haskala rejected organized religion. Some even turned to communism, rejecting Judaism as well.

Why did emancipation in the East take such a different course from that in the West? There were two basic reasons. The first was Napoleonic imperialism, which had dealt a death blow to Western European feudalism. The ghetto, as an independent religious enclave with specific rights and powers of its own, was abolished. But Napoleon's concept of a modern capitalist state had little impact on Russia; feudalism remained in force there and the political status of the Jews as feudal subjects remained unchanged.

The second reason is derived from the first. The modern Western European states regarded all their inhabitants, including the Jews, as equal citizens, though of different religions. Judaism was thought of as another religion, along with Protestantism and Catholicism. In Eastern Europe, however, the Jews were thought of not as a religious sect, but as a minority nationality among other nationalities.

Thus, in the West, where they were considered a religious group, the Jews turned to a religious solution for their predicament. Their revolution against the Orthodox led them to Reform. But in the East, where the Jews were viewed as a nationality, they turned to nationalism as a solution for their predicament. This road led them to Zionism and socialism.

We now come to a swift and chilling end of the Jewish chapter in czarist Russia. Russia was sick unto her Slavic soul. To heal it, Alexander II (reigned 1855–1881) turned to a Russian brand of nationalism known as Slavophilism, which held that Russia should turn her face away from the West and turn to the East to recover her original heritage. Like Hitler's subsequent creed of "one Fuehrer, one Reich, one law," the slogan of the Slavophiles was "one creed, one czar, one fatherland." As in Hitler's Germany, this philosophy was enforced by secret police and judicial torture. The Russian people reacted to terror with terror, and blew up Alexander II with a bomb. But instead of gaining an improvement, the Russians inherited something they had not believed possible—something worse—namely, Alexander III (reigned 1881–1894).

The new Czar appointed Konstantin Pobedonostsev to solve his Jewish problem, which he did with the formula "one third conversion, one third emigration, and one third starvation." To enforce this policy, Pobedonostsev initiated a series of expulsions, and pogroms that turned Jewish life in Russia into a nightmare. The enactment of the May Laws of 1882 triggered a mass emigration which would bring over 3 million Russian Jews to America during the subsequent four decades.

Nicholas II (reigned 1894–1917), Alexander's successor and the last of the Romanov czars, proved disastrous for Russia as well as for the Russian Jews. Dominated by a beautiful but ignorant wife, he led Russia to anarchy by answering with bullets the pleas of his people for bread. His policies brought him the communist Revolution and ultimately his death against a blood-spattered wall in Ekaterinburg, Siberia. And thus the Russian czarist empire came to an end with the bloodbath of the Bolshevik Revolution.

It was with World War I and the Bolshevik Revolution that the young Jews who had traveled the nationalist anti-Talmudic Haskala road split ideologically. One segment affirmed Judaism; the other rejected it. The former espoused Zionism; the latter, communism. Jews like Weizmann, Ben-Gurion, and Jabotinsky, who took the Jewish road, became secular messiahs, leading the Jews back to Palestine to found a Jewish state. Jews like Trotsky, Litvinov, and Kaganovich completely rejected Judaism and led their followers to communism under the delusion that they too were secular messiahs. But instead of leading the Jews to a community of freedom, they led them into the servitude of a slave state.

Those Jews who had turned to communism as a solution to the predicament of being Jewish soon discovered that by casting off their moorings in Judaism and Hebrew culture, they had abandoned the source of their indestructibility. Without Jewish faith, they were like Antaeus, unable to touch the "mother earth" that had given them their strength. These Jewish communists never perceived that under the rock of communist dogma incubated the seeds of anti-Semitism.

The Haskala, which had withered in Russia, was destined to bloom in the United States in the same way that the Reform Judaism that had failed to grow in Germany flourished in America. The arrival of 3 million Russian-Jewish immigrants in America opened a new and most important chapter of American Judaism.

The Great Confrontation

THE DAM BROKE in 1881.

That was the year the Russian Jews were coming. They came not as isolated individuals, but as families, entire villages, towns. They came by the thousands, by the tens of thousands, at the rate of thirty-five thousand a year for the next twenty years, a total of some seven hundred thousand bedraggled souls almost quadrupling the Jewish population in the United States.

Down the gangplanks they came, the confused, bewildered Tevyas and Rivkes, the injured and insulted masses of Russian Jewry, with tears in their eyes and hope in their hearts for a better future, if not for themselves, then for their children. Mixed among them were the odd lots—provincial Hasidim, fearful Zaddikim, arrogant Maskilim, scornful socialists, hopeful Zionists, emancipated intellectuals. From 1900 to the outbreak of World War I in 1914, Russian-Jewish immigrations swelled to a torrent, washing an additional 1,500,000 East European Jews to the shores of America. By 1918, there were over 2,500,000 Russian Jews in the United States, ten times the number of German Jews.

The German Jews in America watched with incredulity as the Russian Jews stepped off the boats. Were they apparitions from the Middle Ages, these wild-bearded, earlocked, black-hatted, caftaned, Yiddish-speaking Jews? The Russian Jews stared with equal incredulity at the well-groomed, clean-shaven, English-speaking German Jews, wondering if they were bona fide Jews or apostates.

As the German Jews continued to watch this ambulant mass of poverty, reeking of oppression, descend upon the land, their incredulity turned into fear, then into apprehension, and finally into pity. What should they do with them? What would the Christians think of this throwback breed of Hebrews? Little did these German Jews suspect that within one generation the children of the Russian Jews would spark an American-Jewish Haskala that would eclipse the intellectual achievements of the German-Jewish elite, and that within a second generation the Russian Jews would wrest dominance from them, just as in the previous century the German Jews had wrested dominance from the Sephardi elite.

The position of the German Jew in late nineteenth-century America vis-à-vis the Russian Jew is analogous to the position of the Western Jew in Israel vis-à-vis the Oriental Jew. Just as in modern Israel a small elite of Western Jews with a democratic tradition has absorbed a mass of illiterate and unskilled Oriental Jews of a feudal background, so the American-German Jews, also of a democratic background, absorbed a mass of equally illiterate and unskilled Russian Jews with a feudal background. And just as the dispersion, education, and integration of the Oriental Jews became the prime concern of Israel, which feared that otherwise they would degrade its civilization, so, for the same reason, the assimilation of the Russian Jews became the prime concern of the German-American Jews.

For a balanced judgment, we must view these events through contemporary eyes. Here arrives an amorphous mass of Russian Jews, directly from a sixteenth-century *shtetl* loaded with antiquated baggage. The mere thought of these Russian immigrants becoming ghetto transplants in America sent a shiver of fright down the well-groomed backs of the German Jews. The Russian Jews had to be dispersed throughout the land, educated in American ways, and integrated into modern society.

To wend our way through the tangled skein of events in

these four immigration decades (1880–1920), we must first briefly examine the economic, social, and educational adventures of these Russian-Jewish immigrants, and then see what happened to their *shtetl* Judaism as it clashed with German-Jewish fears and American-Jewish congregationalism.

For most of these immigants, who had experienced no cultural renaissance, the voyage from Russia to America was a thirty-day leap from a ghetto medieval age into a twentieth-century mercantile jungle. The Western Age of Enlightenment had passed them by almost completely. The names Darwin, Beethoven, and Renoir were as meaningless to them as the terms "democracy," "franchise," and "human rights."

As they stepped off their boats, they were swallowed into the vastness of America. Individually they became the forgotten people of history, the *Luftmenschen* of the world tossed by fate from Europe's Pale and ghetto prisons into America's freedom slums. They were absorbed by the sweatshops of New York, obscurely buried in candy shops, tailor shops, "mom and pop" stores in Boston, Pittsburgh, Cleveland, Chicago. They became cigar makers, pants pressers, buttonhole stitchers, peddlers who worked hard and saved their pennies. But in spite of joking about America as the *goldene medina*—the land of golden opportunities—they believed in the American dream.

Collectively, they quickly became an elite intellectual *lumpenproletariat*. They read not Mutt and Jeff but Marx and Schopenhauer. They discussed not sports but social theories. They did not attend horse races but crowded into night schools. Collectively they gestated a generation of Jews the likes of which the world had never seen. They arrived at a time when the frontier had been officially closed, and America had begun to digest the continent it had swallowed. Instead of being pioneers of the wilderness frontier, they became pioneers of the new urban frontier.

These Russian-Jewish newcomers did not ask for help. They went into the urban wilderness and earned their living through hard work and self-denial, and by storing virtues for the future. They did not "inherit" the Puritan work ethic, which was an outgrowth of the Old Testament. They simply reclaimed their heritage, putting it to work again, three hundred years after the Puritans. As soon as the Russian and Jewish forces that had held them down in Russia were removed, abilities that had been inhibited for centuries exploded in the heady freedom of America. What had taken the ghetto Talmudists centuries to achieve, the American spirit swept away in a decade, often in a year. The new immigrants of the 1890s quickly found the freedom that Rebecca Samuel had discovered in the 1790s when she wrote from Virginia to the folks back in Hamburg: "There is no rabbi in all America to excommunicate anyone. This is a blessing here."

To be Jewish in America, one simply declared oneself Jewish. No rabbinic certification needed; no passport of faith required. *Pilpul* was tossed out with caftans. The immigrants bought themselves store suits and soared into the free market of America, to fail or succeed. And the moment they found that the success word was "education" they stampeded to America's baptismal fonts, located not in churches but in public schools and universities.

While most immigrant parents remained garment workers and shopkeepers, they sent their children to school with the admonition to study hard and "make something of yourself." Thus, in 1908, though Jews constituted but 2 percent of the total population, over 8.5 percent of the college population was Jewish. Jewish representation in professional schools was equally impressive—13 percent of all law students were Jewish as were 18 percent of pharmaceutical students, and 6 percent of dental students. In spite of stringent quotas for Jewish admissions to medical schools, they managed to exceed by 50 percent the 2 percent quota their population "entitled" them to.

But even more amazing than the rapid rise in their educational levels were the new social patterns they established. Jewish slums showed few of the usual patterns of slum life. There were few Jewish paupers in New York City's almshouses. The percentage of Jews in prison populations was far lower than the percentage of Jews in the national population. Jewish homicides were almost nonexistent; infant mortality was well below the average, as was juvenile deliquency. No Jewish children were up for adoption. If a Jewish woman delivered a child out of wedlock, she preferred to suffer shame rather than sell or give away her child. Rarely could one find Jews in bars and poolrooms. They stayed home and played chess or went to museums or attended lectures.

The rabbis in the Pale had been powerful enough to keep the Russian Jews from becoming "Russified," but no rabbinic power could keep the Russian Jews in America from "Americanizing" themselves and "getting ahead." Just as peddling had not been the permanent lot of the German Jews, but a stepping-stone into retailing and banking, so the pushcarts and sweatshops were rungs by which the Russian Jews raised themselves into manufacturing and the professions.

The saga of Abraham Cahan (1860–1951) illustrates the life and death of Jewish socialism, a movement now all but vanished. Born in Vilna, Lithuania, Abraham Cahan was a typical *Talmudbocher* (Talmud student) who had been "corrupted" by the Haskala. After enriching his Talmud education with a university degree, he was swept by the currents of the Haskala out of Jewish religion into socialism, becoming better known among the Jewish radicals in Vilna than in Talmud circles. He loved the Russian language, but fate made him a Yiddish writer. In 1882 he came to the United States.

In the same way that Wise had founded a periodical in German to reach his German-speaking Jewish audience, so Cahan went back to the Yiddish he had rejected to reach the Jewish-speaking Russian masses in America. He founded the *Jewish Daily Forward*, the largest Yiddish newspaper of the time, which wielded great influence on the American-Jewish labor movement. He became an eloquent spokesman for Marxist socialism, and organized the first Jewish tailors' union. But brilliant though he was, he made the same mistake the Maskilim in Russia had made. He discounted the love that the alienated socialist Jews had for secular Judaism. He did not realize it was only their ghetto Judaism they wanted to forsake, not the Jewish spirit buried under its trappings. In the end, like *shtetl* orthodoxy, Cahan's socialism too was rejected.

But in the four decades from 1880 to 1920, Jewish socialism laid the foundation for an important segment of both the American labor movement and much of the social legislation of President Franklin Delano Roosevelt's New Deal. Whereas the communists viewed socialism as scientific materialism, the Jewish socialists thought of it as ethical humanism. They were impelled toward their social goals by moral indignation rather than by rational hate.

The garment district of New York was an ideal place to start a labor-union movement. The garment shops were miniature replicas of ghettos—dank, crowded, unsanitary sinkholes where men, women, and children worked twelve to fifteen hours a day to eke out a miserable existence. And here history played a welcome joke on these exploited Russian Orthodox Jews. The "ungodly" Jewish socialists led the pious toilers from the gloom of the sweatshop into the sunshine of the union hall. Here the new faith of "irreligion" was revealed to them by their socialist redeemers. The Jewish workers joined the socialist-dominated unions and voted the socialist ticket; they read the socialist newspapers, digested the editorials denouncing Jewish religion as the "opiate of the Jews," and then went home and lit the Sabbath candles.

The socialist leaders simply did not know how to counteract the forces of Judaism and American democracy. To neutralize the magic of Yom Kippur, for instance, they held "Yom Kippur balls." Instead of praying, fasting, and penitence, they offered music, dancing, and buffet suppers. But hardly anyone came, for that was the day most socialist party members made their once-a-year pilgrimage to the synagogue. Those who attended neither Yom Kippur balls nor Kol Nidre services went to the Yiddish theater, but booed an actor if he dared smoke on the stage on a Sabbath.

Instead of teaching their children the dogma of the proletariat, these Jewish socialists preached the dogma of capitalist success, and they sent their children to school to become doctors, lawyers, and college professors. The socialist leaders gave up the struggle and became respectably bourgeois. And so eventually died the Jewish socialist movement.

Parallel with the demise of the Jewish socialist movement, but unrelated to it, was the demise of Yiddish as an important language among the descendants of the immigrants. But before it vanished, the Russian Jews who had vegetated in the Pale sparked, almost overnight, a rich Yiddish culture in America. The newspapers and periodicals of the Reform were dull house organs compared to the spirited Yiddish press, vibrating with life and literary merit. The Yiddish theater, through a succession of talented authors, directors, and actors, made a lasting contribution to the American stage.

After World War I, this magnificent Yiddish culture began to collapse. When immigration dried up after 1924, Yiddish began to decline. With the death of an immigrant died a speaker of that tongue, a subscriber to the Yiddish press, and a Yiddish theatergoer. Today, the Yiddish language, press, and stage are almost as dead in America as they are in communist Russia. What Russia achieved with persecution, America achieved with indifference.

In the main, ghetto Judaism and Yiddish died, but not Judaism. The children of the Orthodox did not want to abandon the faith itself; they wanted only to wash away its ghetto taint. They wanted to be modern Jews. They discarded the outer trappings of *shtetl Yiddishkeit* and shopped for a new Jewish faith. While shopping, they reformed the Reform, rehabilitated the Conservative, revolutionized the Orthodox, gave birth to the new sect of Reconstructionism, and swelled the ranks of the "unaffiliated" into the largest Jewish "sect" in America.

The injection of this mass of immigrant hard-core ghetto orthodox Russian Jews into the elite Reform body was to have a major repercussion on American Judaism. The impact would be like a billiard ball run amuck, first striking, then struck, by other balls it had set in motion. Reform Judaism so influenced the children of the immigrants that, to retain their religious affiliation, their parents had to modernize their own observances. But Reform Judaism in turn had to "re-Judaize" itself to avoid being swept out of its dominant position. After a gestation period of sixty years (1880–1940), all the dissident elements of American Jewish society—Sephardi, German, and Russian Jews—coalesced to give birth to the first "American Jews"—Jews who viewed themselves no longer by their ethnic origin but by their common American heritage.

For an understanding of this emerging American Judaism, we must review the Jewish condition in America between 1880 and 1940, beginning with Reform, followed by Conservative Judaism, then Reconstructionism (a new, strictly American religious phenomenon), and finally Orthodoxy.

THE REFORM DILEMMA

We left Reform Judaism in a euphoric mood in 1885, sitting on its shaky Pittsburgh Platform. Not until most of the Reform membership had ideologically hopped off that platform did the Reform rabbis realize they were leaders with few followers. Then, with a reluctant voice, they called for the structuring of a new set of guiding principles.

What had happened?

In the 1880s and 1890s the German Jews had recoiled in horror at the tidal waves of Russian immigration. Not only American Reform, but American-born Orthodox as well, albeit silently, agreed with Rabbi Isaac M. Wise's remark that the immigrations should be stemmed. But when the Reform realized immigration could not be stopped, they rushed, to their credit, to the economic aid of the unfortunate, being careful, however, not to invite this "riffraff" to their homes or temples.

When one considers Reform Judaism in perspective, it must

be conceded that in spite of its shortcomings, it performed an even greater role in the early twentieth century than it did in the nineteenth. Just as Mendelssohn had stopped the emancipated ghetto Jews of Europe from lining up before Europe's baptismal fonts, so American Reform Judaism averted a Russian-Jewish exodus into agnosticism.

The Reform organized fraternal orders and councils to help save immigrant innocents from the pitfalls awaiting them. The National Council of Jewish Women was formed to prevent white slave traders from selling naïve immigrant Orthodox girls into prostitution. The Reform used the Young Men's and Young Women's Hebrew Association they had founded in 1854 to keep sound minds in sound bodies (and to keep those bodies out of the bordellos and gutters). And at the turn of the century, the Reform founded the first Jewish summer camps for the children of the Orthodox to give them a respite from the city slums.

In 1918 a conference of Reform rabbis introduced bold new ideas for social legislation, which anticipated some of the New Deal reforms of the Roosevelt era. In an age when all working hands toiled sixty hours a week, the Reform boldly called for an eight-hour day, a compulsory day of rest for all, and abolition of unrestricted child labor. They called for a fair share of industry's profits for labor, urged legislation for sanitary working conditions, and demanded arbitration in crippling labor disputes. Twenty years before the Social Security program, the American Reform rabbis also called for a government program of unemployment insurance and pension benefits for the aged.

Reform also proposed a sweeping ecology program. Quoting the Psalms (24:1), "The earth is the Lord's and the fulness thereof," they interpreted the words to mean that man was but a tenant on earth and had no right to despoil it. They called for ecological legislation to end the ruthless exploitation of the earth's resources by the robber barons of industry, and asked for humane treatment of animals and humane slaughter of cattle as demanded by the Torah. It is interesting to note that almost fifteen hundred years before, the Talmud had prohibited destroying food and banned other ecological crimes.

But though it was in the vanguard of Jewish social, moral, and ethical thinking, Reform Judaism had sunk into an empty spirituality, a victim of its own rationalism. It had all the proper transmitters—Hebrew Union College, Union of American Hebrew Congregations, Central Conference of American Rabbis—but little to transmit. Just as the excesses of the Protestant Reformation had led to a sterility within Protestantism as reformers threw out the good with the bad, so the excesses of the Radical Reform led to a sterility within Reform as its zealots discarded the beautiful with the archaic in Orthodoxy.

The first post-Pittsburgh Platform generation did not sense the coming spiritual emptiness of that platform, for it still had its memories of tradition to draw upon. But the children of that new generation lacked such memories. They had grown up in a barren religious world where all phenomena—spiritual, moral, physical—had neat scientific explanations that satisfied neither mind nor spirit. Here, paradoxically, the Russian Jews came to the rescue of the Reform, recharging their empty religious batteries.

The Reform Jews, who shunned the Russian Jews socially, came in contact with them professionally—as their doctors, lawyers, teachers, counselors, social workers. Through these contacts they were reintroduced to many Jewish customs the Russian immigrants had retained. A new generation of Reform began to find virtues in many of the ceremonies their parents had discarded. Sabbath candles again flickered in Reform homes, the sound of the Kiddush reverberated in Reform temples, and the bar mitzvah ceremony began making cautious, new debuts. This did not mean that Orthodox *shtetl* Judaism had won a victory and that Reform was in retreat. On the contrary. The new Reform generation had come to realize that their parents had thrown the baby out with the bathwater. Though they continued to let the *shtetl* water drain, they now rescued the baby. Reform congregations began to demand that their rabbis inject more warmth into Reform's "scientific" services.

By 1935 it had become clear to the Reform rabbis that they stood on a practically empty platform. Their people had long ago deserted it, and the Reform hierarchy realized the time had come to structure one that mirrored reality. Thus, in 1937, the Central Conference of American Rabbis convened in Columbus, Ohio, to bring ideology and people together.

We must pay homage to the versatility of Reform. It managed to bury the Pittsburgh Platform without declaring it dead. It did it with semantics. Whereas the principles of the Pittsburgh Platform were stated in negative terms, the *New Guiding Principles of the Columbus Platform* were stated in positive terms—*what to believe in*, not *what not to believe in*.

The Columbus Platform consisted of three parts: the nature, the ethics, and the religious practices of Judaism. The euphemistic terms "Israelite" and "Hebrew" were dropped for the succinct term "Jew." The harmony of Judaism with scientific truth was reaffirmed, while it was graciously conceded that man had a soul. While acknowledging the Torah, the Platform also acknowledged that the Talmud had some validity as a source for Reform Judaism. It also redefined the Jews as a nation as well as a religion—a people who, though loyal citizens of whatever land they lived in, were obliged to help rebuild Palestine as a Jewish state. Thus Zionism was officially recognized as an authentic Jewish movement.

The second part of the platform reaffirmed in modern language what Moses had proclaimed at Sinai—protect the children, the infirm, and the aged; uphold individual freedom; demand justice for the underprivileged and minority groups; insist on high moral standards; work diligently for the abolition of poverty, tyranny, and prejudice; be generous in charity.

The third section quietly demolished the Pittsburgh Platform. It reaffirmed the value of prayers, customs, festivals, and traditions and called for a greater and more dignified observance of the Sabbath.

Like most committee prose, the Columbus Platform prose was also dull. It contained no poetic expressions to stir the soul, no Isaiah-like allegories to lend it grandeur. But its ideas surmounted its pedestrian writing.

THE CONSERVATIVE EXPERIMENT

For many Jews in the Gilded Age of the late nineteenth century, Reform was traveling too fast and too far to the left. Many Jews who had fled to Reform before 1880 because they felt uncomfortable in the tents of the Orthodox began to feel queasy in the aftermath of the *trefah* banquet, and chilled in the shadow of the Pittsburgh Platform. It was all right, they felt, to eat a hamburger at a downtown lunch counter, or a steak at Delmonico's, but eating ham, pork, or snails—that was going too far. Discarding phylacteries and fringed garments might be pardonable. But holding main religious services on Sunday still seemed a desecration.

As these dissidents could not go back to Orthodoxy and did not feel at home in Reform, they solved their problem in a typically American Congregationalist fashion—they founded their own denomination. Thus was born Conservative Judaism, the hybrid progeny of a most unlikely triad of Jews: Sabato Morais (1823–1897), an Italian rabbi of Portuguese descent who had held a post in a London synagogue; Cyrus Adler (1863–1940), son of an Arkansas cotton planter who became professor of Assyriology at Johns Hopkins University; and Solomon Schechter (1847–1915), a Rumanian-born rabbi who taught Talmudics at Cambridge University.

Conservative Judaism began right at the top with the founding in 1887 of the Jewish Theological Seminary in New York City for the training of Conservative rabbis. Its chief founder, Sabato Morais, was as much a conglomerate product as the movement itself. Born in Leghorn, Italy, he was a cantor in a Spanish synagogue in London before coming to Philadelphia in 1851 to succeed Isaac Leeser in Mikveh Israel. A reluctant tolerator of Reform, he was one of the rabbis who had stormed out of the *trefah* banquet in 1883 and had been completely turned off by the Pittsburgh Platform. The time had come, he felt, to found a Jewish sect more modern than Orthodox and less radical than Reform.

By the sheer force of his personality, Morais obtained distinguished support for his Conservative seminary. But, though it had the proper humble beginning—a basement room in Congregation Shearith Israel in New York City and a first class of only eight impoverished students—it failed ten years later with Morais' death. Conservatism was an empty religion—a movement in search of both a creed and followers. Mere opposition to Reform and disdain of Orthodoxy does not a religion make.

But Conservative Judaism was to have a miraculous rebirth. The midwife in that resurrection was Reform Judaism, with the Russian Jews as the precipitating irritant. The Reform snubbed the Russian Jews socially because of their gauche manners and low economic standing, but they feared the radicalism the Russian-Jewish socialists were introducing to the American Jewish community. They also feared that all Jews in America would be tainted, in Gentile eyes, by this radicalism. This apprehension was not totally unjustified.

The Russian-Jewish immigrations caused a noticeable increase in social anti-Jewishness in the United States. The German Jews, who had moved with aplomb and relative freedom in Gentile circles as members of their clubs and guests in their homes, now found doors closed. As more and more Russian-Jewish immigrants poured into the country, more American Jews became identified with the Russian Jews. The "better" neighborhoods, clubs, hotels, and resorts became increasingly "restricted" to keep out Jews. The fear that this social anti-Jewishness would mature into anti-Semitism was real.

The need to tame and Americanize the "hordes" from Russia became increasingly apparent to the establishment Jews. As one social leader phrased it, "We have to teach them to distinguish between the Judaism of Isaiah and that of some obscure kabalistic maggid." But how was this Americanizing to be achieved? The solution was presented by Cyrus Adler, an intellectual semi-Orthodox Jew, to Jacob Schiff, a millionaire Reform Jew of Orthodox parentage.

Cyrus Adler had all the proper antecedents to represent the new, emerging American Jew. He was born in the unlikely place of Van Buren, Arkansas, son of a German-born cotton planter. Adler studied Assyriology at Johns Hopkins University in Baltimore, and after graduation compiled a long entry in Who's Who in America—instructor in Semitic languages at Johns Hopkins, director of the Ancient Near East Department of Washington's National Museum, and Librarian of the Smithsonian Institution. He was the founder of the American Jewish Historical Society, the Jewish Publication Society and the Jewish Welfare Board, and co-founder of the American Jewish Committee; he was editor of the *Jewish Quarterly* and the American Jewish Yearbook and was a member of the editorial board of the Jewish Encyclopedia. His success as a mediator resided in his ability to bridge the worlds of Orthodoxy and Reform.

Adler saw in the faltering Conservative movement the vehicle for the "redemption" of the Russian Jews, for he, as much as the Reform, feared their radicalism and obscurantism. Conservative Judaism, he felt, would be able to contain the large center of Russian Jews between the extremes of socialism and Hasidism. Just as Israel uses its army to "Israelize" the immigrant Oriental Jews, so Adler planned to use German Reform Jews to finance Conservative Judaism, which would serve as a tool to Americanize the Russian Jews.

Adler took his plan to Jacob Schiff. Being a good capitalist, Schiff shuddered at the thought of Russian-Jewish socialists; being a good Reform snob, he shuddered at the thought of Russian Jews in Reform temples. He wanted the Russian Jews Americanized, but not in his backyard. Schiff agreed with Adler's ideas, and with a group of other Reform notables (among them David and Simon Guggenheim, Leonard Lewissohn, Mayer Sulzberger, and Louis Marshall), collected a half-million dollars (equivalent to 4 million today) for the Adler project. The Conservatives now shopped for the best brains and talent this money could buy, and bought the best— Dr. Solomon Schechter—to shore up the faltering Jewish Theological Seminary.

Born Shneur Zalman in Rumania, of strict Orthodox parents (his father was a Hasid and the town's kosher slaughterer), Solomon Schechter went to a Hebrew school in Vienna and to Berlin University for Judaic studies. In 1890 he was appointed lecturer in Talmudics at the University of Cambridge, England, where he earned fame not only for introducing wit into his lectures but also for the identification of a fragment of an early manuscript of Ecclesiastes found in Egypt. His subsequent identification of thousands of fragments of Hebrew religious writings found in a Cairo synagogue brought him great renown.

Accepting the Conservative invitation, Schechter came to the United States as head of the Conservative Jewish Theological Seminary. He astutely concentrated on recruiting a distinguished faculty—among them Louis Ginzberg, author of *Legends of the Jews;* Alexander Marx, noted Jewish historian; Israel Friedlander, distinguished Arabist; and Mordecai M. Kaplan, the future "heretic" in the Schechter den of Conservatives. Schechter's own writings, especially his three-volume *Studies in Judaism* and his essays in the *Jewish Quarterly Review,* helped explain Conservative Judaism to the Jewish intellectual community.

Theoretically, Schechter's Conservative Jewish philosophy was founded on that of the German schools of Zunz, Frankel, and Graetz; but in spirit he was closer to the American concept of a practical accommodation of Judaism to contemporary life. Consciously or unconsciously, Schechter helped create a religious Judaism that suited the American environment, not the European. A traditionalist, he nevertheless admitted the possibility of change. In his view, such changes in religious outlook as were needed by the times would come through "the consecration of general use." Conservative Judaism would honor the historic, religious concepts of Judaism, the centrality of the Torah, the sanctity of the Talmud, the use of phylacteries, the keeping of dietary laws—but necessary modifications could be made. In simple language, this meant that the most popular elements in Orthodoxy would be retained, but all the rest would be negotiable by committee vote. Thus, in many respects, American Conservatism in 1910 resembled Reform in Germany in 1810—prayer in the vernacular was permitted, a modified prayer book was used, decorum was enforced, services were shortened, mixed seating was allowed. But fealty was also paid to Orthodoxy. Head covering was used, the *talit* was mandatory, *kashrut* was insisted upon. Schechter appeared to have steered Conservatism skillfully between the Scylla and Charybdis of Orthodoxy and Reform.

Everything Adler and Schiff had hoped for from Conservative Judaism was ostensibly realized. The vast majority of the membership of this newly structured sect was Russian-Jewish. Conservative Judaism tempered and ultimately transformed the *shtetl* orthodoxy of the Russian-Jewish immigrants. It funneled them into Conservative synagogues and kept them out of Reform temples and socialist meeting halls. In 1913 the Conservative movement became so strong that it broke away from its Reform benefactors. It went into business for itself by establishing the United Synagogues of America, which united the Conservative congregations the way Reform had united its temples.

With the death of Schechter in 1915, Conservative Judaism suffered a setback. The era of Conservative expansion was over, and, no longer sustained by Schechter's wit and fame, the leadership had to campaign hard to retain its members. While the Reform congregations were demanding more traditional Judaism in their religion, forcing their rabbis to become more "Jewish," the Conservative congregations were pressuring their rabbis for less orthodoxy and more reform. What emerged was a curious, unstated compromise between the orthodox-oriented Conservative rabbi and his reform-minded flock. The Conservative congregations listened to their rabbis with reverence on the Sabbath and then went on to ignore those laws they thought were out of step with the times. The average Conservative congregant who ate non-kosher food in restaurants, kept a semi-kosher home, and drove to the synagogue on the Sabbath had the best of both worlds—the world view of the Orthodox and the freedom of Reform.

Though the Conservatives were closer to Reform than to Orthodox in religious matters, there was still a vast social gulf between them. Most Conservatives were Russian-Jewish immigrants and their children. Reform was still the religious ideology of German, Austrian, and other Western European Jews. The blurring of the difference, and intermarriage between the two, did not occur at an appreciable rate until after World War II. But with the foundation of the Theological Seminary, the Conservatives had laid the basis for the renaissance of Jewish learning within the Western tradition.

THE RECONSTRUCTIONIST FANTASY

In curious ways do new Jewish religious sects elbow their way into history. Conservative Judaism, founded by an Italian Jew, funded by a German Jew, and expounded by a Rumanian Jew, was destined to give birth to a new Jewish sect, Reconstructionism, conceived by a Lithuanian Jew, Mordecai Menahem Kaplan (1881–   ). Kaplan took diverse strands of Judaism and wove them into a practical philosophy, a uniquely American Judaism that was to earn him the adulation of the alienated intellectuals and excommunication by the Orthodox. Born Orthodox, he was "heterodox" by the time he went to high school. Ordained a rabbi by the Jewish Theological Seminary, he was appointed dean of that seminary's new Teachers' Institute in 1909.

Kaplan got his inspiration for Reconstructionism from the Young Men's and Women's Hebrew Association. In them he saw a model for the future synagogue as a Jewish center for the integration of all Jews into one organization. In 1922 he put his ideas into action and founded the Society for the Advancement of Judaism, which served both as a synagogue and as a podium for his ideas. The publication in 1934 of his magnum opus, *Judaism as a Civilization,* created a sensation. In this book, Kaplan argued that Judaism had evolved to a point where it was no longer a mere religion—it had matured into a religious civilization. But the religious community, as the Jews had known it for the past two thousand years, said Kaplan, had broken down. A reconstruction was needed, a unifiction of all activities—cultural, civic, charitable, social, religious. The growth of Talmudics—"theological deadwood" as he termed it—had to be pruned from the living branch of Jewish culture to allow this new civilization to bloom. Religion, in Kaplan's view, had to be deemphasized and Jewish culture stressed.

Kaplan also held that the idea of a Covenant had been relevant only in the days of Moses, when the Jews were a nomadic tribe. It had no meaning for the present-day urban intellectual Jew. Kaplan felt that the Jews should accept the myth, mystery, and magic of the Jewish past and make them part of a new ritual cult, along with the Torah. Together, these would constitute the "sancta," the sacred objects of Judaism.

In Kaplan's world, one could be a rabbi without believing in the God of Abraham, Moses, or Isaiah. The Reform rabbinate had abrogated Talmudic law so that Judaism could be a denomination among other denominations. Kaplan abrogated Mosaic law so that the Jews could be just a people among other people. In his civilization, there was no faith, no supernatural, nothing divine, just ordinary folk improving God's handiwork.

In 1941, Kaplan published his own concept of what *halakah*—the Jewish Law—ought to be. His *Guide to Jewish Ritual* presented Mosaic Law as a "prepared table" from which each individual Jew could help himself to those laws he felt most necessary for his survival as a Jew. The Orthodox greeted this travesty of the Torah with silence. But Kaplan's Sabbath prayer book, published in 1945, was more than they could take. The Orthodox excommunicated him, a gesture that had as little effect on him as an excommunication by the Pope would have on a Baptist minister in the American Bible Belt.

Reconstructionism had little success because most of its best ideas were quickly appropriated by the Conservative and Reform. Although the Reconstructionists established a rabbinic college in Philadelphia in 1968, by 1976 they had but ten congregations.

And yet, within Kaplan's philosophy of Judaism as a civilization, with the synagogue as a Jewish secular center, may be the seed for a new American and world Judaism, a possibility that will be discussed in the final chapter.

THE FALL OF SHTETL ORTHODOXY

Never has so disastrous a defeat in so short a time been suffered by any Jewish religious sect as that suffered by *shtetl* orthodoxy in America. In less than six decades, from 1880 to 1940, 3 million Jews of Russian and Eastern European background, representing 90 percent of the Jews in America, lost the orthodoxy of their forebears, abandoned their *shtetl* culture and discarded their Yiddish language. It was not the Reform who toppled the *shtetl* religion of these immigrants, but something far worse. The final ignominy of *shtetl* orthodoxy was that the Russian Jews themselves just walked away from it. By *shtetl* definition, not more than 5 to 10 percent of these immigrant Jews or their descendants in America today would qualify as acceptable Orthodox Jews. The Orthodox hierarchy, like Belshazzar, saw the handwriting on the wall, but either it did not read it properly or paid it no heed until too late.

Until now we have viewed the Russian-Jewish immigrants as one group rather than as a cluster of different interests. In the freedom of America, this mass exploded along its political, nationalistic, and religious sutures into three large fragments. The socialist Jews became, as we have already discussed, a respectable bourgeois. The nationalist Jews, of whom we shall speak later, became the Zionists. The segment that concerns us here is the Orthodox Jews, and what happened to them.

What prevented America from becoming a fertile ground for *shtetl* Judaism was not the Reform or Conservative movements as much as the Congregationalist spirit of America itself. Just as the Western European rabbis had disdained coming to this *trefah* land until the mid-nineteenth century, so the elite hierarchy of the *shtetl* rabbinate disdained coming to America in the early phases of the Russian-Jewish immigrations. By the time they did come, most Americanized Russian Jews no longer viewed them as saints but as anachronisms.

The *shtetl* rabbis who did emigrate watched with astonishment their formerly docile congregants slipping from their sphere of influence. They watched sadly as beliefs nurtured through three centuries vanished in a decade. In the Pale, thanks to the feudal system, rabbis had had the power to control Jewish life. But in the American democracy, they had been rendered powerless by Article 3 of the United States Constitution. There was no pope or prince, no governor or czar, to complain to. And there was no way to prevent the Jews from entering those evil gardens of worldly knowledge—public schools and colleges.

American Jewish history repeated itself. What had happened in 1700 and 1800 recurred in 1900. Without a rabbinate from 1650 to 1850, the Jews in America had used an improvised, unstructured American *minhag* long before Wise published his structured one. As the Russian Jews began arriving without rabbis, they emulated their predecessors. When the Pale rabbinate arrived, it was too late. "Family purity had been erased from our lives," lamented a rabbi from Lithuania upon finding few Jewish women trekking to a *mikvah*. A generation later, odds were that neither did his daughters, who probably headed for college instead.

Unlike the Reform Jews, who simply ignored prohibitions they found irrelevant, many of the American modern Orthodox Jews unofficially reinterpreted prohibitions that had become overly burdensome. Previous Talmudists had defined driving a car, turning on electric lights, and answering the telephone as work, and thus these activities were forbidden on the Sabbath. The "modern Orthodox" think of them as pleasures, thus transforming former "sins" into *mitzvot* duties. For had not the Lord given the Sabbath to man for rest and pleasure?

These redefinitions were effectuated unobtrusively without learned Talmudists holding court. One Orthodox rabbi moved his small synagogue from the city of Cleveland to Cleveland Heights because of the influx of Blacks. However, since his congregants now lived miles away from their new synagogue and were therefore not within walking distance, few came to Sabbath services. Saddened by the sight of empty pews, the ingenious rabbi had a parking lot built three blocks from the synagogue so his congregants could drive on the Sabbath to the parking lot, but walk from there to the synagogue. Attendance jumped.

This is the way the new American *halakah* works—just as it did in the days of the Revolution. This was also in the spirit of the ancient Jewish sage who had stated, "Go see what the people are doing," by which he meant that a law which no longer is observed by the majority of Jews must be regarded as irrelevant. The motto, however, applies only to matters in which there is controversy about the Law, not to acts clearly forbidden by the Torah.

A fictional character, David Levinsky,* illustrates the rapid Americanization of the Russian Jews better than hundreds of individual word portraits could, for his story is their collective biography. David, a young yeshiva student, pious and learned, mostly in Talmudic minutiae, emigrates from Russia to the United States. He almost starves on the boat because he will eat only kosher food. On arrival he searches for and finds a

* Abraham Cahan: *The Rise of David Levinsky.*

Jewish synagogue, one that expounds the Judaism taught by the sages of his home town. Then begin the transgressions, one by one. First he cuts off his earlocks. Next we see him clean-shaven and dressed like a Reform Jew. Soon he finds night school more to his liking than the synagogue, and newspapers more interesting than the Talmud. His total inheritance of *shtetl* Judaism is cast aside, even before he becomes a successful garment manufacturer. But he never renounces his Jewishness.

The most revealing aspect of David Levinsky's story is how easily this transformation is achieved. There is no soul searching, no agonized second thoughts. It also illustrates how little staying power ghetto orthodoxy had, crumbling almost overnight in its first encounter with democracy and Western civilization.

Why were so many immigrants able to abandon ghetto orthodoxy with such ease?

Perhaps David Levinsky and his 2.5 million peers had no real faith to lose. For the multitude, the Judaism of the Pale was mostly a ritual of "do this but don't do that." All too often that was the sum and substance of the religious teaching for millions of David Levinskys. It endured for three centuries in the Pale because so few Jews dared ask or thought of asking "Why?" But in America the children of the immigrants did ask "Why?" As soon as this question was asked and the traditional answer, *Mi'tornisht* (It is forbidden to ask), given, the armor of six hundred and thirteen commandments, negative and positive, disintegrated.

The main blow to Orthodoxy came in a clash over education. The Orthodox had hoped to establish *heders* in America on the ghetto model. But most Orthodox parents, who had experienced the horror of the *heder* in Europe, refused to send their children to such institutions, even though myth still extolled them as a paradise of *Yiddishkeit*. And if the parents did not refuse, the children themselves did.

The diehard Orthodox had begun with high hopes. At the turn of the century, there were three European-style yeshivas clustered on Henry Street in lower New York. The first, Etz Hayyim, founded in 1886, had six teachers and an enrollment of approximately two hundred. The second was the Rabbi Isaac Elchanan Seminary, organized in 1897, with about eighty students. In the third, also founded in 1897, eight teachers taught two hundred and fifty students. When one considers that there were over a million Orthodox Jews in New York at the turn of the century, one realizes the enormity of the failure of Orthodoxy to attract less than five hundred students a year to its schools.

History was about to sweep these three dismal schools out of existence, when the totally unanticipated happened—not reform from the outside but a revolt from the inside. Between 1906 and 1908, Orthodox students at the Isaac Elchanan Seminary staged a series of strikes against the teachers, objecting to the antiquated teaching methods, to the narrowness of the curriculum, and to the obscurantism of the institution. They forced an assembly of rabbis to meet and adjudicate between them and the teachers.

The rabbis knew that they were witnessing the dying of the *shtetl* spirit. To the consternation of the diehard Orthodox the rabbinic board members voted for the students. It was a victory of American Judaism over that of the ghetto. It was freedom from religious tyranny. The stage had been set for a counter-Reformation and for the entry of the most unlikely character upon the Orthodox educational scene. He was Bernard Revel (1885–1940), a Lithuanian-born rabbi, who, after having made his fortune in oil in Oklahoma, returned to reform the *heder* in the name of Orthodoxy.

Revel had disdained a mere *heder* education. Arriving in New York at age twenty-one, in 1906, he enriched his yeshiva education by supplementing it with studies at New York University and Dropsie College. After "making it" in the Oklahoma oilfields, where he ran a refinery, he returned to New York in 1915 to serve as the head of the Isaac Elchanan Seminary. Having been a successful businessman, he had practical knowledge of modern organizational methods. His "baptism" in oil had washed away some of his fundamentalist ideas. His "sight" had been miraculously impaired—he could no longer see a danger to Jewish faith in the cohabitation of Judaism with science. He became a "subversive" who bored from within. He toppled the fundamentalists and made himself a power in the new modern American Orthodoxy.

After merging the Elchanan Seminary with the Etz Hayyim Academy, Revel undertook to enrich the new school's curriculum with Western science and humanities. The new school grew in prestige as an educational institution where Orthodox students could pursue a dual program of Talmudic and secular studies. In essence, Revel was pursuing the very same politics in twentieth-century America for which Levinssohn and Lilienthal had been reviled in nineteenth-century Russia.

In 1928, in the face of vociferous imprecations by the last of the European-style Orthodoxy, Revel founded Yeshiva College (now University) as an extension of the seminary. It became the first Jewish liberal arts college in the United States, thus trumping both the Reform and Conservative, which had no such institutions of their own. In 1927, the indefatigable Revel organized the Graduate School of Jewish Studies to confer ordination upon its students. No longer did the American Orthodox have to import its rabbis from Europe.

If Revel achieved the impossible, his successor, Samuel Belkin (1911–1976), achieved the improbable. Ordained an Orthodox rabbi in Poland, Belkin emigrated to the United States in 1929, receiving his doctorate from Brown University in 1939. His credentials now read like that of a Reform rabbi from Germany—he was an authority on the Talmud, Philo, and Hellenistic literature. Elected president of Yeshiva College in 1943, he enlarged the institution from a college with 850 students and 94 faculty members to a university with 8,000 students, a faculty of 2,200, and teaching centers throughout New York City, including graduate schools in science and social studies. Perhaps his most impressive achievement was the establishment of the Albert Einstein College of Medicine. In spite of dire predictions of disaster, he invited faculties of Jews and non-Jews, and even Reform Jews, without the walls of Judaism tumbling down.

Several attempts were made to quash the Revel and Belkin version of American Orthodox Judaism. In the forefront of the fight was the American branch of Agudat Israel, founded in Poland in 1912 by hard-line Orthodox of Germany, Hungary, and Poland. But the American Orthodox, divided as they were on what constituted God's word in every phase of Jewish activity, never achieved the organizational unity of the Reform and Conservative. Instead, the Orthodox splintered into three main groups.

The most important of the three is the Rabbinical Council of America, established in 1923. Over half of its members are graduates of Yeshiva University. It is concerned mainly with family problems and rulings on policy for its nine hundred affiliated synagogues. The second largest is also the oldest, the Union of Orthodox Jewish Congregations (1898), claiming nine hundred affiliated and eight hundred satellite synagogues, which it services with advice. Most of its members are, however, quite small. The Union is also involved in questions concerning *kashrut*. It is a nonforce in American-Jewish cultural life. Finally, there is the Union of Orthodox Rabbis of the United States and Canada (1902), also with about nine hundred members. Militantly Orthodox, it opposes any cooperation with the non-Orthodox, and provides rabbinic leadership for the surviving synagogues with an Eastern European flavor.

The Orthodox European-oriented rabbinate was doomed by the American spirit of congregationalism. In Orthodox synagogues, as in Reform and Conservative, the power was usually held by the president, not the rabbi. These lay leaders realized that if they did not Americanize their institutions, their congregants would leave. They had to innovate or go out of business, and innovate they did. Decorum in Sabbath services was enforced. The sale of the privilege of being called up to give the Torah blessing was banned. The liturgy was modernized, prayers shortened, and sermons given in the vernacular. Many congregations that adopted these changes continued to call themselves Orthodox, but technically they are closer to Conservatism. In spirit, many are akin to the first Reform synagogues in Germany.

But the Orthodox counterreformation in the 1920s and 1930s came too late. Massive defections had already taken place. The extent of this abandonment of Orthodoxy can be judged by some statistics on education. Only about 20 percent of Orthodox children were receiving any kind of intensely religious education, and only 10 percent were receiving a European-style Yiddish education.

It is unlikely that more religious education would have stopped the flight from Orthodoxy. Statistics show that those with a Talmud Torah education dropped out of Orthodoxy at the same rate as those without it. The hundreds upon hundreds of synagogues established by immigrant parents were abandoned by their children. Had it not been for tens of thousands of new arrivals each year, European-style Orthodoxy would have all but disappeared before World War I instead of after World War II.

The policy of unrestricted immigration, which allowed Orthodox Jews from Europe to refill the ever-shrinking American Orthodox ranks, could not continue indefinitely. The day of reckoning came shortly after World War I. Statistics reflect America's general concern with the policy of unrestricted immigration. From 1820 to 1870, about 6,700,000 Europeans had emigrated to the United States. Of these, 1 percent were from Eastern Europe, and 99 percent (mostly of Anglo-Saxon and Nordic origin) from Western Europe. But from 1870 to 1930 a total of 25,500,000 European immigrants arrived on America's shores. Of these, 57 percent were from Eastern Europe.

Though antipathy to the flood of Jewish immigrations was also apparent in the sentiment against unrestricted immigration, anti-Semitism and racism were not the only motives. Americans were worried about the ethnic "character" of their nation. Should it be preponderantly Slavic and Catholic, or Nordic and Protestant? This is a legitimate concern of a country. Just as Israel wishes to remain a Jewish nation and therefore holds other religions to a minority status, just as Finland wishes to remain a Protestant Finnish nation, and Italy a Catholic Italian one, so America, by and large, preferred to be an Anglo-Saxon and Nordic nation.

But could the United States continue to absorb an unrestricted number of immigrants and maintain its ethnic character? The frontier was gone. No longer could it act as a catalytic agent in the transformation of Europeans into Americans. But a new concept—the "melting pot"—had risen to replace the idea of an integrating frontier. Would such a melting pot actually obliterate European habits of thought? Or would the immigrant Hungarians, Poles, Yugoslavs, Italians, Ukrainians, and Jews refuse to be Americanized? Would they insist on retaining their Old World cultural patterns, thus creating a balkanized nation where ethnic and religious groups would remain distinct and irreconcilable? *

In 1921, sentiment against unrestricted immigration forced Congress to pass the Quota Law, limiting immigration in any year to 3 percent of the number of each nationality according to the census of 1910, with a maximum quota of 357,000 per year. The Johnson Act of 1924 limited the number of each nationality to 2 percent, rolled the census back to 1890 and reduced the total immigrants for any one year to 164,000. As most Western European nationals had arrived before 1890, and most Eastern European nationals after that date, the Johnson Act achieved its intent—the preservation of America's Anglo-Saxon character. The act of 1924 effectively dammed

* Indeed, the melting pot did not work for long. After World War II, the ethnic minorities, both immigrant and native, began asking for "rights" not inherent in the Constitution and demanding government subsidies to perpetuate their ethnic minority cults. This gave rise to the "salad bowl" theory, which holds that though the lettuce, tomatoes, and cucumbers retained their "ethnic" individuality in the bowl, the salad itself would still be "American." But sociologists now ask what if the result is not an "American salad" but remains an "ethnic mix"? Could the continued unity of America be then taken for granted, or would it crumble in an encounter with hard times, as did the "salad bowl" Austrian Empire?

the stream of Oriental, Slavic, Mediterranean, and Jewish immigration.

With the stemming of Orthodox immigration, the Americanization process of those already in the United States took over with a rapidity none had foreseen. By the end of World War II the terms Spanish, German, and Russian Jews began to lose their former social impact. Though these terms are still used, few take such national origins seriously. Though some German Jews still consider themselves the social elite of American Judaism, intellectual superiority has actually passed to the children and grandchildren of the Russian-Jewish immigrants.

Between 1933 and 1939 the Johnson Act provisions were waived to permit 157,000 Jewish refugees from Hitler's Europe to enter the United States. This group was to exert a great influence on American life, inasmuch as it represented a large section of Germany's intellectual elite—world-renowned academic leaders and scientists—symbolized by Albert Einstein. Their entry marked the transfer of the world's intellectual leadership from Europe to America, as evidenced by the increase of Nobel Prizes awarded to Americans.

From 1944 until 1959 immigration restrictions were again waived for an additional 192,000 Jewish refugees and other displaced persons from devastated Europe.

The third and smallest of these post-Johnson Act Jewish immigrations occurred between 1960 and 1970, this time consisting of 73,000 Jews fleeing Castro's Cuba and the Arab Near East.

These fewer than a half million new immigrants were quickly absorbed into the mainstream of American Jewry and quickly lost their "ethnic" tags. Most came with nothing but their memories and brains. But, like earlier immigrants, they were confident that if they did not succeed in America, their children would. Like their predecessors, those who spoke Yiddish soon abandoned it. The Old World Orthodoxy many brought with them was soon lost.

So far we have touched little upon the institutionalized religious life in the six decades between 1880 and World War II. In 1880 there were 270 synagogues in the United States, of which over 200 of the largest and most important were Reform. By 1895, the number of synagogues had increased to over 1,900; by 1937 it had mushroomed to 3,700. However, this proliferation was not necessarily a proof of Jewish piety. Henry L. Feingold has remarked that "The increase in religious buildings appears to be inversely proportionate to the quality of religious feeling therein."

By 1938, however, in spite of an increasing Jewish population, the proliferation of synagogues came to a standstill. Of the 4 million Jews in America at the time of World War II, Reform, Conservative, and Orthodox could each claim about 18 percent as members of their respective synagogues and temples. Allowing for the Reconstructionists, this left about half the Jews "unaffiliated"—or about 2 million people—as the largest Jewish "denomination" in the United States.

Yet these statistical labels are misleading; they do not disclose the real beliefs of the members. The terms Orthodox, Conservative, Reform, as far as religious practices are concerned, are merely proper names, not evaluations.

If an Orthodox Jew is defined as one who lives by the *halakah*, then such Orthodox Jews would constitute only 5 percent of all American Jews. The other 95 percent of those labeling themselves "Orthodox" are what Marshall Sklare has described as "nonobservant Orthodox." They are members of an Orthodox synagogue because they prefer an atmosphere of traditionalism. They are Jews who call themselves "Orthodox" not out of religious choice or observance, but out of social and cultural preferences. A truer definition of this group of Jews would be Conservative.

The situation is much the same among those labeled "Conservative." Most of the present members of Conservative congregations do not meet the prescribed requirements of the Jewish Theological Seminary, and they are therefore not

"Conservative" in the true definition of that term. In daily behavior they are actually imbued with the spirit of Reform.

The "Reform" label for the Reform is equally inaccurate. The number of members in Reform congregations is not a true indication of their religious beliefs. Many are unaffiliated in spirit, but have affiliated themselves with a Reform congregation for social ties and as a positive affirmation of their Jewishness. But, on the other hand, should the unaffiliated ever affiliate, it is usually estimated that 75 percent would choose Reform rather than Orthodox or Conservative.

The figure of 3,700 congregations is also deceptive. Some 2,000 of these congregations are classified as "Orthodox." Actually they are among the smallest and of little significance to Jewish life today, and few of them qualify as truly Orthodox. Since World War II, most have been relocated from the cities to the suburbs. As one wag expressed it, the Orthodox who had stayed away from their synagogues in the cities had fled to the suburbs, and now they had to build new synagogues in the suburbs before they could stay away from them, too.

Yet, in spite of this seeming disaffection from "faith," attachment to the synagogue persists. The function of the synagogue in American-Jewish life at this juncture of its history could almost be compared to the function of the "musical banks" in Samuel Butler's satirical novel *Erewhon*.

The country of Erewhon had two types of banks, the "commercial" and the "musical." The former were ordinary structures, bustling with business. The latter were epics in marble and gold, and always nearly empty. Here all transactions were executed with solemnity, accompanied by music. Though everyone in Erewhon dealt with the currency of the commercial banks, everyone pretended that the currency of the musical banks had a higher value, though nothing could be bought with it. The musical bank managers constantly complained that though their currency had higher spiritual value, less than half the Erewhonian population frequented their banks. The pillars of society mournfully sided with them, worked mightily in drives for new membership, yet kept most of their money in the commercial institutions.

"Yet, we do something not so very different from this even in England," observed Butler. Such a comparison could also be made today, not only of the relation of the Christian to his church but of the Jew to his synagogue.

Yet it is this mass of Jewish "unbelievers" who support most of the 3,700 synagogues and temples. These "membership Jews," believe they should be members, if not for themselves, then for their children.

"Has the synagogue become a graveyard where prayer is buried? Are the spiritual leaders of American Jewry members of a *chevra kadisha* (burial society)?" Abraham J. Heschel once asked. "Is it that the people don't care, or is it that the rabbis don't know how . . . to kindle a spark in the darkness of the soul?"

But perhaps today's Jews do care, and perhaps enlightened rabbis are now questioning the efficacy of old ways of keeping Jews within the orbit of Judaism. Perhaps they, along with their flocks, are in search of new paths to God. Perhaps Judaism is at the same crossroads today that it was two thousand years ago, when the old Sadducee Judaism was challenged by new economic, social, and cultural conditions. Then it was not Judaism that died, but Sadduceeism. Today, other economic, social, and cultural challenges confront the Jews. Could it be that now it is not Judaism that is dying, but Pharisee, or rabbinic Judaism as practiced in the past.

The frontier stripped the European Jewish immigrants of their Old World traditions and transformed them into Congregationalist Jews. The melting pot took over the job started by the frontier and obliterated the ethnic distinctions between Sephardic, German, and Russian Jews. These, however, were external, Gentile forces acting upon the Jews. In the twentieth century, a new force, totally Jewish in origin and aims, molded the Jews. This new force was Zionism—a Jewish messianism disguised as nationalism.

Before we can speculate on what future American Judaism may become, we must first trace the origins of Zionism in Europe, then follow its flight to the United States, where, paradoxically, the Reform will lead the Orthodox back to Zion. Though it will be European agnostic Jews who ignite and fuel the Zionist Revolution, it is the American Reform Jews who will play an important role in creating the state of Israel. With that victory, American Jews will enter a new road to Judaism.

V

ZIONISTS ON THE MARCH
(1850–1950)
The Romantic Revolution

Revolt in the Shtetl

"Long live the King!"

That shout by one of the two hundred and one delegates attending the first Zionist Congress in Basel, Switzerland, in 1897, broke the silence as Theodor Herzl majestically walked to the podium. Then tumultuous applause greeted the founder of modern political Zionism. That night Herzl wrote in his diary, "In Basel I founded the Jewish state. Maybe in five years, certainly in fifty . . . everybody will recognize it."

Herzl was wrong. It took fifty-one years.

Before the conference in Basel, there had been a half-century of Zionist ideology; after it, there was a half-century of politics. But neither the thinkers nor the doers who achieved the miracle of a reborn state of Israel were the kind of people pious Jews had envisioned as assistants to the messiah.

History had disrespectfully chosen a most unlikely cluster of Jews for this holy task—alienated intellectuals, disenchanted Talmudists, romantic agnostics. The final ignominy, however, was the fourth Zionist musketeer on this "unholy" messianic team—the American Reform rabbi. No wonder some Orthodox, who believed that only a messiah sent by

God could lead the Jews back to Zion, first cursed and then vehemently denounced these worldly Zionists, before grudgingly accepting the *fait accompli* of a Jewish state.

Historically, the Zionists were the accidental progeny of a trilogy of events—an intellectual revolt in the *shtetls*, a new nationalism in Europe, and the emergence of anti-Semitism in Western civilization. In a theological sense, however, Zionism is as old as Jewish history. Seven hundred years before the Babylonian exile (586 B.C.), God had promised a return from that exile. Time and again the Prophets had also predicted an exile for the Jews and a return. And sixty years after the Babylonian exile, the Prophets Ezra and Nehemiah did indeed lead a band of Jews from Babylonia back to Jerusalem, thus constituting the first "Zionade" in history.

What the Prophets Jeremiah, Isaiah, Amos, Micah, and Zephania had prophesied had seemingly come true. Thus, when Jerusalem fell a second time, in 70 A.D., and a second dispersion took place, the Jews confidently looked for another redemption, this time by a messiah. This time, however, they had to wait not sixty but two thousand years.

While the Jews were waiting for the arrival of their tardy messiah, as promised in the Old Testament, the Christians were waiting for the return of their departed messiah, as promised in the New Testament. But as the first coming of the Jewish messiah materialized no more than the second coming of the Christian messiah, the Jews became impatient. They now tried to hurry history to fulfill their expectations. This created unanticipated consequences.

For fifteen centuries, the Jews were to be afflicted by a succession of colorful false messiahs—saints, charlatans, and fanatics who could not fulfill the hopes they had raised. Diverse though they were, all these messianic pretenders promised they would reunite the Diaspora Jews in the Holy Land. Without this central theme, no messianic pretender could even achieve a hearing.

That is, until the Ghetto Age. The startling fact about this period is that in three hundred years it produced no messianic aspirant with the avowed aim of leading the Jews back to Israel. However, ghetto Jews did have their messianic hopes raised twice—once by Sabbatai Zevi, and the second time by Baal Shem Tov himself. But Sabbatai Zevi was not a product of the ghetto—only his followers were. As for Baal Shem Tov, his followers did proclaim him a figurative messiah, but he never laid claim to that title nor felt a need to advocate a messianic return to Israel. In fact, the ghetto era was the only period in Diaspora history which produced no messianic pretenders. The Ghetto Age was completely Diaspora-oriented.

But in the end, the Jewish experience with the mysticism of Sabbatai Zevi and Baal Shem Tov had a beneficial effect. Sabbateanism and Hasidism, with their frenzied faith and flights from reality, had led the Jews into blind alleys with disastrous results. This caused an ever-greater segment of Europe's Jews to become suspicious of religious panaceas and redemption roads. They began to look for new, realistic escape routes out of the hell of their ghettos. Any secular Pied Piper would do. Even a Christian one.

And a Christian Pied Piper it was. When redemption from the ghetto came, in the late eighteenth and early nineteenth centuries, it came, as we have seen, through the new Enlightenment that swept the Western world. Culture-seeking Jews grabbed the outstretched helping hand of this Western Enlightenment that breached the walls of the ghetto and heeded its voice bidding them welcome into Western civilization. They did not wait for a Czar Peter to come and cut off their ghetto earlocks; they did it themselves. Side by side with the Christians, Jews flocked to the banners of Mazzini to free Italy from her foreign oppressors, and called themselves Italian Jews. Jews joined the revolutions and counterrevolutions in Germany, and called themselves German Jews. In Austria, Jews joined their Christian brethren, helping them to foment the Revolution of 1848 against the reactionaries, and called themselves Austrian Jews. The French Revolution freed the Jews from the ghettos of France, and they fought

as "French Jews" in the rebellion against the restoration of
the Bourbons. This experience of nationalism added a new
element to the Jewish consciousness. If Jews could fight and
die for Germany, Austria, and France, why could they not
also fight for a country of their own, for Palestine?

But this idea did not immediately explode into action. With
the fall of the ghetto, it seemed as though the millennium had
arrived for the Jews without the help of a messiah. Alas, it
was a mirage. The new paradise of nationalism contained the
virus of racism, which, after a fifty-year incubation period,
broke out in a deadly rash of anti-Semitism.

The carrier of this deadly virus was a seemingly innocuous
movement known as Romanticism (circa 1800–1850). It was
a revolt of poets, painters, philosophers—a revolt of artists
—against an increasingly mechanized and industrialized civilization in which individuals were treated as cogs in a social
machine. The Romantic movement was characterized by a
return to mysticism, to a dream world of unspecified yearn-
ings, a mystique of the soul rather than the reason of the
mind. This dream world was seized by rabid apostles of
nationalism, who wished to give their ideologies roots reaching into the distant past, back into legend and myth, back to
racial origins, the mystique of "blood."

Thus modern racism was born. In the racist philosophy,
citizenship is not determined by a birth certificate but by
racial origin. In the past, anti-Jewishness had been based on
religion and could be overcome by conversion; but the Jews
could do nothing about anti-Semitism because they could not
exchange their "Semitic" origin for a "Nordic" one. Racism
offered no options to the Jews—the "final solution" was death.

Thus nationalism, the hope of the humanists, was transformed within one century into racism. A totally new challenge had been hurled at the Jews, demanding a totally new
response. It would eventually demand the firing of the old
Jewish peace messiah and the hiring of a militant messiah—the
reverse of an action taken some two thousand years before
when another catastrophe had faced the Jews.

In Biblical days, the Jews had been scrappers who lived by the sword, ready to draw it at the hint of a threat. Their God had been an *Ish Mil'hama*, a Man of War. Fearlessly the Jews had fought Canaanites, Phoenicians, Assyrians, Babylonians, Egyptians, Greeks, Romans—losing now and then, but always bouncing back, sword in hand, shield at bay. A turning point in their history had come, however, in the first century A.D., after the destruction of Jerusalem in 70 A.D. by the Romans and the fall of Masada three years later.

It was at this point in their history that the Jews yanked the sword away from the "Man of War" and turned him into a Jewish "Prince of Peace." Jochannan ben Zakkai, leader of the Peace Party and opposed to the War Party, which advocated a do-or-die stand against the besieging Romans, defected to the Romans, making a deal with them. He, ben Zakkai, would work for peaceful coexistence with Rome if the Romans would grant him permission to open an academy for religious studies at Jabneh. Masada was the only Jewish island of resistance after the fall of Jerusalem, and the battle there ended with the death of every defender. Had the Peace Party not surrendered, all would have perished, as did the defenders at Masada. At that time, surrender was the correct response to the challenge of history, for, as noted, the Romans had not threatened total extermination, but demanded only political surrender.

For close to two thousand years, during the Diaspora phase of Jewish history, this accommodation had worked—a political surrender for religious freedom. The Jews lived stateless, successively in the Roman, Parthian, Sassanid, and Islamic empires, and in the Christian medieval world, suffering by and large the same disabilities endured by all minorities during those centuries. They had not been threatened with total extermination for being "Jewish." But in the nineteenth century, with the advent of racism, accommodation was no longer possible. Racism, unlike Romanism, offered the Jews no choice except death.

Modern history is recapitulating the drama of Masada with

a different cast of characters. Israel besieged is like a new Masada. Like the Romans, the hostile Arabs surrounding her threaten her political autonomy. What course should Israel take—that of Masada and hope for military victory, or that of Jabneh and hope for mercy? The Peace Party, in modern Israel, believes that Israel should surrender and trust to the goodwill of the Arabs; but today's Zionists believe that the only chance for Israel's survival lies in firm resistance and battle if necessary. At this juncture of events, history has shown that a messiah armed is called for—that the correct response is to stand on one's feet and fight instead of falling to one's knees to pray. As Israel has found out, the enemy of today, unlike the Romans in the past, gives no choice but ignominy and death.

What would the Jews, freed from the ghettos after a three-century imprisonment, do? Would they walk like lemmings to their death, following an obsolete peace messiah who did not hear the threats of anti-Semites, or, if they did, paid them no heed? Or would they snatch the olive branch from their two-thousand-year old Diaspora "peace messiah" and restore the sword of old to a younger, more militant successor?

Few, very few, Jews in the 1850s saw the coming danger. But those few who did laid the foundations for Jewish political Zionism. There would be no messiah, they said, until the battle was won. After the Jews themselves had regained Palestine, then, and only then, might the messiah arrive.

Three most unlikely Jews took the first steps to defrock the Diaspora "peace messiah," strip him of his olive branch and restore to him his sword. These three were among the first to perceive that there was an anti-Semitic doorkeeper at the gate of the Western paradise of Enlightenment. They were Moses Hess, (1812–1875), a disenchanted Marxist, who disabused the messiah of his rationalist hopes; Leo Pinsker (1821–1891), a dispirited assimilationist, who stripped the messiah of his illusions of a future brotherhood; and Theodor Herzl (1860–1904), the disillusioned dilettante, who lifted the messiah from the kneeling position to the standing, ordering him to get out and work for freedom instead of praying for it.

And suddenly, shorn of his earlocks and bereft of his caftan, the messiah was no longer a meek savior but the proud *Ish Mil'hama* of old. He heeded the lesson from Moses that not until force was applied did anything happen. Instead, this new Zionist messiah said, "Come let us go up to the mountain of the Lord, to the house of the God of Jacob and He will teach us of His ways." And the Jews followed him into Israel, and they built Hebrew University, and the Weizmann Institute, and the Hadassah Hospital, and they healed the sick and taught the lame to walk, and they again transformed a barren, cactus-infested patch of desert into a land of milk and honey.

Jewish liberals of the 1850s viewed the new anti-Semitism they were encountering as the final convulsion of a dying feudal order. Moses Hess thought otherwise. He was among the first to perceive that this nascent anti-Semitism had nothing in common with the old anti-Jewishness; that anti-Semitism was an outgrowth of the new nationalism and was maturing into racism. "Reform, conversion, education, and emancipation," he wrote, " . . . none of these will open the gates of society to German Jews." A Jewish state was needed, Hess said, "both as a spiritual center and as a future base of operations for political action."

Few heeded Hess's warning. His book, *Rome and Jerusalem*, published in 1862, attracted no attention; one hundred and sixty copies were sold, and then it was forgotten.

Leo Pinsker, after having flirted with assimilation, was the first to divert anti-Semitism out of the stream of normalcy and channel it into the diagnostic clinic of psychiatry, identifying it not as a political opinion but as a pathological condition. He viewed with contempt those Jewish liberals who thought prejudice could be cured with reason. Anti-Semitism, he said, was not a reaction to something the Jew did or did not do, but was the result of an aberration in the anti-Semite. Jews, he said, were fools to ask for justice, mercy, humanity;

such appeals were meaningless to anti-Semites. Nor should the Jews look to non-Jews for help; none would be forthcoming. It was time for them to save themselves. Pinsker's book *Auto-Emancipation* (1882) suffered the same fate as that of Hess's.

It remained for Theodor Herzl to liberate Zionism from the intellectual drawing room and thrust it into the arena of politics. He was a man with a magnificent obsession. He took Zionism away from the intellectuals and gave it to the people.

Theodor (Binyamin Ze'ev) Herzl was born in Budapest, Hungary. In 1878 his family moved to Vienna. Culturally he was a product of the German Enlightenment. He studied not Talmud but Roman Law; he aspired to be a playwright, not a rabbi. But history made him the leader of the Jewish people.

Herzl was a complex syndrome. He was intolerant, domineering, egotistical. He cut a majestic figure with his Oriental appearance and brooding eyes. His strength was his total ignorance of Judaism; his views were unclouded by interfering facts. Imperiously he swept all obstacles out of his way. He won because he was oblivious to all he was not. He once told Baron von Hirsch contemptuously, "You are a money Jew; I am a Jew with spirit. Your methods breed beggars." He once complained, "I am a general of *shnorrers* (beggars)." But his spirit made soldiers of them.

In his book *The Jewish State* he outlined his aspirations in precise details, including the design and color of the national flag for his as yet nonexistent state. He expected to be ridiculed, and he was. But he did not need his book for his task. His spirit paved the path. Just as the Maskilim had stirred the intellectuals into a rebellion against Talmudism, so Herzl stirred the Jewish masses into a revolt against the *shtetl*. He did not regard the ghetto Jew as a fount of *Yiddishkeit*. He wept for their state of beggary and held out to them the image of the proud people they had once been. He held out to them not hope but certitude that they could once again attain statehood if they willed it. With Herzl, one did not have to sing for one's supper. He offered redemption, not piecemeal but in one fell swoop. Herzl knew the Jews could not wait. He was "a prophet in a hurry" who imperiously swept history along to his will and conceit. With him, modern political Zionism was born.

After Herzl's death and the outbreak of World War I, Zionism seemed doomed. But two most likely candidates for the job of saving the movement appeared at the right time and met at the right crossroads. One was Chaim Weizmann, the twentieth-century relay runner carrying the Jewish Zionist gospel. The other was David Lloyd George, the twentieth-century relay runner carrying the Christian Zionist gospel—a belief that Christian, "especially British," destiny was intertwined with the fate of Palestine. Out of that encounter came the Balfour Declaration, which granted the Jews a homeland in Palestine.

Chaim Weizmann (1874–1952) was born amidst the *blote* of Motel, a godforsaken plot of mud near Minsk. Educated in Talmudics in the Pale, he later studied at German and Swiss universities. In 1904 he was appointed lecturer in biological chemistry at Manchester University in England, and he became the director of the British Admiralty Chemical Laboratories in 1916. Deeply influenced by the Haskala, Weizmann discarded his *shtetl* Orthodoxy, but in his heart burned a love of Jewishness. He joined the Zionist movement as a youth and by 1914 was the undisputed leader of one of the most insignificant movements in Jewish history at that time. There were only eight thousand Zionists in England, twelve thousand in the United States, and a few thousand in the rest of the world, fragmented and isolated because of the outbreak of World War I.

David Lloyd George (1863–1945), the British statesman who served as prime minister of England from 1916 to 1922, was a Welsh Nonconformist who had been brought up on the Bible. "I was taught far more about the history of the Jews than about the history of my own people," he wrote. As a millenarian, he believed that British destiny was to liberate Palestine from the Turks and to invite the Jews to settle there under British protection.

What drew Weizmann into the inner circle of the British government and involved him with the Balfour Declaration was his discovery of a process for producing acetone, a solvent desperately needed for the production of munitions, because German U-boats had virtually halted the import of Chilean nitrates.

There are four main versions of how the Balfour Declaration came into being: the Arab, the anti-Semitic, the Jewish, and the historic. According to the Arabs, the British handed Palestine to the Jews to get desperately needed dollars from the United States, which, they claimed, was controlled by Jewish financiers. According to the anti-Semites, the Jews outsmarted the British by tricking them into the deal. The popular Jewish version holds that the British presented Palestine as a gift to Weizmann for his discovery of the acetone process. The historic view is more complex. Though Weizmann's contribution did create a tremendous amount of goodwill toward both him and the Jews, many other political considerations went into the formulation of that declaration. An important one was the fact that so many members of the cabinet were also millenarian in spirit. Weizmann himself expressed amazement at these Anglican "crypto-Jews" who had discovered a Zionist policy of their own. Fortuitously for the Jews, the needs of the day permitted the British to combine that sentiment with politics.

When the Balfour Declaration was signed on November 2, 1917, and shown to Weizmann, he said, "We can hear the steps of the messiah." Actually, he heard the steps of his own doom. For with the signing of the Balfour Declaration, the Zionist scene abruptly shifted from England to the United States, where the slumbering Zionist party had come to life, seizing the leadership from the European Jews.

The main cause for this shift of power was perhaps Weizmann himself. He was a dashing, impressive man, with regal appearance and impeccable manners, a Semitic social lion who loved the ladies of high society. And he loved British democracy as much as he did Zionism. But he had a fatal astigmatism —he could not see beyond the drawing rooms of British aristocracy. He could not see the British Tommies, standing with naked bayonets on the periphery of empire, protecting that democracy. Weizmann put all his Zionist eggs in the British imperialist basket, and cracked them. He was torn between his total love of Zionism, and his total commitment to the British way of life. He could not contemplate that one day his beloved Jews might have to fight his beloved British. He was a Jewish Hamlet, immobilized by these two loves, unable to give up one for the other.

In the end, the decision was torn from him by David Ben-Gurion (1886–1973), an upstart from Plonsk, a dreary factory town in Poland. He was a pragmatic lion in the den of intellectual Zionist Daniels—tough, single-minded, unmoved by brilliant arguments that had no roots in reality, a man possessed with an instinct for the political jugular.

His father, a fervent Zionist, started his son on the road to Zion. At the age of fourteen, Ben-Gurion founded a Zionist youth group, was arrested twice during the Russian uprisings of 1905–1906, and when safe no longer, headed for Palestine in 1906. Here he joined the labor movement, helping to formulate its platform in a Marxist spirit. However, Marx would have rejected this "Marxist." Ben-Gurion demanded that his labor party members speak only Hebrew. He preached the doctrine not of an international proletariat settling in Israel, but only true Zionists. All else to him was empty verbiage.

With World War I, Ben-Gurion's name became inextricably interwoven with the struggle for Palestinian independence, and he worked unceasingly to create a party organization that could take over and run the state when freedom arrived. His creed was bold and direct—unlimited immigration for Jews into Palestine, the creation of a Jewish army to defend the rights of the colonizers, and the unification of all Palestine into a Jewish state. As one Zionist candidly expressed it, "Whenever the Arabs listened to Weizmann, they heard the drums of Ben-Gurion."

After World War I, Ben-Gurion saw that Zionism had shifted to the United States. That was where he headed with the Zionist ball, and where he almost lost it.

Ben-Gurion never visualized that it would be the Reform Jews who would seize the initiative, Americanize the Zionist ideology, and carry it first to the White House, then successively to the League of Nations and the United Nations, and in the end become the political implementers of an independent state of Israel.

That was and is the genius of the American Jews—to turn the ideological word into the pragmatic deed. Zionist history was now being made in America. And history did not even have the decency to blush at such a turn of events.

The Great Awakening

POLITICAL ZIONISM drifted into the United States in the 1880s, flotsam on the waves of the Russian-Jewish immigrations. At first, no one paid it much heed. Isaac M. Wise, usually so perceptive, missed its significance, calling it "Ziomania." His colleague Kaufmann Kohler regarded Zionism as a degeneracy, though nothing to worry about.

But by 1897 some five thousand American Jews were taking this new ideology seriously. That year, the Central Conference of American Rabbis passed a resolution denouncing Zionism. In spite of it, American Zionism became a national movement in 1898 when two Reform rabbis, Stephen S. Wise and Gustav Gottheil founded the Federation of American Zionists. From eight thousand members in 1900, it grew, in spite of formidable opposition, to over a million after World War II.

Opposition to Zionism came from one minor and two major sources. The minor source was the Jewish radicals, mostly socialists, who viewed the Zionists as reactionaries. Zionist nationalism was a threat to the Socialist philosophy of internationalism. With the rise of Nazism in Germany, however, the Jewish socialists defected to Zionism in large numbers.

A far more serious threat to the growth of Zionism in America was the opposition of Orthodox and Reform. Their stand against Zionism is similar to that taken by the Vatican against recognition of Israel. For close to two thousand years the Church has held that the Jews would not possess their homeland until they converted to Christianity. But in 1948 the Jews established the state of Israel without having converted. This placed the Vatican in a dilemma: Should it change its dogma to suit the facts, or should it hope for an Arab victory to substantiate its dogma?

Just as popes awaited the conversion of the Jews as a prerequisite for a return of the Jews to Palestine, so the purist Orthodox waited for the messiah as a prerequisite to lead the Jews back to the Holy Land. But instead of a messiah came the "ungodly" Zionists to mock their prophecy. To the purist Orthodox, Zionism was an evil conspiracy, a plot to substitute the will of man for the will of the Lord. It had to be resisted.

However, the advent of Hitler instead of a messiah, the arrival of a holocaust instead of a millennium, changed the minds of most purist Orthodox. They came up with two "escape clauses" permitting them to do so. Israel, they argued, had come into being not as a result of the Zionists, but as a gift from heaven. Furthermore, they averred, the new state of Israel did not represent the actual redemption; it was merely a beginning, which would be concluded by the real messiah when he came. Today, only a small segment of extreme right-wing Orthodox still refuse to recognize the legitimacy of the state of Israel.

Reform, meanwhile, was the prisoner of its Pittsburgh Platform, which had discarded the messianic concept of a return to Israel. Reform, too, was in the same dilemma as the Vatican: Should it cling to its dogma or renounce it? Reform lacked the wisdom of the Church to keep silent. Instead, it issued missive after missive denouncing the Zionists.

By the 1930s, the official Reform position had become even more untenable. Hitler had as profound an effect upon the Reform as he had upon the Orthodox. Few new members flocked to Reform banners. In 1935, a shaken Central Conference of American Rabbis, though not repudiating the Pittsburgh Platform, in effect nullified it by taking a neutral stand on the Zionist question. Finally, in 1937, the Pittsburgh Platform, which had denied the exile, denied Palestine, denied the messianic aspirations of the Jews, was repudiated.

Myths are hard to slay, however, and one unslain myth is that Zionist leadership came mostly from East European Jews, while American-born Jews, especially all Reform, closed their hearts to the Zionist cause. The truth is that without the American Jews—especially a segment of Reform Jews—there might not be a state of Israel today.

In the United States, as in Europe, the main Zionist leadership did not come from the Orthodox. It came from those who had given up Orthodoxy. But in the United States, top leadership also came from a source not present in Europe— from Reform rabbis who defied the Pittsburgh Platform and joined the Zionist ranks.

From the welter of American Zionist leaders, we have chosen four who, in our opinion, contributed the crucial statesmanship for final success. One is a Conservative, two are Reform, and one is unaffiliated. They are Henrietta Szold, who brought American women into the Zionist movement and made her organization, Hadassah, a dominant force in contemporary Jewish life; Rabbi Stephen S. Wise, whose impassioned oratory swept the Zionist question into the

White House of President Woodrow Wilson and before the League of Nations; Louis D. Brandeis, whose prestige gave Zionism a new respectability and opened to it the doors of men who make history; and Rabbi Abba Hillel Silver, whose magnetic oratory took the Zionist question into the White House of President Harry S. Truman and before the United Nations.

Henrietta Szold (1860–1945) is a unique product of the American soil, for, had she had been born and remained in her parents' Hungary, she might have matured into a kitchen matriarch. Fortunately for American Judaism, she was born in Baltimore, grew up in America, and became the general of an army of Jewish women who paved the way for Jewish women into other leadership roles in American Judaism.

Henrietta, the eldest of eight daughters, had an adoring father who lavished on her the attention Jewish fathers of that time usually reserved for their eldest sons. Though highly romantic, she never married. For fifteen years she taught French, German, mathematics, and botany at an elegant academy for girls in Baltimore, in addition to teaching religion in her father's synagogue.

The Russian-Jewish immigrants changed her life. She moved to New York City to help educate them and in 1907 joined a small Zionist Women's Auxiliary study circle, devoted to sewing garments for the settlers in Palestine. Two years later she visited Palestine. Enthralled by the country's beauty, but cast into despair by the misery of its people, Henrietta returned to the United States and in 1912 organized the Hadassah Chapter of the Daughters of Zion. In 1914, it became simply Hadassah, an independent organization of which she was elected president. In 1916 she organized medical units of doctors and nurses in a program to improve the health, medical care, and education of the people of Palestine. More than anyone or anything else, Hadassah has been responsible for Israel's hygienic, medical, and health standards, which are the equal of most advanced Western nations.

Hadassah served one other function—it transmitted Jewish culture. Under Henrietta Szold's guidance, the Hadassah assumed an educational responsibility to transmit the Jewish cultural heritage to Jewish children. It is probable that in the latter half of the twentieth century, under the impact of Hadassah and other women's organizations emulating it, Jewish women in general are better versed in Jewish history and culture than are Jewish men, and that most Jewish children receive whatever knowledge they have of Jewish culture by dint of their mothers' efforts.

While Henrietta Szold was affecting all American Zionism as well as American Judaism, our three male Zionists were concerned mainly with a Jewish state. Stephen S. Wise (1874–1949), the "first apostle to the Gentiles," * and Louis D. Brandeis (1856–1941), a "Puritan in spirit and conduct," were intellectual Zionist twins from 1910 to 1930. The marriage of Wise's oratory with Brandeis' prestige gave Zionism a legitimacy that opened hitherto closed social and political doors.

Born in Budapest, Hungary, of a famed rabbinic father, Wise was brought to the United States as an infant. Graduating with honors from Columbia University at the age of eighteen, and ordained in Vienna, Wise founded the Free Synagogue in New York, holding its rabbinic post until his death. In spite of his European ordination, his cultural equipment was American. He was a co-founder of both the National Association for the Advancement of Colored People and the American Civil Liberties Union. He founded the Jewish Institute of Religion in opposition to Hebrew Union College,† and the American Jewish Congress in opposition to the American Jewish Committee.

Wise was a formidable orator, incomparable in invective. He did not venerate logic and never aimed for total accuracy. Passion was his métier, and he could whip an audience into a

---

* He was the first American Jew to take the Zionist cause to Christian audiences.

† In 1954, that school merged with Hebrew Union College.

frenzy of concurrence. Wise was the Achilles of Zionism—always sulking in his tent, at odds with his colleagues. He had little tolerance for "cultural Zionists" like Ahad Ha-Am, whose pontificating essays he viewed as an opiate for the Zionists. Above all, Wise was a passionate Zionist. He was the co-founder of the first American national Zionist organization and a participant in every important Zionist infight. He made enemies wherever he could, and broke with Weizmann in the 1920s and with Abba Hillel Silver in the 1940s. But he was farsighted enough to seek non-Jewish support. Together with Louis D. Brandeis and Felix Frankfurter (a future Supreme Court Justice), he helped in the formulation of the Balfour Declaration text.

More than any other American Zionist, Louis D. Brandeis, because of his prestige, lured American Reform and the unaffiliated into Zionism. His parents had fled Bohemia in 1848 and settled in Louisville, Kentucky, where he was born. He attended high school in Germany, and was graduated from Harvard Law School. Brandeis made his fame by defending the common man against "the curse of bigness"—the utilities, insurance companies, and railroads. His crusades eventually helped secure the passage of this country's first minimum wage and maximum hours law. In 1916 he was appointed to the Supreme Court; he served as an associate justice until his retirement in 1939.

Brandeis saw himself as a product of American, not Jewish, history. Until he became a Zionist late in life—in 1912 at the age of fifty-six—he had never belonged to any Jewish organization, not even a synagogue or temple. His first official contact with Jews came when he undertook to defend the International Ladies Garment Workers Union, at which time he laid the foundations for the principles of mediation and arbitration in labor disputes.

Like Alexander the Great severing the Gordian knot with his sword, so Brandeis severed the Gordian knot that tied so many influential Reform Jews to the Pittsburgh Platform. His prestige was such that when he asserted that "there is no inconsistency between loyalty to America and loyalty to Jewry," it was accepted as a fact without debate. "Loyalty to America demands . . . that each Jew become a Zionist," he declared. And because the great Justice Brandeis said so, it became so. Together with Wise, Brandeis made Zionism "American." Together, they laid the Zionist cause on the desk of President Woodrow Wilson, a descendant of Presbyterian parsons on both sides, and a millenarian in spirit.

In December 1918, Wise, with a delegation of Zionists appointed by Wilson, headed for Paris and the peace talks at Versailles. At San Remo, Italy, where the conference on Palestine took place, the American delegation won—the Balfour Declaration was incorporated in the peace treaty with Turkey, with Britain as the mandatory power. If not for that confirmation, the Balfour Declaration would have been no more than a scrap of paper, for the British were having second thoughts about it. Deeply moved by the news of the treaty, Wilson exclaimed, "To think that I, the son of a manse, should be instrumental in restoring the Jews to the Holy Land."

The stage had now been set for the entry of our fourth giant of American Zionism, Abba Hillel Silver, the "Mufti from Cleveland," as Chaim Weizmann called him. A towering personality and a great leader of people, Silver was the chief architect of Zionist policy from World War II until the proclamation of the State of Israel in 1948.

Abba Hillel Silver (1893–1963) was born in Lithuania, the son of a Hebrew teacher who emigrated to New York in 1902. An ordained rabbi from Hebrew Union College in 1915, Silver took the pulpit of the prestigious The Temple in Cleveland.

Silver too was a passionate Zionist for whom Zionism and Judaism were one. "Zionism is not refugeeism," he preached. "Philanthropy alone is not the answer." The official stand of Reform against Zionism infuriated him, and in a speech that shook the planks in the Pittsburgh Platform, Silver exhorted,

"A messianic hope not bound up with the restoration of Israel in Palestine is simply not found in Jewish religious literature anywhere from the time of the Second Isaiah to our own time, except of course in the writings of these Reformers."

When Abba Hillel Silver thundered in wrath, even the "ass in its crib" and the Reform in their then Cincinnati headquarters took heed. The subsequent Columbus Platform absolved the Reform, like a political Kol Nidre formula, from all previous anti-Zionist vows. Total recantation, however, did not come until after the establishment of the state of Israel.

Silver had the mass of nonestablishment Jews behind him —Orthodox and Conservative, and some Reform. More than any other Jewish leader, he sensed the still-strong Puritan element in many American Christians and their belief that the Jews had a right to a homeland of their own. Deliberately he set out to mobilize this pro-Jewish Christian sentiment. More than anyone else, he was instrumental in the passage of Congressional resolutions favoring the Zionist cause. He reached the apex of his career as a Zionist leader in 1947 when he presented the case for an independent Jewish state to the United Nations. And he was among those who influenced President Harry S. Truman's decision to become the first head of state to recognize the state of Israel.

A casual incident shows how steeped Truman was in the millenarian spirit. In 1953 he visited the Jewish Theological Seminary and was introduced to its chancellor, Louis Finkelstein, as "The man who helped create the State of Israel." Truman responded heatedly, "What do you mean 'helped create'? I am Cyrus, I am Cyrus!" evoking the Biblical Cyrus, King of Persia, who made possible the return of the Jews from Babylonian captivity.

Zionism had triumphed. But Zionism had been more than just a response to a new anti-Semitism. It was also a Romantic revolt of the Jews against the dogmatism of the Talmud and the dry rationality of German-Jewish Reform. It was a revolt against the image of the "exiled Jew," the "ghetto Jew." It was a longing for a return to the roots of their own history, a yearning back to myth and legend, back to ancient Palestine where Jews were heroes, not *shlemiels*.

Instead of being led by artists,* as was the Christian Romantic revolution, the Jewish Romantic revolt was led by intellectuals who did not want to be "birth-certificate" Jews, that is, Jews certified by Gentiles as Russian Jews, Polish Jews, or Austrian Jews, by virtue of having been born in those countries. They wanted to be "Jewish Jews." Zionism gave them a sense of identity with their own past. Zionism was in fact the political extension of the Haskala in the same way that Gentile nationalism was a political extension of Western Enlightenment.

Though the Zionists in Europe and America had different motivations, they were both equally affected by this Romantic revolt. As the Orthodox religious spirit shrank, the Jewish national spirit expanded. Zionism filled the vacuum in the minds of those Jews who had rejected Orthodoxy but not Judaism. And thus came about the curious condition whereby the least religious Jews were often the most ardent Zionists, and the most religious Jews were often the most ardent anti-Zionists.

Both European Reform Judaism and Zionism were products of the West European Age of Enlightenment. Both provided escape hatches from Orthodoxy. Reform Judaism was the religious escape hatch of the Jews in Western Europe, and Zionism the political escape hatch for the Jews in Eastern Europe.

Reform Judaism was adopted in the main by those West

---

* The Jews had no artists of renown in the first half of the nineteenth century. But parallel with Zionism, there occurred the first Jewish revolt against Talmudic strictures on art. Art by Jews, which for eighteen hundred years of Diaspora life was a barren desert, suddenly, within half a century of the initial Zionist revolt, bloomed with such names as Pissarro, Soutine, Chagall, Modigliani, Epstein, Zadkine, Antokolsky, Lipchitz—all European Diaspora Jews who defied their peers and fled into art.

European Jews who had rejected Orthodoxy, but not Judaism. Having found acceptable religious values in Reform, they did not need the values of political Zionism. But those Jews in Western Europe who thought of themselves as secular Jews embraced Zionism for its political vistas. They wanted to establish a Jewish state modeled on the Western democratic state where they could cultivate their own secular garden, free of anti-Semitism.

The East European Jews had a different motivation. Because Reform Judaism had never penetrated into Eastern Europe, they had no religious avenue of escape from Orthodoxy, only the political road of Zionism. But the East European Zionists wanted more than a state free of anti-Semitism. They wanted a Jewish state where they could develop into authentic "Jewish Jews," not European Jews.

In America, none of this applied. American Zionists, by and large, were motivated by altruistic impulses and a sense of justice. Zionism as a return to Israel was not for them but for other Jews, the unfortunate ones. It was not the intention of American Zionists to settle in Israel, but they would fight for its right to exist and help those who wanted to go there.

Thus we see that the Western European Zionists were motivated by a desire to escape anti-Semitism and to live with dignity; the East European Zionists were motivated by a desire to create a place where they could be "authentic Jews"; the American Zionists were motivated by a desire to help both achieve their aspirations.

The Zionist situation in the United States, however, was even more complex because of the four Jewish sects of Reform, Conservative, Orthodox, and "unaffiliated."

The unaffiliated, who maintained their Judaism by "assertion" rather than by temple membership, found in Zionism a perfect ideology for strengthening their ties to Judaism. They could become Zionist leaders because they could affirm their Jewishness in this way without being bound to a religious sect or creed.

Jews who passionately embraced Reform had no need for the nationalist therapy of Zionism and therefore rejected it. For those Reform, however, who found establishment Reform too sterile, Zionism gave their Judaism a greater Jewish content. They became Zionist leaders.

The Conservative, who had no messianic dogmas to defend and no anxieties about their religious beliefs, produced few leaders of note, but they became passionate followers.

The purist Orthodox, ritually against Zionism but emotionally for it, were immobilized, thus producing neither leaders of distinction nor followers of note. As in Reform, the most vociferous Orthodox opposition came from within its rabbinic leadership.

The Mizrachi organization of religious Jews was a notable exception to the hard-line Orthodox opposition to Zionism. Founded in Vilna in 1902 to make peace with the Zionists, it created nothing but strife with its demands that the Zionists should have a voice only in political matters, not cultural. Peace was finally achieved in 1920, when the World Zionist Organization granted them autonomy in the field of education in Palestine. The Mizrachi thus became the base for the future religious party in Israel. The first American Mizrachi chapter was founded in 1911, but the movement in general had little significance until the 1930s brought the threat of Hitler and his brown-shirted Myrmidons. At this time an increasing number of religious purists joined Zionism via the Mizrachi. But it produced few leaders of distinction in the national Zionist organization. Most were reluctant followers, committed only to political and religious goals, not to social and cultural ones.

The "nonobservant Orthodox," on the other hand, became passionate Zionists, without the aid of the Mizrachi. With the Conservative, they formed the bulk of the Zionist membership. And thus came about an ironic twist in Jewish history. In the First Zionade, in the fifth century B.C., led by Ezra and Nehemia, it was the "godly" who led the "ungodly" masses back to the Promised Land. In the twentieth-century "Zion-ade," it was the "ungodly" Reform and unaffiliated who led the "godly" masses of Orthodox and Conservative in the drive for the restoration of Zion.

There is one more reason, however, why American Reform developed Zionist leaders, while both the European and American Orthodox did not. There was and is no such thing as "European Orthodox" or "American Orthodox." Both are "Jewish Orthodox" and would be so no matter in what civilization or age they resided, for the purist Orthodox still live in virtual isolation from all other cultures and are totally impervious to them. To them, therefore, the Zionist slogans of self-help had the sound of heresy. Their Talmud world called for them to let the messiah do the job of leading the Jews back to Israel. To the Reform Jews, on the other hand, the Zionist creed that if you want a country of your own, you should fight for it seemed eminently American. Thus the philosophy of the purist Orthodox tied them to inaction, whereas the philosophy of Reform led to action.

The birth of the state of Israel solved all problems for all sects. One no longer had to make up one's mind; history had made the choice. The Reform discovered, as Brandeis had assured them, that there was no conflict of dual loyalty—one could be American and pro-Israel. The Orthodox dis-covered, as their own rabbis now assured them, that no con-flict of dogma was involved—one could have the state of Israel first and the messiah later. Only two fringe groups were left out in the cold—the extreme right-wing Orthodox, still denying the legitimacy of Israel, and the extreme right-wing Reform, still proclaiming that Judaism was only a religion.

Whereas Zionism was a lifesaver for the European Jews, to the American Jews it was an emotional stimulant that awakened them to the centrality of Israel to Judaism. Though Zionism did not obliterate the divisions in America among the Orthodox, Conservative, Reform and unaffiliated, the catalytic effect of Zionism did accelerate the trend toward unification. It set American Judaism on a course toward a unity that will, as in the days of old, include all hues of Jewishness, from mild agnosticism to modern Orthodoxy. As for the radical right and left fringes, Judaism has always had the pleasure of their company since the days of Moses.

VI

THE UNIQUE AND THE UNIVERSAL
(1950 into the Future)
The Shaping of American Judaism

The Great Fusion

HAVING PARTICIPATED in America's Colonial history, in her Revolutionary birth in 1776, and in her expansion from the Appalachians to the Pacific; having participated in the War of 1812, in the Civil War, in World Wars I and II, and in the commemoration of her Bicentennial, how fare America's Jews today?

The twenty-three Portuguese Jews who arrived in New Amsterdam in 1654 have proliferated into 6 million. America has become the main Diaspora center, containing more Jews than all the rest of the world. American Jews have become the leaders of Diaspora Jewry. Their leadership helped secure an independent state of Israel; their resourcefulness helped Israel survive the initial shocks an independent state is heir to. In every phase of Jewish international life, American Jews occupy seats of leadership.

What is the economic status, the educational and cultural standing of these remarkable American Jews into whose hands history has placed the scepter of world Judaism? Are they drifting away from Judaism? Are they returning to the Judaism of their forebears? Or are they evolving new modes of expressing ties to a Judaism they cannot and do not wish to forsake?

Of all the transformation periods in American-Jewish history—the Colonial, the antebellum, the German Reform, the Russian-Jewish flood tide—the period following World War II is perhaps the most momentous. In a curious way it recapitulates an aspect of the American experience from the time of the Revolution to the closing of the frontier. Just as trappers fled the settlers who fled the townspeople as America expanded westward, so the white Christians fled the Jews who fled the Blacks in the upward-mobility race from city to suburb.

The immigration saga of the Jews in Cleveland, Ohio, illustrates this flight. When the first Russian-Jewish immigrants with their limited knowledge of lawn care settled among the Gentiles around Scovill Avenue before World War I, horrified Christians, watching their neighborhoods deteriorate, fled to the 105th Street area between Superior and St. Clair avenues. The next generation of Jews, swollen by new immigrants after World War I, fled the Scovill area as the Blacks pressed in upon them. To the horror of the 105th Street Gentiles, Scovill Avenue Jews resettled in their midst. This time the white Christians fled to Cleveland Heights and Shaker Heights.

But while the 105th Street neighborhood was blighted by immigrant Jews who did not know how to maintain property values, their children brought learning to the neighborhood Glenville High School, making it number one in scholastic honors but plunging it to the bottom of the football standings. After World War II, however, the children of the first 105th Street generation moved to Cleveland Heights and Shaker Heights as the Blacks crowded into the 105th Street enclave. But this time the Gentiles did not flee. The new generation of Jews were as conscious of property values as their Gentile neighbors; dressed in slacks or Ivy League suits, they were indistinguishable from them.

What happened in Cleveland's Glenville High School happened all over the United States. The percentage of Jewish high school students enrolled in colleges and graduated was twice that of the national average. The upward mobility of the Jewish immigrants was remarkable because they took such tremendous strides on such a broad front in such a short time.* Perhaps never anywhere else in the world has there existed a minority group with the status, diversity, and affluence of the Jew in the second half of twentieth-century America.

The statistical profile of the American Jew differs radically from the statistical profile of the nation as a whole.† Only 1.3 percent of America's 6 million Jews are farmers, and none are listed as farm laborers, as compared to 10.8 and 2.0 percent respectively for the nation. Another 1.3 percent of Jews are listed as blue-collar workers, none as "service workers," contrasted to 6.1 and 7.6 for the nation. Moving to the opposite end of the social scale, we find the reverse—only 27.4 percent of the nation's workers are listed as individual entrepreneurs, professionals, and in corporate management, but 68.6 percent of the Jewish labor force falls into one of these three categories. Only the Episcopalians surpass this Jewish achievement.‡

In income, too, the Jews (again with the exception of the Episcopalians) surpass all other ethnic or religious groups in America. Only 19 percent of America's household heads earn over $10,000 a year, but 33 percent of Jewish household heads are in this category. There is a similar discrepancy on the lower economic scale—21.1 percent earning less than $3,000 for the nation as a whole, but only 16 percent of Jews fall

---

* *Newsweek*, March 1971, gives the following statistics: College age youth in college: 80 percent for Jews, 40 percent for nation. College graduates: 17 percent for Jews, 7 percent for nation. Graduate Schools: 13 percent for Jews, 4 percent for nation.

† The statistics are based on "Economic Status," an article by Nathan Reich in *The American Jew: A Reappraisal*, edited by Oscar I. Janowsky, 1959—the latest available figures of this nature.

‡ *Newsweek*, March 1, 1971, has the following breakdown—in manual occupations: 22 percent for Jews, 57 percent for nation. White-collar occupations (including sales): 22 percent for Jews, 10 percent for nation. Professionals: 20 percent for Jews, 10 percent for nation. Managers, officials, proprietors: 35 percent for Jews, 13 percent for nation.

into that income bracket. By 1965, nearly half of the Jewish families in America enjoyed solidly middle-class status, having annual incomes between $7,000 and $15,000. By contrast, 44 percent of the total American population earned only $3,000 to $7,000.*

Jews populate faculties of colleges and universities at three times their proportional population quota. In the professions of law and medicine, this 3 percent ethnic minority represented 17 and 33 percent respectively.

But even more astounding than this advance in status has been the Jewish entry into the political, intellectual, and artistic fields—in law, politics, science, music, art, drama, literature—fields in which the American Jew was conspiciously absent until after the arrival of the Russian Jews. There had, of course, been exceptions, but by and large the cultural contribution of the Jews to the American scene from Colonial days to World War I was meager.

A generation after the arrival of the Russian Jews, however, Jewish political and cultural activities exploded. Suddenly there appeared Supreme Court justices, a host of governors and senators, cabinet members and presidential advisers who won fame in jurisprudence and politics. American-Jewish scientists became Nobel Prize winners. Jewish conductors, musicians, and playwrights dominated stage and screen. Jews composed the songs Americans hummed, wrote the novels they read, made movies they saw. Jews became painters, sculptors, and art critics. Few of these headline personalities were German-Jewish in origin. The overwhelming majority had an East European background. But even more noteworthy is the fact that few of them remained within the Orthodoxy of their parents; the overwhelming majority chose Reform or drifted into the unaffiliated.

How can one explain this one-generation jump from obscurity to stardom, from slum to affluence? What enabled them to achieve this eminence? One reason is that in spite of the constricted world of the *shtetl*, its ethics and emphasis on

* *Newsweek*, March 1, 1971.

learning implanted a thirst for knowledge in its denizens. The immigrants brought this attitude with them and implanted it in their children. Though Jewish values in America shifted from the Talmud to the worldly philosophers, learning itself was held in high esteem. In the Russian-Jewish family in America, a doctorate in physics was held in higher esteem than an executive title in the business world. Ironically, too, the very Talmud that Jewish youth were escaping had sharpened their minds and honed their wits. The burst of creativity was stimulated by the sudden release of the three centuries of pent-up energy in the heady freedom of American democracy.

Another reason was an economic one. The children of the immigrants wanted to escape the slums their parents were mired in. But where could they go at the turn of the century? By the time the Russian-Jewish immigrants began arriving, most of the top posts in steel, railroads, banking, and finance had been claimed by the Christians, and what was left had been staked out by the German Jews. The new opportunities were in retailing, entertainment, and the academic and artistic worlds—and that is where the children of the Russian immigrants rushed with their talents.

The flight to the suburbs and the invasion of the college campus played a crucial role in the erosion of the religious barriers between Reform, Conservative, Orthodox, and unaffiliated, and in the tearing down of the social barriers between Russian and German Jews. On campus and in suburb, the children of all Jewish sects met and married and begat children for whom the religious beliefs and social pretensions of their grandparents and parents meant little or nothing.

A fictitious Jacob Kantor family could epitomize the East European Jewish experience in America much as the Warburgs and Rosenwalds symbolize the German-Jewish saga. Jacob Kantor, born in Kaunas, Lithuania, fluent in Hebrew and well versed in the Talmud, migrated to America in 1890, settling in Chicago. Hearing fortunes were to be made in the South, he headed with his peddler's tray to the rural towns of

Hilo and Olney, Texas, where he found the roads paved with dust, not gold. One reason for his failures was that Jacob Kantor preferred to argue a *blatt* Gemara (a page in the Talmud) rather than make an extra sale.

But his three sons, though respecting their father's learning, preferred the extra sale. In 1920 they opened a dry goods store in Dallas, and their innovations in retailing caused their enterprise to grow into a national chain. The three Kantor brothers exchanged their parents' Orthodoxy for Reform and became community leaders and philanthropists. Their children, in turn, stepped mostly into the ultra-Reform or joined the unaffiliated; some intermarried, but none renounced their Jewishness. Some of Jacob Kantor's great-grandchildren are lost to Judaism, but more are rediscovering their Jewish identity through Jewish community activities, Hebrew culture, and aid to Israel.

We have seen how there has always been a reform element in Judaism that challenges the orthodoxy of its times. And there have always been dire predictions by the votaries of the status quo that Judaism would collapse if anything in it was changed. But, as we have seen, Judaism survived the successive abandonments of animal sacrifice, polygamy, and other practices. These customs, and others equally deeply rooted in past tradition, were easily cast off without affecting the humanistic, moral, and ethical core of Judaism.

Thus, after three centuries of experimentation, Judaism in America has not expired in spite of the majority of American Jews praying in the vernacular, not separating the sexes in synagogues, and not using phylacteries. Reform, which instituted most of these changes as a rebellion against *shtetl* practices, gradually assumed an existence of its own, evolving without a prepared program, into new forms.

According to Marxist dialectics, when a society changes its economic structure two events occur. First, relationships between social and economic groups begin to change, no matter what their ethnic origin or religion. When that happens, old institutions crumble because they are not geared to serve the

new demands. Then new institutions arise to serve the new
needs of new group interrelations. So, too, with Reform Judaism. The new modes of worship and the new institutions
serving Judaism in America were brought about by the new
social and economic conditions existing in America. Those
who opposed the changes became known as the Orthodox;
those who kept some of the old and accepted some of the new
became known as the Conservative; and those who favored
(and initiated) the changes became known as the Reform.

Thus it was axiomatic that Reform would be in the vanguard of almost every new development in American secular
Judaism. Reform innovated, founded, or paid for almost all
new American Jewish institutions or ideas—the Jewish Publication Society, the National Council of Jewish Women, the
American Jewish Committee, the American Jewish Congress,
the Synagogue Council of America, the Joint Distribution
Committee, the Young Men's and Women's Hebrew Associations, and innumerable others. Since these and others play
a central role in our assessment of what the future of American Judaism might be, we need to examine the origin and
growth of a few of these organizations to discern an important trend.

In 1820, an indigent Jewish Revolutionary War veteran
fell ill in New York City and some Jews decided to look
after him. After his death there was three hundred dollars
left. So the money would not be wasted, the benefactors decided to open a Hebrew Benevolent Society, independent of
their synagogue. The idea spread throughout American cities
with large Jewish populations. Rebecca Gratz had been in the
forefront of this movement. Jewish orphanages, old folks'
homes, burial societies began to mushroom all over the country.

The first all-Jewish hospital was founded in 1857, not by
accident but in self-defense. Zealous nuns, working in hospitals, loved to baptize dying Jews to ensure their "salvation."
Living Jews did not take kindly to this thoughtfulness. In
1870 the chain of Mount Sinai hospitals was begun not only

to prevent the baptism of dying Jews but also to provide Jewish medical graduates a place for internship denied them by most non-Jewish hospitals.

The years between 1865 and 1880 saw the greatest growth of these benevolent institutions. Behind this phenomenal growth was a "lodge mania." The Independent Order of B'nai B'rith was founded in 1843 by twelve poor, rather than the usual rich, German Jews. As B'nai B'rith grew, it needed ever more activities to keep its restless members occupied. The decision was made to "go into charities." This attracted more members, which in turn forced a greater expansion into further charities and good deeds. In 1882 B'nai B'rith went international, with a chapter in Berlin.

The first Young Men's Hebrew Association (YMHA) was started in 1854, without so much as a "thank you" to the Young Men's Christian Association (YMCA) on which it was modeled. Its chief function was to serve as a cultural conveyor belt for the transfer of Jewish immigrant youth from shtetl obscurantism into "Americanism." These YMHA's also proved to be a practical way of keeping Jewish youth off the streets, preventing them from becoming absorbed in the ranks of pimps and gangsters.

The National Council of Jewish Women, founded in 1893, combined social action with local service, sponsoring a wide variety of activities to help hapless immigrants. As early as 1911 it outlined a social legislation program—regulations for child labor, slum clearance, pensions for mothers, and pure food and drug laws. After World War I it helped refugees stranded in internment camps; during World War II and after, it helped victims of the holocaust.

To prevent the denial of civil and human rights to Jews all over the world, Reform Jews founded the American Jewish Committee in 1906. This organization was instrumental in alerting the world to the danger of Nazism and helping refugee Jews resettle.

The American drive for efficiency impelled the Jews to merge their small, proliferating welfare organizations into larger conglomerates. The first such merger took place in Boston in 1895, where funds were raised and disbursed jointly for all Jewish agencies in that city. This trend toward larger groupings of welfare agencies culminated in 1932 with the founding of the Council of Jewish Federation and Welfare Funds, or, simply, the Federation, which was soon recognized as the disbursing organization for social welfare for the total American Jewish community. Through the United Jewish Appeal, the Federation provides support for overseas Jews in distress, making it the single most powerful and effective civic world organization in Jewish history.*

But as Jewish organizational life grew stronger, Jewish religious life weakened. By America's Bicentennial, most American Jews did not attend synagogue regularly, though 60 percent were dues-paying members. Nor, except for Rosh Hashana, Yom Kippur, and Passover, did they observe Jewish holidays. They did not read the Torah, study the Talmud, or seek "Jewish solutions" to everyday problems.

Yet America's late twentieth-century Jews say they are Jewish, and they want their children to have a Jewish-oriented education. But they do not want to be identified with *shtetl* symbols, though they pay them nostalgic deference. They want new, relevant Jewish symbols. They are searching for a new survival script.

Of the three main Jewish sects in America, Reform Judaism has thus far been the prime force in getting things done, supplying most of the ideas, money, and leadership. Reform has remained in the vanguard of everything new in secular American Judaism. But it is no longer foremost as a Jewish religious sect. Nor is it any longer foremost in Jewish scholarship. Here the unaffiliated and Conservative have overtaken it.

Little change, however, has taken place in the Conservative community at large since World War II. In the 1960s, a group of Jewish Theological Seminary graduates did stage a minor revolt in an attempt to force sharper distinctions be-

* *The American Jewish Yearbook,* 1976, lists 328 national Jewish organizations and 235 Federation offices.

tween Conservative and Orthodox, but failed. Later, however, the "rebels" won some minor victories. Angered by the refusal of the Orthodox to recognize as valid divorces granted by Conservative rabbis, the Seminary sanctioned driving to the synagogue and switching on electric lights on the Sabbath, a case of *post hoc, ergo propter hoc*, inasmuch as the vast majority of its members were already doing so. In 1969, the second day of all festivals (except Rosh Hashana) was eliminated, thus putting the Conservative in line with Reform and the practice in Israel. The tendency among the Conservative has been for the leadership to become more orthodox and for the lay people to become more reform.

The purist Orthodox establishment has continued to maintain that it is the only authentic form of Judaism. Ironically, the Orthodox, who are most insistent that they have direct authority from God to interpret His intent, have been most plagued by conflicting claims among competing rabbis about just what the true word of God is. Thus all efforts to establish a central authority among the Orthodox have failed, each sect claiming it alone possesses the revealed truth.

Of the 6 million Jews in America, one fifth are classified as Orthodox, but this classification has no clear meaning. Two thirds of the Orthodox belong to what we have already termed "nonobservant Orthodox" who proclaim their holiness on the Sabbath, but do not practice many of the *mitzvot* a duly certified Orthodox member should. As in frontier days, the nonobservant Orthodox structures its own *halakah* by ear and convenience. Though they do not admit it, most in this group have already passed into Conservative ranks.

The remaining third is splintered into two factions, one ideologically headquartered at Yeshiva University, and the other clustered around small sects, mostly Hasidic. The intellectual leader of the first is Rabbi Joseph Dov Soloveitchik, professor of Jewish philosophy and Talmud at Yeshiva, who has captured the imagination and devotion of the young Orthodox intellectual elite. Soloveitchik represents the progressive wing of Orthodoxy, which holds that the Jewish Orthodox commitment calls for neither a withdrawal from the world nor for hostility between Torah and Western culture—as long as the two are kept separate.

The second faction, under various leaders, espouses different and mutually hostile paths to God's grace. Adherents number barely 25,000 to 50,000. Several Hasidic sects have captured the imagination of some young American Jews, some formerly mixed-up adolescents, drug addicts, and left-wingers. In this new Hasidism, they have found the escape they previously sought in asocial activities.

But purist Orthodoxy in America is in an untenable position. On the one hand it is attacked by its own right-wingers for condoning too much deviation from strict *halakah*. On the other hand there is a growing restlessness among Jewish youth who wish to be "modern" Orthodox but are disheartened at the slowness with which even Yeshiva Univeristy refuses to come to grips with the problems of the world. They charge the university with "moral isolationism" and an undue preoccupation with many meaningless aspects of the Talmud.

Thus, except for small losses or gains in membership, Reform, Conservative, and Orthodox are locked in about the same membership stalemate they were in before World War II.

A stalemate also prevails in the field of Jewish secondary education—from Sunday schools to day schools. Before World War II, enrollment (about 25 percent of all Jewish school-age children) barely kept pace with the increase in population. After World War II, however, enrollment increased by over 50 percent. Statistically everything looked beautiful. But there was a snake in this educational garden of Eden. Behind the façade of the smiling statistics lurked a grim truth. Though numbers had multiplied and quality improved, results declined.

Jewish education failed to keep Jewish youth Jewish. In fact, the more intense the Jewish orientation, the greater the rate of defection seemed to be. So, for instance, religious school enrollment plummeted from its high-water mark of

600,000 in 1960 to 400,000 in 1975, a loss of one third in fifteen years, and this at a time when the Jewish population in America increased from 4 million in 1938 to almost 6 million in 1975. The Jewish day school, held up as the ideal in Jewish education in the post-World War II era, did most poorly. Here, the largest segment of the student body comes from Orthodox homes; here the most intensive Jewish education is given. But after graduation only a small proportion remain ritually Orthodox.*

Why is Jewish youth unresponsive to the new education— smooth, modern, brilliant? Why is Jewish youth rejecting these efforts? We must recall that of the 2.5 million David Levinskys who came to the United States between 1880 and 1940, over 2 million abandoned Orthodoxy without forsaking Judaism. Yet the Jewish educational establishment is still trying to hammer into the grandchildren of the David Levinskys the articles of faith their grandparents and parents abandoned. Could this be what Jewish youth is rejecting?

All manner of reasons have been put forward to explain the rejection of Jewish educational institutions by Jewish youth—self-hatred for being Jewish; unwillingness to assume the burden of Jewishness; and even the absence of a little anti-Semitism to steel Jews for adversity.

Some sociologists do ascribe self-hatred to Jews who reject any aspect of outdated Jewish life. We believe, however, that a Jewish youth may dislike Orthodox ways yet love Judaism just as an Amish youth may dislike Amish ways yet love Christianity. In our view, neither one is consumed by self-hate.

It often seems as if Orthodoxy goes out of its way to prove that Judaism is a burden by adding more unnecessary burdens —a sort of Jewish mortification of the mind, in contrast to the Christian practice of mortification of the flesh. This was

---

* For an interesting and authoritative study on the subject, we refer the reader to *Analysis: Jewish Education for Naught: Educating the Culturally Deprived Jewish Child*. Institute Jewish Policy Planning, Washington, D.C., September 1975.

bewailed amusingly in the fourteenth century by Kalonymous bar Kalonymous of Italy, a scion of the famed Kalonymous family. In a social statire, *Even Bohan* (*Testing Stone*)
he wrote:

> Cursed be he who told my father the news . . . a son is born
> to you. Woe to him whose children are males. What a
> grievous yoke awaits them. Whole armies of prohibitions and
> commandments lie in wait for them—all the 613 command-
> ments, positive and negative. Who can fulfill all these? No
> man, no matter how diligent he may be, can withstand whole
> regiments. It is impossible to save oneself. One remains a sin-
> ner and lawbreaker.

Kalonymous did not know how lucky he was. In the next
four centuries, Talmudists would formulate thousands of new
commandments.

Kalonymous' works represent a genre of Jewish literature
ignored until modern times by Jewish history because it deals
with nonreligious aspects of Jewish life. Kalonymous, a master
of the Talmud, studied medicine and philosophy and was
conversant with Hebrew, French, Latin, Italian, and Arabic.
His goal was to introduce Arab scientific achievements to
Jews and Christians. He became a friend of King Charles of
Anjou, who sent him on a scientific mission to Rome, where
he became a popular figure among worldly Jews and Christians for his high spirits and satiric pen. The rabbis, enraged
at his Purim parody *Massachet Purim*, had the work burned.
It is an irony of history that one of the few surviving original
copies is to be found not in Israel or a Western democratic
country but in the Asiatic Museum in Leningrad.

All too many Jewish historians also portray the sum of
Jewish history as a dirge of anti-Semitism. Some have even
suggested that anti-Semitism has helped to preserve Judaism
because in times of trouble Jews tend to be "more Jewish."
Therefore, they contend, a little anti-Semitism might be good
for the Jews. But if an external force is needed to preserve
Judaism, is it worth preserving? Holding such a view would

be an admission that Judaism does not contain ideas which command loyalty, respect, and devotion. If so, Jewish children could, with justification, ask, "Why be Jews? What's so great about being despised, persecuted, derided? Why should we subject ourselves to all this for the sake of a tag if it signifies nothing?"

Judaism has persisted neither because of nor in spite of anti-Semitism. Judaism has endured because of its ideas and the impact those ideas have had on the world. Judaism has attracted anti-Semites precisely because its ideas are a threat to totalitarians everywhere, a threat to the enemies of democracy. Jews have remained Jews not because of self-hate, or burdens imposed upon them, or anti-Semitism, but because they are imbued with the values of Judaism. Jews realize intuitively that Judaism is greater than the definitions of ghetto scholars, grander than the content of Sunday-school curricula.

But Jewish youth are caught between two concepts of education. On the one hand they are offered what they do not want; on the other hand they are denied what they are looking for. Let us examine this paradox.

Whereas the task of rabbinic Judaism in the first fifteen centuries of the Christian Era, from ben Zakkai to Joseph Caro, had been to insulate the Jews from contact with the Gentile world, such insulation is not only impossible but undesirable in the modern world. Then it had been the correct response; now new challenges demand a new response. Today's Jews do not wish to be "protected" from Western civilization; they want to be a part of it.

This exclusion of secular knowledge from Jewish life was begun as an effort to insulate the Jews from the dreaded "enemy," Hellenization, which stood for worldly knowledge, for involvement in world affairs. There is, for instance, no rabbinic historic account of the Hasmonean Wars, the life of the Jews in the Hellenistic world, the Jewish War with Rome, or of the Jewish secular intellectual achievements in the Islamic Empire and feudal Europe, until the nineteenth century. Philo, though acknowledged by the world as a great philosopher, and Josephus, equally renowned as a historian, were unknown to the Jews until modern times. Because their writings were outside the rabbinic scope of thought, their names were not mentioned and their works not taught. This philosophy of isolation is still prevalent today among the strict Orthodox, who still believe that Judaism can survive only if isolated from all other ideas.

Nineteenth- and twentieth-century Jewish philosophers like Hermann Cohen, Franz Rosenzweig, and Martin Buber strove to evolve a Jewish philosophy within the Western tradition. Whereas the modern Jew leans toward their universalist philosophies, the Jewish educational system too often tends toward the opposite, the isolationist paths of the past.

Jewish history, for instance, is still too often taught in Sunday Schools in total isolation from world history. In this view, the world is divided in two parts—the bad, bad Gentiles, and the good, good Jews; only martyrs and makers of the Talmud are shown as the great men of Jewish history, and Judaism itself is reduced to a dirge of suffering, the Jews eternally prey to anti-Semitic wolves. When Jewish youth goes to college, this entire structure crumbles; Jewish history is seen in a new perspective, and what has been taught is rejected.

In America, the process of alienation of Jews from the formal Jewish educational programs proceeded more swiftly than in Europe because here innovation was an ongoing process. With few Talmuds in sight for a couple of thousand miles, the Colonial Jews became their own Talmudists, deciding what was needed to keep them Jewish without the benefit of yeshivas and rabbis. Many of these impromptu innovations were discarded when they no longer served a function, or simply perished when they did not achieve hoped-for ends. They were not preserved in sacred texts as a burden to future American generations. But many did survive, like the Bat Mitzvah, women's participation in services, Jewish summer camp activities—all American concepts that had no counterparts in Europe.

Innovations within American Judaism will continue. Though most will be discarded, some will survive to become part of a new Jewish heritage. The Jewish camp movement— Orthodox, Conservative and Reform—will be one of those survivors. One of the most innovative is the Brandeis-Bardin Institute in Brandeis, California, founded in 1941 by Dr. Shlomo Bardin (1898–1976) as "an adventure in curing alienation."

Born in the Ukraine and steeped in the Hasidic tradition, Bardin was first drawn to Russian socialism. But, soon disillusioned, he went to Palestine in 1919. There he founded a technical school in Haifa (now part of Haifa Technion), and the Haifa Nautical School, the first known school in Jewish history to train Jewish seamen.

Two events changed Bardin's life. The first was a trip to Denmark in 1930 to study its educational system. Here he conceived the idea of teaching Jewish youth the spirit of Judaism within a four-week period rather than trying to teach the total body of Jewish knowledge over a series of years. The second was an encounter with Supreme Court Justice Louis D. Brandeis.

The Danes had innovated the Folk High School system to block the intensive Germanization program of Bismarck's Prussia. Through the artful combination of folk dancing, folk art, folk singing, and working with the soil, the Danes succeeded in preserving their culture. At a chance meeting with Justice Brandeis, the emancipated Ukrainian Hasid Bardin outlined to this Jewish Brahmin his idea of producing dedicated Jewish youth in four weeks—by grafting the kibbutz concept of community life onto the Danish idea of cultural survival, and enriching this blend with American camp activities. The Hebrew schools, contended Dr. Bardin, could not do the job of imbuing Jewishness in Jews because they were modeled on the *heders* in isolated Eastern European *shtetls*; therefore they were not appropriate for America, where the Jews were an integral part of society. Bardin's concept rested upon *touching* the human being rather than teaching him, as temples, synagogues and Sunday schools tried to do. Brandeis enthusiastically embraced Bardin's ideas and lent him his support.

Basically the Bardin idea is to hand Jewish youths the Torah, the Sabbath, a medley of Jewish rituals and see what they do with them. Campers participate in Jewish music, Jewish dance, Jewish dramatic expression, and are given the opportunity to express concepts of Jewishness through art. All these activities are carried out in an intellectual atmosphere. Nothing but kosher food is served, but there is no compulsion for campers to keep kosher. The Sabbath is a day of joy and relaxation. There is no manual work, but everything else is permitted— baseball, swimming, dancing, tennis.

The Sabbath service is the memorable event. A layman reads the week's Torah portion, then three laymen expound on its meaning. Most of them have never given a thought to the contents of the Torah. Yet, thus challenged, their expositions are relevant, and perhaps more in the spirit of Moses than most theological interpretations.*

Before his death, Bardin realized another dream—the creation of the House of the Book, the first facility for a four-year Jewish preparatory school, and patterned after the great prep schools of New England. Arising like a sculpture carved by time atop one of the Santa Susana mountains, the House of the Book is so ingeniously designed that it can be transformed quickly from a house of study into a house of prayer or a house of assembly—the three functions of the original synagogue.

History may yet decree that the Brandeis-Bardin Institute is a new Jabneh. Ben Zakkai at Jabneh hammered out survival tools in terms of isolating the Jews from the world around them. Bardin innovated ideas to help the Jews survive as Jews by showing them how to swim without drowning as Jews and world citizens in the scented pools of Western civilization, be-

---

* Some of these expositions have been published in a book entitled *Torah: The Layman Expounds at Brandeis Institute*, Tasmania Press, 1976. Some are extraordinary in their perception.

cause that is the called-for response in the modern world. This Bardin "cure for alienation" has taken root in such countries as Denmark and Israel.

The strength of America Judaism is that American Jews are constantly trying, testing, experimenting, innovating.* We have seen American Judaism shaped by many forces—by the frontier, by freedom of religion, by Protestant Congregationalism, by the American genius for organization, by both native and German reform movements, by Zionism—but thus far, very little by *shtetl* Orthodoxy.

Collectively, the American Jews are one of the most remarkable groups in the world. A society of 6 million Jews has attained the highest economic, educational (non-Jewish), and social levels in Jewish history, and enjoyed a degree of freedom never before attained by Jews in any country, in any civilization, in any age, including the kingdoms of Judah and Israel in ancient days, and the state of Israel today.

Zionism fused the diverse strains of American Jews into a closer "community of Jews," united in its support of Israel. Campus and suburb erased the social barriers between German and Russian Jews; equal education erased the economic barriers between the two. Kaddish has been intoned over the *shtetl* brand of Orthodoxy, and a new, modern Orthodoxy is replacing it. Conservative and Reform are blending into each other. Though religious affiliation is greater than ever, religion as we have known it is growing weaker. American Jews realize they no longer live in a ghetto milieu, that their Jewish heritage no longer needs its ghetto wrappings. America has become the Diaspora center of world Judaism. A new Jewish history is being written in America.

But what will this chapter hold for American Judaism? Will the concepts of American Judaism be adopted by the Jews in the world Diaspora and by the Jews in Israel? Will

* Deep in the heart of Mississippi, for instance, lies the Henry S. Jacobs Camp, founded by Macy Hart, to save Southern Jewish youth from vanishing into Gentile hinterlands. His pioneering concepts, along with those of Bardin, and the Ramah camps of the Conservatives, have become blueprints for other such camps from the Orthodox to the unaffiliated.

this Jewish paradise in America endure forever, or will it, too, pass? What is the future of America's Jews and American Judaism?

Jews, God, and Destiny

CAN A HISTORIAN predict what will happen in the future on the basis of what has happened in the past? Scientists do not hesitate to do so. The Russian chemist Mendeleev, for instance, predicted the properties of as yet unknown elements, based on the behavior of known ones.

Similarly, metahistorians—historians who venture "beyond history"—have formulated theories about the course of future civilizations by evaluating the behavior of past ones. So, for instance, in *Decline of the West* (1918), Oswald Spengler predicted that Western civilization was declining, while two new civilizations, the Sinic in China and the Slavic in Russia, were on the rise. Laughed at by historians in the 1920s, he is taken more seriously today.

Metahistory is not a new discipline. As early as the third century A.D., kabalists wrote metahistorical works that concentrated on the metaphysical and spiritual meaning of history rather than on the chronological. In the sixteenth century, Isaac Luria, one of the great kabalists, fashioned a fascinating metahistoric evaluation of the Jewish experience.

Luria, whose insights we shall use for a view into the future of American Judaism, thought of all human experience as passing through three stages. In the first stage, Luria sees a twofold action—as all events of Jewish history are brought into a thesis of history, God withdraws himself into an exile within himself. In the second stage, everything that was brought together is shattered, and the Jews are dispersed throughout the world. In the third stage, which Luria calls the "restoration," all that was shattered in the second is unified into a new thesis of history that will herald the return of the Jews to Zion. This event, says Luria, will prepare the way for the redemption of mankind.

Through this Lurian lens of history, the Jewish saga can be viewed as a kabalistic drama in three acts, each act two thousand years long. The first act, from Abraham to Jesus, corresponds to Luria's first stage; the second act, from Jesus to Ben-Gurion, corresponds to his second stage. The third act, from Ben-Gurion to the anticipated redemption of mankind, corresponds to Luria's third stage.

In the first act, the Jews are trained, programmed, and prepared for a specific mission. In a series of six scenes, God, it seems, hands out a succession of scripts to six Jewish dramatis personae, each fulfilling a specific role in a Jewish predestination drama. Abraham proclaims a monotheistic God; Moses gives the Torah to the Jews; King Josiah starts the canonization of the Torah; the Prophets make the Jewish concept of God universal; and with the sixth and last script two Jewish nationalists, Ezra and Nehemiah, introduce a program to preserve the Jews as Jews. Toward the end of this act, the Romans occupy Judea and the Jews rise in a futile rebellion. Jerusalem falls, the Temple is destroyed, and the Jews are exiled. Amidst this desolation, the first-act curtain falls on the first two thousand years of Jewish history.

During a brief intermission, the Jews debate what to do. Should they deny the past and integrate, or should they reaffirm the past and continue as Jews? As the curtain rises on the second act, the Jews choose to reaffirm the past. Consonant with Luria's thesis that God has withdrawn, the Jews have to write their survival script for the second act.

In this act, the Jews are catapulted from civilization to civilization, and confronted by six challenges. They respond successfully to the first four—the impact of the Greco-Roman world (200 B.C.–200 A.D.), the tolerance of the Parthian-Sassanic society, which the Jews call Babylonia (200–600), the grandeur of the Islamic Empire (700–1200), and the rise and fall of the feudal civilization (1000–1500). But with the fifth challenge, the Ghetto Age (1500–1800), comes the first setback in Jewish history. Freed from the ghetto, in the sixth scene, the Jewish Modern Age (1800–2000), the Jews discard their caftans, reenter the mainstream of Western history, and stand side by side with their Christian brethren, blessing the new trinity: Logic, Reason, and Science.

Alas! Whereas the Feudal Age of Faith consigned the Jews to ghettos, the Modern Age of Reason consigned them to concentration camps. Whereas the Talmudists had written the survival scripts for the previous five challenges, it was secular Zionists who now rushed to the rescue. In this sixth scene, the Jews rise like a phoenix out of the ashes of Hitler's concentration camps and return to Zion as if summoned by the Prophets to recreate the state of Israel right under the nose-cones of atomic bombs. On this triumphant note, the curtain falls on the second two thousand years of Jewish history.

Has our kabalistic drama ended with the return of the Jews to the vortex of their history? Or is this also an intermission while they wait for the third act? Are the Jews once again confronted with the same existentialist choice their ancestors were confronted with two thousand years ago, after the first act? And who will write the script for the third act?

But while waiting for the third-act curtain to rise, the Jews have time to reflect on four parallelisms that have become apparent. In the first act there was a Jewish state, but no Diaspora. In the second act there was a Diaspora, but no Jewish state. And now, as the third act is about to unfold, there is both Diaspora and a Jewish state. What role will the American Diaspora Jews play in this new challenge?

The first act was dominated by Sadducee Judaism, the Judaism of sacrifice in the Jerusalem Temple tended by priests. The second act was dominated by Pharisee (or rabbinic) Judaism, the Judaism of rabbis, prayer, and synagogues.

Does this succession indicate that rabbinic Judaism will like-wise be replaced in the third act by some new form of Judaism in which American Jews might play a dominant role?

In the first act, the Torah served the Jewish state. In the second, it was mainly the Talmud that served the Diaspora. What will be the function of Torah and Talmud in the third act, with both a Diaspora and a State of Israel existing side by side? Will American Jews have a role in fashioning a new function for the Talmud as an instrument of survival for the Jews?

And finally, the fourth parallelism. In the first act, the armies of Babylonia removed Judaism from its Jerusalem headquarters (586 B.C.) and resettled it in its first miniature Diaspora, from whence it spread into the Semitic and Medi-terranean worlds. In the second act, through the conquering Cross,* Judaic ideas were spread into the second segment of the world, the Aryan. Will a new force in the third act scatter the Jews into yet another segment of the world, the Asiatic?

As the curtain goes up on the third act, the spotlight is on the American Jews, into whose hands capricious history has placed the scepter of Diaspora Judaism. Will this heritage entrusted to them by the blind permutations of historic events wilt into a wasteland of anti-intellectualism, or will an Ameri-can-Jewish renaissance assure its continuity?

Does American-Jewish history today, in fact, bear a faint resemblance to past events? Reflecting on recent world and American-Jewish history, one has a sense of *déjà vu*. In the sixth century B.C., toward the end of the first act, we saw the Babylonians destroy the Palestinian centers of Judaism in the same way Hitler destroyed the European centers of Judaism in the twentieth century toward the end of the second act. The former shattered the centrality of Judaism anchored in

---

* It took the Christians a thousand years to Christianize Europe. Between 300 and 1300 A.D. the victorious Christian armies forced both the New and Old Testaments on the vanquished pagans and barbarians on the European continent. Thus Judaic ideas were introduced by Christians into barbaric Europe before Jewish settlements began.

Judea and shifted it to Babylon; the latter shattered the centrality of Judaism anchored in Europe and shifted it to America. When Cyrus the Great, king of Persia, presented the captive Jews of Babylonia a passport to return to Palestine, most of them declined that invitation. American Jews in the 1950s similarly declined an invitation from Ben-Gurion to return to a reconstituted state of Israel.

Has America become the new Jewish Babylon—a laboratory for new ideas? Are we perhaps already seeing the emergence of a new Judaism on American soil, just as some two-and-a-half millennia ago a new Judaism began to emerge on Babylonian soil? Is American Judaism destined to play the same dominant role in the third act that Sadducee Judaism played in the first and Pharisee Judaism in the second?

Everything points to such an outcome. In the waning centuries of the first act, the Pharisees subtly undermined and finally did away with the Sadducee Judaism of priesthood, sacrifice, and Temple. The American Jews, in the waning centuries of the second act, are similarly vitiating the Pharisee institutions of rabbi, prayer, and synagogue. Have these three institutions, in fact, already begun to assume new—non-Pharisee—functions?

In Pharisee Judaism, the rabbi was the decision maker. He was a teacher of Judaism and a certifier of values; he was a judge who determined right and wrong according to Talmudic law. He could enforce his decision not only because he was a scholar and a saint but because the Gentile host nations in Europe, until the fall of feudalism, gave him the power to enforce them.

But with the transition to America came the collapse of the feudal and ghetto system of self-government. Jews no longer went to rabbis for Talmudic decisions on law; they went to civil courts. Lay professionals—lawyers, social workers, leaders of Jewish secular community organizations—usurped most of the rabbi's former functions. Even as American Jews rendered the "Pharisee rabbi" obsolete, the American situation created new functions for him. As we have seen, the rabbi in

America became a preacher, a theological psychiatrist, a motivating spirit in the Sunday school system, an interfaith mediator.

In the days of old, many believed salvation could be achieved through prayer, but few today believe praying will bring about miracles. Nevertheless, many still feel an inchoate yearning for salvation, which they know a psychiatrist cannot give them. So Jews go to synagogues, or feel they should go, in the same spirit the Erewhonians went to their musical banks. Has the synagogue in fact become a symbolic museum? Can the Jews rejuvenate themselves spiritually in the synagogue by touching their past in the same way Antaeus could recharge his strength by touching the earth?

Again, Jewish history has provided a parallel. For over three centuries (200 B.C–100 A.D.), the Temple in Jerusalem and synagogues existed side by side; priestly Judaism did not fade out until after rabbinic Judaism had taken hold. Thus the synagogue as a "museum" may persist in Jewish life for another century or so, until the new institutions destined to replace it have gained the confidence of the Jews.

This shift is already beginning to take place. American Judaism no longer expresses itself mainly through the culture of the synagogue but through the culture of organizations. Mordecai Kaplan, as we have noted, perceived this trend in the 1930s and advocated that the synagogue itself become the Jewish community center for religious, social, and cultural activities, shifting its central theme from congregational worship to "social togetherness." In Kaplan's view, the synagogue should contain not only a sanctuary, library, and classrooms, but also a gymnasium, auditorium, and swimming pool.

Kaplan was derided for his view and the synagogues were slow to act. The Jewish Federations stepped into the vacuum, seized the leadership and provided the "social togetherness" programs the synagogue would not. The emphasis has thus shifted from the rabbi, who strives for results with prayer, to the institutional director, who achieves results through organizational action, backed by people of wealth who achieve status through leadership roles. Power is thus shifting from the synagogue to the "agencies"—the Jewish Federation, the United Jewish Appeal, the Jewish Welfare Board, the Jewish Community Centers Associations.

"The more things change, the more they remain the same," said Montaigne. The highly organized American Jewish community of today is indeed beginning to resemble more and more the organized Jewish communities in the high Middle Ages (1000–1500). But the counterlaw to Montaigne's epigram is the axiom that the more events resemble those of the past, the more they differ from them. The difference between the Jewish community in the medieval world and in America today is that in the former the synagogue was central and in the latter the synagogue is becoming peripheral. The trend is for Jewish community power to be concentrated in the Federation; the synagogue may eventually become one of its many satellite member organizations.

In essence, this would be the reverse of Kaplan's version. Not the synagogue but the future Federation complexes with sanctuaries, gymnasiums, swimming pools, libraries, classrooms, and welfare offices would all be unified into new Jewish *sancta*. These *sancta* would radiate religious and secular Judaism much as Greek cities in the Hellenistic world radiated Hellenization through their *sancta* of gymnasia, temple, stadium, bath, and theater.

This concept of a *kehilla*—a total Jewish community of activity—is not completely new in American-Jewish life. It was tried, unsuccessfully, from 1908 to 1922, in New York City. The New York *kehilla* was founded by a Reform rabbi, Judah Leon Magnes (1877–1948). Born in San Francisco, and an avid baseball and Horatio Alger fan, Magnes was ordained in 1900 at Hebrew Union College. To everyone's surprise, this maverick who ate only kosher food and was an ardent Zionist, obtained a rabbinic post with Temple Emanu-El in New York City, an institution noted for its extremely Reform stance. To no one's surprise, he did not last long; he was a casualty in the inevitable clash over tradition. By 1922 he was at odds with everyone—Orthodox, Conservative, Reform, Zionists, and pacifists.* That year he emigrated with his family to Jerusalem, where he helped found Hebrew University, becoming its chancellor and first president.

But during his New York rabbinic internship, Magnes did manage to found the New York *kehilla*. The need for such an institution exploded on the New York scene in a most unexpected way. The prevalent stereotype is that if there are any "Jewish criminals" they are never children of the Orthodox, who are too full of genuine *Yiddishkeit* to turn to crime. But such was not the case in New York at the turn of the century, when most Jewish criminals were children of the Orthodox. Vexed by this problem, New York's police commissioner wrote an article (1908) in which he claimed that 50 percent of the criminals in New York were Jews. Though this figure was exaggerated, it nevertheless caused Magnes to conceive of a *kehilla* of New York to curb this Jewish "crime wave." (This was actually only a minor episode in American-Jewish history, confined to New York City. In general there was remarkably little crime among the Jews as a group, especially considering their poverty and uprootedness.)

The *kehilla* was composed of a federation of Jewish organizations representing Reform, Orthodox, and Conservative, and its energies were directed toward education, morals (a euphemistic term for crime control), labor relations, and charitable activities. Effective for a while, it soon began pulling apart, mainly because of the unwillingness of the Orthodox to see anything but the Orthodox view of things, especially in education. The experiment collapsed.

Past failures have often blazed paths to new successes, and it appears that the Jewish Federation and its auxiliary organizations will succeed where Magnes and Kaplan failed. But

* He was a pacifist in all except Jewish matters. He vehemently opposed America's entry into World War I, but helped smuggle arms to Jews in Russia to help them defend themselves against Czarist pogroms, and he called for war against Nazi Germany, ardently supporting World War II.

should such a takeover of the synagogues come to pass, who will its leaders be? Secular Jews with degrees in theology, or rabbis, who might give themselves a new name to suit new functions?

Such a change of name by the rabbinate would be nothing new in Jewish history. In the past, with each challenge, the rabbis did assume different names to suit new functions. In the Mishna period (Greco-Roman challenge, 200 B.C.– 200 A.D.), rabbis were known as *Tannaim*, the "Repeaters." In the Gemara period (Parthian-Sassanid challenge 200–500), they were called *Amoraim*, the "Reasoners." In the Islamic challenge, (700–1200), they were titled *Gaonim*, the "Eminences." In the period of the codifiers (medieval challenge, 1000–1500), they were referred to as *Poskim*, the "Decision Makers." All were Talmudists. All had sought new uses for the Talmud *—augmenting it, codifying it, commentating on it—in the search for new responses to new challenges. These centuries (200 B.C. to 1500 A.D.) constituted its greatest period—from Hillel, who elevated the Mishna to scientific status, to Caro, the last of the great codifiers.

Not until the ghetto period (1500–1800) were the rabbis simply known as rabbis, perhaps because, in the ghetto, their task was reduced to counseling ghetto inmates with hope of keeping their spirits alive during this three-century incarceration. As life did not significantly change in the ghetto for three centuries, neither did the Talmud. Here the spirit of the universal Talmud vanished. The rabbis could no longer innovate—they merely served the past. Yet, this was perhaps the only viable response to the ghetto situation.

Thus it was that the leaders who responded to the next challenge, the Modern Age, were not rabbis in disguise as *Tannaim* or *Amoraim*, or *Gaonim*, or *Poskim*, but secular Jews disguised as Zionists. This was the first time in the two

* The name "Talmud" (Hebrew word for learning) is of late origin. It was not until the fifth century A.D., after the Mishna and Gemara were fused into one discipline, that these two works as a unit became known as the Talmud.

thousand years of the second act that worldly, not ordained men were the rescuers, and the only time in the second act when the Talmud was not the vehicle for the rescue.

But whether secular men or rabbis seize power in a "Federation Community" in the third act, two questions arise. First, is a Judaism centered in a Federation instead of a synagogue "Jewish"? Second, what vehicle can be used for the transfer of "spiritual charisma" from synagogue to Federation?

A Jew educated in the ghetto tradition might very well ask how a Federation Judaism could possibly be Jewish. A similar question was asked by Sadducee Jews of the Pharisees two thousand years ago, when they were asked to pray in a synagogue under the direction of a rabbi instead of going to the Temple to sacrifice a heifer under the supervision of a priest. But just as the Pharisee rabbi could say without qualm to the Sadducee priest, "Yes, this is authentic Judaism—majority vote makes it so," the Federation Jew likewise can answer the Pharisee Jew, "Yes, this, too, is authentic Judaism—majority vote makes it so."

The real problem is the preservation of the Jews and Judaism, not whether it is done within the confines of a Jerusalem Temple, a Diaspora synagogue, or a universal Jewish Federation. Hillel the Elder (first century B.C.) summed up the essence of Palestinian Judaism in his Golden Rule. "Do not do unto others that which you would not have them do unto you. All else is commentary." A modern-day American Hillel might sum up American Judaism with this Golden Rule: "Do not forget you are a Jew; do not forget Israel; do not forget the Sabbath; and do not forget not to do unto others that which you would not have them do unto you. All else is commentary."

History may yet decree that the American rabbis may again be at the helm of Jewish history. There are indications that they are girding themselves for a future confrontation with the secular leaders. They may add a degree in business administration to their doctorate of ordination. They may also give themselves a new title (like *Manhig*—director—, for instance), seize the leadership of the secular Establishment and transfer it into a spiritual institution. But this would not change the fact that the central power would still be vested in the Federations, not the synagogues.

The second question, How would spiritual, charismatic power be transferred from synagogue to Federation? is a more vexing one. The Torah was the script for the first act, the Talmud for the second. A new script is now needed for the third act. The paradox is that though the majority of Jews—not just in America but the world over, including the Jews in Israel—have abandoned the Talmud of the Orthodox as a survival script, the Talmud itself as an idea may have to be resuscitated. The Talmud, which so brilliantly served the Jews in the first four challenges of the second act, may have to be modernized and made to serve the Jews in the future as it had in the past, prior to the Ghetto Age.

The Talmud was an indispensable vehicle for survival in the Diaspora. If it did not exist, it would have to be invented, for without it, even the Torah would have been an unworkable document. With the exception of a few commandments, the Torah's statutes are so vague that they could not be applied intelligently without interpretation and amplification in Biblical times. Even the Sadducees, who opposed the early Mishna, had a "talmud" of their own, a commentary to tell them what a Torah law meant and how it was to be applied and enforced.

Perhaps the Jewish Modern Age (1800–2000), with its secular Jewish leaders, is but an interim period to permit the Jews to recover from the torpor of the Ghetto Age. Perhaps the time has come for American Jews to go back to the Talmud, modernize it to meet the needs of the times, so that it can again serve the Torah and the Jewish people as it did in pre-ghetto days. This perhaps is the great challenge for American Jews, to start the universalization of the Talmud to serve the Jews the world over in the third act.

But which sect would or could take the lead in such a

move? The Orthodox, who are smothering the Talmud with an excess of veneration. The Conservatives, who are keeping it barely alive with a timid Law Committee? The Reform, who have formally renounced it? Or could Jewish women emerge as a new force and seize the initiative?

The Orthodox are stalemated. As the Orthodox law now stands, they are powerless to act because they are entrapped in a cul-de-sac of their own creation. Once it has been enacted, a Talmudic law, no matter how limited in scope, assumes a life and holiness of its own. According to the Orthodox, any law, however insignificant or absurd, can be annulled only by a court greater than that which instituted it, or by definite proof that it constitutes a grave danger to the entire Jewish community. Since the Orthodox will not acknowledge any court superior to that which passed the law, and since it is impossible to prove, for instance, that a prohibition against switching on an electric light on the Sabbath is dangerous to Jewish existence, the mass of obsolete Orthodox laws will linger on.* Can the Orthodox, victims of their own legislation, be counted on for creative leadership?

The Conservatives are in a similar bind. On occasion they do "amend" or reinterpret" the Talmud, but they still regard it as scripture coequal with the Torah, and thus their intellectual currents often "turn awry, and lose the name of action."

But could such leadership come from the Reform, who have abandoned the Talmud? This is neither farfetched nor impossible. It would only be a recapitulation of history. The first Reform rabbis were defectors from Orthodoxy; now they would become defectors from Reform. The mistake the Reform made in the nineteenth century was in not heeding David Einhorn's dictum that the Talmud was the medium through which the divine might be understood, but without the Talmud itself being considered divine. Instead of modernizing the Talmud and making it serve their ends, these

---

* These two arguments have also been used, thus far successfully, to stop all efforts by the non-Orthodox to annul the excommunication of Spinoza.

superb nineteenth-century Jewish scholars carelessly discarded their greatest potential asset.

For those who view Russian-Jewish *shtetl* Judaism as the zenith of Jewishness, American Reform is a wasteland. But for those who see *shtetl* Judaism as the nadir of the two-thousand-year history of Diaspora Judaism, American Reform offers hope for a renaissance. Thus far few Jews can see Reform as the savior of Judaism. The fashion is still to view Orthodoxy as a repository of true Jewishness.

Another source for future leadership in a modernization of the Talmud might come from Orthodox or Conservative women. A small segment is already in revolt over male dominance in religious ritual. These women have formed minyans of their own and conduct their own Sabbath service in defiance of tradition. A revolt is also brewing against the completely male-oriented interpretations of the role of the woman in Jewish life. Especially galling to the religious but emancipated Jewish woman are the present Talmudic rulings concerning the *niddah*, the menstruous woman, which, in spite of all apologetic literature on the subject, still depict women as unclean and bestow humiliating sexual restrictions upon them as a consequence of that judgment.* Ever more Jewish women are attending Yeshiva University, the Jewish Theological Seminary, Hebrew Union College, and other such institutions of higher Jewish learning. The sudy of Torah and Talmud are no longer closed subjects to them. There is no reason why a future Hanasi, Rashi, or Caro would not be a woman.

But even if Reform should return to the Talmud and make it serve the needs of the third act, it is more likely that, once

* The Torah devotes but fourteen sentences to the subject (Leviticus 15:19-32). The Talmud, however, expands it into ten chapters and numerous commentaries, including nine chapters in the Tosefta. Many of the injunctions in the Talmud contradict those in the Torah, and scholars have unsuccessfully tried to harmonize the statements of the sages with existing knowledge. For an illuminating essay on the subject, see *Niddah*, The Encyclopedia Judaica, Vol. 12.

the modernization process has started, the liberals in the Orthodox and Conservative camps will wrest the initiative away from the Reform who are not as well equipped scholastically for that task as are the Orthodox or Conservative. Just as the fictional character David Levinsky epitomized the 2 million Orthodox Jews who shed *shtetl* Judaism for American ways, so another fictional character, David Lurie,* may foreshadow a struggle in the making among American Orthodox and Conservative for the leadership of modern American Judaism.

David Lurie, born in America of Orthodox East European parents, attends a yeshiva in New York. Here his life recapitulates those of Max Lilienthal, David Einhorn, and Samuel Hirsch in Germany, who in their youth began to question the Orthodoxy they were born into. Like them, David Lurie is interested not only in Bible and Talmud but also in worldly philosophy and higher Biblical criticism. The head of the yeshiva senses David's fears that he may not receive ordination because he has questioned the opinions of Talmudic sages. The rabbi tells him he will give David his final tests whenever he is ready.

"The Rebbe will give me ordination despite what I told him?" asks an incredulous David, and the rabbi answers, "I will not investigate your ritual fringes, Lurie. That is between you and your obligations to the past. Are you telling me you will not be an observer of the commandments?"

"I am not telling the Rebbe that."

"What are you telling me?"

"I will go wherever truth leads me. It is secular scholarship, Rebbe; it is not the scholarship of tradition. In secular scholarship there are no boundaries and permanently fixed views."

"Lurie," answers the rabbi, "if the Torah cannot go out into your world of scholarship and return stronger, then we are fools, and charlatans. I have faith in the Torah. I am not afraid of the truth." In these words, true Judaism is encapsulated.

But whether the Reform, Conservative, or Orthodox—male or female—seize the ultimate leadership, American Judaism

* Chaim Potok, *In the Beginning,* Fawcett Publications, Inc., 1975.

would need fearless leaders like Judah Hanasi (c.135–c.220), who affirmed those portions of Mishna he thought relevant and ignored those sections he felt were obsolete; or innovators like Abba Arika (early third century), who "invented" the Gemara as a way of augmenting the Mishna to pave a path for new laws to serve Jews confronted with new challenges; or trailblazers like Rav Ashi (352–427) who, in the face of bitter opposition from the orthodox of his day, labored to fuse the Mishna and Gemara into the future Talmud, which became the "bible" of the same Orthodox who had opposed its creation. When such leaders appear on the American scene, Judaism will again be infused with the spirit of excitement and discovery. Even more, America could become the new Babylonia, where a universal Judaism for the third act would be hammered out. Such a new American Judaism anchored in a revitalized, modernized Talmud with a valid *halakah* for the modern Jew, could become an exportable Judaism of value to both Israel and a world Diaspora.

This brings up the question of the roles of Israel and of the Diaspora in this third act. Twice in history the Jews have been exiled from their homeland—once by the Babylonians and once by the Romans. Each time Diaspora Jews not only preserved Judaism in exile but also eventually restored the Jewish state. The leaders who restored Jerusalem in the fifth century B.C. were all born in the Diaspora. And so were the Zionist leaders who restored the state of Israel in the twentieth century A.D. Without the Diaspora to preserve the Jews, there would have been no Jews either two thousand five hundred years ago or today to rebuild the ancient homeland. The Diaspora Jews made both events possible.

Thus the past shows that if the Jews wish to continue to be actors on the stage of history, they must continue to cultivate their Diaspora as well as to preserve the Jewish state. Each must nurture the other, because each is dependent upon the other. And if there is to be a Lurianic third act for both Jew and Gentile, the world itself may need both Israel and the Diaspora. The new Space Age that heralded the third act may have made this need a necessity. With the Space Age, the national state is becoming obsolete, foreshadowing the formation of new, international entities.* The world itself is slowly becoming one vast Diaspora for man, with man himself on his way to becoming "diasporized" as he is pried lose from his former moorings in one ecumene and catapulted into new, larger ones.

Two thousand years ago, at the end of the first act, we saw Jews evicted from their homeland into the world at large and becoming the world's first diasporized people to survive in a world Diaspora. Jewish survival was possible because the Jews did not become a rootless people—they had spiritual roots in Jerusalem.

Could it be that the diasporized Jews will serve mankind as a master pattern? The new, diasporized man, compelled to live in a diasporized world, will also be compelled to search for a new, universal ideology that will give his life a spiritual meaning. Why could not Jerusalem, now the spiritual homeland of the diasporized Jews, become the spiritual citadel for the new diasporized man, with ethical Judaism—the Judaism of the Prophets—the universal creed for the universal man in the third act?

Is this too farfetched? In the tenets of Christianity, Islam, capitalism, socialism, communism, we can still behold the Jews who begot or inspired these ideas. Just as Hellenism (from Pericles to Alexander the Great) evolved into a universal Hellenistic civilization that dominated the Mediterranean world for five centuries (300 B.C.–200 A.D.), so the ideas contained in Judaism could evolve into a universal ethic for all mankind. Is it the destiny of the Jews to proselytize the universal aspect of their faith to a diasporized world that is sick unto its scientific soul? Are the people of the world as ready to begin embracing universal, ethical Judaism today as the pagans in the Roman Empire were ready to embrace Christianity in the fourth century A.D.?

* For a fascinating account of this future global imperialism, see *The Coming Caesars*, by Amaury de Riencourt.

Is it by accident that it was three Diaspora Jews who introduced three documents, one for each act, that shaped Jewish destiny and shook the world—Moses, the "Egyptian" Jew,[*] who bequeathed the world the Torah in the first act; Jesus, the Galilean Jew,[†] in whose name the world received the Gospels for the second act; and Karl Marx, the German Jew,[‡] who presented the world with *Das Kapital*, for the third act?

With prescient clarity, anti-Semites realize that Christianity is Judaism for the Gentiles. As the racist historian Houston Stewart Chamberlain wrote, "The Jew has spoiled everything with his Law and his Cross." [§] With the Decalogue (the Ten Commandments) and the Beatitudes (the Sermon on the Mount) the Jews have indeed stated their bill of human rights—a challenge to the totalitarians. The Bolsheviks, too, saw the same danger in these Jewish human rights that Chamberlain did, and took Jewish humanism out of Marxism, substituting heartless Leninism.

Modern Israel is in a spiritual dilemma. She can live neither by the Orthodoxy of the past nor by the nationalism of the present. Overwhelmingly the Israeli, like the American David Levinskys, have rejected their *shtetl* and ghetto past. As in America, but a scant 10 percent of the population live purist-Orthodox lives. This in spite of the fact that unwanted Or-

---

[*] Moses could be termed a "pre-Diaspora" Diaspora Jew because he died before the first Jewish state was established, and thus his entire life was lived outside the Jewish state.

[†] Galilee, conquered by the Assyrians in 732 B.C., was separated from the Jewish state for over 600 years, until reunited with the Kingdom of Judah in 104 B.C. During its six centuries of captivity, Galilee was almost bare of Jews, and already known in the days of Isaiah as *Gelil ha-Goyim*—Circle of the Heathens. When reconquered by Judah, the Galileans were forcibly converted to Judaism. It is ironic that when Jerusalem was destroyed in the war with Rome, the homeless rabbinical schools sought refuge in despised Galilee, and that it was here in the land where Jesus was born, that most of the Mishna and Jerusalem Talmud were written.

[‡] Though Marx was born of Jewish-born parents who had converted to Christianity, he is nevertheless viewed by history as a Jew, for he came out of a Jewish milieu, not a Christian one. Christianity bequeathed him no heritage.

[§] Houston Stewart Chamberlain was mindful of the fact that Jesus was a Jew.

thodoxy is forced on the majority by the minority because the Orthodox hold the political balance of power in a badly splintered Israeli parliament.

Israel finds herself in a most embarrassing situation—75 percent of her laws are based on British common law, 20 percent on Talmudic rulings, and 5 percent on Turkish law. It certainly does not bespeak well for the Talmud when a Jewish state bases 80 percent of its laws on Christian and Turkish legal precepts because the Talmud refuses to accommodate itself to the modern world.

Inasmuch as life in Israel differs from life in America, there might be a need for two Talmuds, one to serve the needs of the Jews in the Diaspora and a second to serve the needs of Israel. Interestingly enough, there is a precedent for this. For two centuries (from about 200 to 400 A.D.) there existed two Gemaras, one in Palestine and one in the Diaspora, and later, two Talmuds. One, known as the Jerusalem Talmud, interpreted life and law for Jews living in Palestine. The other, known as the Babylonian Talmud, interpreted life and law for Jews living outside Palestine. When organized Jewish life ceased in Palestine after the sixth century, the influence of the Jerusalem Talmud faded and the Babylonian Talmud took over as a universal code for the Diaspora Jews.

A modernized Talmud could come out of Israel—she has the tradition and scholarship to do it. It is possible. But the American Jews have the three-century heritage of voluntary and congregationalist Judaism and the resiliency to accept change. In spirit the Israeli Jew is closer to the Colonial American Jew than to European *shtetl* or ghetto Jews. Already American Judaism—Reform, Conservative, and modern Orthodoxy—is beginning to make inroads in Israel, despite fierce opposition by the Israeli Orthodox.

But what would be so "American" in such an American Talmud beyond the fact that it was conceived on American soil? For one, it would be totally different in spirit from that of the old Babylonian and Jerusalem Talmuds. American Judaism is the first and only noncoercive Judaism in Jewish history. It was conceived in liberty and survived total indifference and permissiveness. In the crucible of the American experience, only those aspects of Judaism that the Jews wished to retain survived. It will be in this spirit of freedom that an American Talmud would respond to new challenges. Such a Talmud could also serve as a force to establish social freedoms in societies where they previously did not exist. In the Middle Ages, for instance, those parts of the Talmud dealing with nonreligious subjects such as individual rights, labor laws, and social welfare, eventually seeped into the laws of the Gentile nations among whom the Jews lived.*

But what if metahistorians like Spengler, who predict the death of Western civilizations, are correct? If the West declines, what will happen to American Jews and their Judaism? Will the American Jews stagnate culturally, as the Jews in the Islamic Empire did when it expired? Or will they find sanctuary in new Diaspora centers?

Based on past experience, new Diaspora centers would probably emerge in a new civilization. But where would such a new civilization most likely arise? Spengler, as already noted, postulated the growth of two new civilizations, one in Russia and one in China. Metahistorically it would be no more unlikely for the Jews to establish Diaspora centers in Russia or China than it had been for them to flourish in such diverse social, religious, and economic milieus as Babylonia, Persia, Greece, Rome, Parthia, Sassania, and the Islamic Empire, as well as in Catholic and Protestant nations. Why not Russia or China? Moses never dreamt that Jews would one day create a Golden Age of Judaism in Moorish Spain, nor did Maimonides ever envision a Diaspora center in America.

One could argue against the possibility of a Diaspora center in Russia because of its present anti-Jewish policies. But history teaches that one cannot count on the present to per-

---

* For an interesting account of such a diffusion, see the articles "The Influence of Jewish Law on the Development of Common Law" and "Judaism and the Democratic Ideal," in Louis Finkelstein's *The Jews: Their History, Culture, and Religion.*

petuate itself. Spain, which fostered a Golden Age of Judaism, expelled the Jews. England, which once expelled the Jews, later became a haven for them. Communist Russia, which at first granted equality to the Jews and was the second nation to recognize the state of Israel, reversed its policies. Future needs may force Russia to reconsider her position. But should Russia some day expel all the Jews, might they not be welcomed by China? And might not this possible consequence force Russia to grant the Jews within its borders those freedoms conducive to the establishment of a Diaspora center there?

History could, of course, deal other alternatives. The present-day Jewish communities in South America or South Africa or Australia could erupt as new Diaspora centers, although in the past all new Diaspora centers have arisen in new, emerging civilizations. We must recall that our first act took place in the Semitic sector of the world, and the second act unfolded in the Aryan segment. Parallelism would indicate that the third act should take place in the Asiatic part of the world (as yet untouched by the Jewish ethic), with the Jewish Diaspora capital perhaps centered in China.

Meanwhile the Diaspora world center will most likely continue to be anchored in America for the next century or so, long enough for the American Jews to start writing the survival script for the third act. As the first and second acts foreshadow, American Judaism seems to be destined to become the new world Judaism, no matter where future Diaspora centers may be anchored.

With American Judaism we have seen how the three Babylonian-made institutions of rabbi, prayer, and synagogue have already begun to assume new, non-Pharisee functions. Just as rabbinic Judaism two thousand years ago discarded those parts of Torah and Talmud that dealt with priesthood and sacrifice because they no longer served actual needs, so American Judaism (though only Reform thus far acknowledges it) is discarding "laws" it considers as outdated as those pertaining to sacrifice. This still leaves the heart of Torah and Talmud intact—their codes of ethics, morality, and justice. Festivals and traditions will continue to serve as meaningful symbols to help Jewish identity survive.

It is our contention that American Judaism, as finally shaped by Jews, God, and American history, will be the Judaism which will affect the world, the vehicle whereby Luria's affirmation that the redemption of the Jews will herald the redemption of the world will be brought about.

Is this too farfetched? Is American Judaism really destined to be the Judaism of world Jewry? Is there really a manifest destiny in Jewish history? Suppose the Jewish idea of chosenness has been a grand illusion, that Abraham's encounter with God was but a paranoid delusion, as Freudians would have us believe? Even if so, we see no objection to it. Ideas, not facts, create history. Facts are only footnotes that adorn it. From the historical view, it is meaningless to argue whether the virgin birth or the trinity are facts. But believing in these concepts, millions of Christians were willing to die in their defense, and in the name of Christianity they created Western civilization. Likewise, it is equally meaningless to argue whether Abraham actually met God, or whether Moses received the Torah at Sinai. Believing in, or choosing to believe in, the authenticity of Abraham and Moses and the grandeur of the Torah, the Jews have captured the imagination of man and toppled empires with their ideas. These are the real facts. In history, illusions become reality and shape destiny. In the words of the Proverbs: "Where there is no vision, the people perish."

If the Jews have been acting under the spell of an illusion for four thousand years, then history has already made that illusion a reality. One does not lightly discard a four-thousand-year history like that of the Jews; there is no other history in the world to compare to it in nerve, energy, and grandeur. Who else has dared give the world God, Abraham, Moses, Isaiah, Job, Jesus, Spinoza, Marx, Freud, Einstein? Jews have been and are part of the greatest cultural and moral adventure story in the history of man. It is only fitting that the Jews should be around to say *Shalom* to the messiah when he comes, in the finale of the third act.

This is the history, culture, and heritage which has been entrusted to the American Jews either by the blind permutations of events or by a manifest destiny. We prefer to think it is the workings of a manifest destiny. We also believe that history has chosen well in selecting the American Jews for the task of preserving and perpetuating the Jewish *paideia.*

Bibliography

COMPILING A BIBLIOGRAPHY for this book has been a difficult task because a great deal of the material has come from magazines, periodicals, and monographs too numerous to list. But we do wish to acknowledge the debt we owe these authors, and to pay our compliments to periodicals like *American Zionist, Commentary, Conservative Judaism, Judaism, Jewish Observer, Jewish Social Studies, Midstream, Reform Judaism, Reconstructionism, Tradition,* and many, many others that publish so many brilliant essays on the Jewish condition.

We also wish to pay our respect to three excellent encyclopedias—the one-volume Standard Jewish Encyclopedia (published 1959), remarkable for its spirited prose and compression of material; the twelve-volume Jewish Encyclopedia (published 1901), remarkable for its distinguished editorial board, its scholarship, and outspokenness on religious matters; and the sixteen-volume Encyclopedia Judaica (published in Jerusalem, 1972), praiseworthy for its comprehensive content, personality sketches, and depth of research. The Jewish Encyclopedia, however, is more forthright on religious matters and boldly wades in where Encyclopedia Judaica hesitates to tread.

General Jewish History

Abrahams, Israel. *Jewish Life in the Middle Ages*. New York: Meridian Books, Inc., 1958.

Adler, Morris. *The World of The Talmud*. New York: Schocken Books, 1963.

Altmann, Alexander, Ed. *Studies in Nineteenth-Century Jewish Intellectual History*. Cambridge: Harvard University Press, 1964.

———. *Moses Mendelssohn: A Biographical Study*. Philadelphia: The Jewish Publication Society of America, 1973.

Arkin, Marcus. *Aspects of Jewish Economic History*. Philadelphia: The Jewish Publication Society of America, 1975.

Ashtor, Eliyahu. *The Jews of Moslem Spain*, Vol. 1. Philadelphia: The Jewish Publication Society of America, 1973.

Baeck, Leo. *The Pharisees*. New York: Schocken Books, 1947.

Baer, Yitzhak. *A History of the Jews in Christian Spain*. 2 Vols. Philadelphia: The Jewish Publication Society, 1961.

———. *Galut*. New York: Schocken Library, 1947.

Baron, Salo W. *History and Jewish Historians*. Philadelphia: The Jewish Publication Society of America, 1964.

———. *The Russian Jew Under Tsars and Soviets*. New York: The Macmillan Company, 1964.

———. *The Jewish Community*. 3 Vols. Philadelphia: The Jewish Publication Society of America, 1948.

———. *A Social and Religious History of the Jews*. 16 Vols. New York: Columbia University Press, 1952–1976.

Ben-Sasson, H. H., and Ettinger, S. *Jewish Society Through the Ages*. New York: Schocken Press, 1971.

Bentwich, Norman. *For Zion's Sake*. Philadelphia: The Jewish Publication Society of America, 1954.

———. *The Jews in Our Time*. Baltimore: Penguin Books, 1960.

Blau, Joseph L. *Modern Varieties of Judaism*. New York: Columbia University Press, 1966.

Bonsirven, Joseph. *Palestinian Judaism in the Times of Christ*. New York: McGraw Hill Book Company, 1965.

Cohen, Henry. *Justice, Justice.* New York: Union of American Hebrew Congregations, 1968.

———. *Why Judaism?* New York: Union of American Hebrew Congregations, 1973.

Cronbach, Abraham. *Reform Movements in Judaism.* New York: Bookman Associates, Inc., 1963.

Dimont, Max I. *Jews, God and History.* New York: Simon and Schuster, 1962.

———. *The Indestructible Jews.* New York: The World Publishing Company, 1971.

Dinur, Ben Zion. *Israel and the Diaspora.* Philadelphia: The Jewish Publication Society of America, 1969.

Dubnow, Simon. *An Outline of Jewish History.* 3 Vols. New York: Max N. Maisel, 1925.

Elazar, Daniel J. *Community and Polity.* Philadelphia: The Jewish Publication Society of America, 1974.

Elbogen, Ismar. *A Century of Jewish Life.* Philadelphia: The Jewish Publication Society of America, 1944.

Finkelstein, Louis. *Jewish Self-Government in the Middle Ages.* New York: Philipp Feldheim, Inc, 1964.

———. *The Pharisees: The Sociological Background of Their Faith.* 2 Vols. Philadelphia: The Jewish Publication Society of America, 1962.

———, Ed. *The Jews: Their History, Culture and Religion.* New York: Harper & Brothers, 1960.

Fried, Jacob, Ed. *Jews in the Modern World.* 2 Vols. New York: Twayne Publishers, 1962.

Ginzberg, Louis. *On Jewish Law and Lore.* New York: Meridian Books, 1962.

Glazer, Nathan. *American Judaism.* Chicago: The University of Chicago Press, 1957.

Gordis, Robert. *Judaism in a Christian World.* New York: McGraw-Hill Book Company, 1966.

———. *The Root and The Branch: Judaism and the Free Society.* Chicago: The University of Chicago Press, 1962.

Graetz, Heinrich. *History of the Jews.* 6 Vols. Philadelphia: The Jewish Publication Society of America, 1956.

Grayzel, Solomon. *A History of the Contemporary Jews from 1900 to the Present.* New York: Meridian Books, 1960.

Hapgood, Hutchins. *The Spirit of the Ghetto.* New York: Schocken Books, 1966.

Heller, James G. *Isaac M. Wise: His Life, Work and Thought.* New York: The Union of American Hebrew Congregations, 1965.

Herford, R. Travers. *The Pharisees.* New York: The Macmillan Company, 1924.

Hertzberg, Arthur. *The French Enlightenment and the Jews.* New York and London. Columbia University Press, 1968.

Heschel, Abraham J. *The Insecurity of Freedom.* Philadelphia: The Jewish Publication Society of America, 1966.

Kamen, Henry. *The Spanish Inquisition.* New York: The New American Library, 1965.

Katz, Jacob. *Tradition and Crisis.* New York: Schocken Books, 1971.

———. *Exclusiveness and Tolerance.* New York: Schocken Books, 1961.

Kaufman, Reuben. *Great Sects and Schisms in Judaism.* New York: Jonathan David, 1967.

Laqueur, Walter. *A History of Zionism.* New York: Holt, Rinehart and Winston, 1972.

Lewisohn, Ludwig. *Theodor Herzl.* Cleveland: The World Publishing Company, 1955.

Maimon, Solomon. *An Autobiography.* New York: Schocken Books, 1947.

Marcus, Jacob Rader. *The Jew in the Medieval World.* Philadelphia: The Jewish Publication Society of America, 1960.

Parkes, James. *The Conflict of the Church and the Synagogue.* New York: Meridian Books, 1961.

Patai, Raphael. *Tents of Jacob.* Englewood Cliffs, N.J.: Prentice-Hall, Inc., 1971.

Raisin, Max. *Great Jews I Have Known.* New York: Philosophical Library, 1952.

Rivkin, Ellis. *The Shaping of Jewish History.* New York: Charles Scribner's Sons, 1971.

Rosenthal, Gilbert S., Ed.: *Banking and Finance Among Jews in Renaissance Italy*. New York: Bloch Publishing Company, 1960.

Roth, Cecil. *Short History of the Jewish People*. London: East and West Library, 1953.

——. *A History of the Marranos*. New York: Schocken Books, 1974.

——. *The Jews in the Renaissance*. Philadelphia: The Jewish Publication Society of America, 1959.

——. *A History of the Jews in England*. Third Edition. Oxford: Oxford University Press, 1964.

Sachar, Abram Leon. *A History of the Jews*. New York: Alfred A. Knopf, 1930.

Sachar, Howard M. *The Course of Modern Jewish History*. Cleveland and New York: The World Publishing Company 1958.

Schwarz, Leo W., Ed. *Great Ages and Ideas of the Jewish People*. New York: Random House, 1956.

Smith, Morton. *Palestinian Parties and Politics That Shaped the Old Testament*. New York: Columbia University Press, 1971.

Steiman, Sidney. *Custom and Survival*. New York: Bloch Publishing Company, 1963.

Vorspan, Albert. *Jewish Values and Social Crisis*. New York: Union of American Hebrew Congregations, 1973.

——. *Giants of Justice*. New York: Union of American Hebrew Congregations, 1962.

Weinryb, Bernard D. *The Jews of Poland*. Philadelphia: The Jewish Publication Society of America, 1975.

Weizmann, Chaim. *Trial and Error*. New York: Schocken Books, 1966.

Wirth, Louis. *The Ghetto*. Chicago: The University of Chicago Press, 1956.

Zborowsky, Mark and Herzog, Elizabeth. *Life Is with People*. New York: International Universities Press, Inc., 1952.

American Jewish History

American Jewish Committee. *American Jewish Yearbook.* 56 Vols. (1899–1976). Philadelphia.

   An indispensable record for which the American Jewish Committee deserves the accolades of all American Jews.

Baron, Salo W. *Steeled by Adversity.* Philadelphia: The Jewish Publication Society of America, 1971.

Birmingham, Stephen. *The Grandees.* New York: Harper and Row, Publishers, 1971.

———. *"Our Crowd".* New York: Dell Publishing Co., Inc., 1967.

Blau, Joseph L. *Judaism in America: From Curiosity to Third Faith.* Chicago: University of Chicago Press, 1976.

Blau, Joseph L., and Baron, Salo W., Eds. *The Jews of the United States, 1790–1840: A Documentary History.* 3 Vols. New York: Columbia University Press, 1963.

Bleiweiss, Robert M., Ed. *The Layman Expounds the Torah.* Brandeis, California: The Brandeis Institute, 1976.

Borowitz, Eugene B. *The Mask Jews Wear: The Deceptions of American Jewry.* New York: Simon and Schuster, 1973.

Davis, Moshe. *The Emergence of Conservative Judaism.* Philadelphia: The Jewish Publication Society of America, 1963.

de Sola Pool, David and Tamar. *An Old Faith in a New World. Portrait of Shearith Israel 1654–1954.* New York: Columbia University Press, 1955.

Eisenberg, Azriel, and Goodman, Hannah Grad, Eds. *Eyewitness to American Jewish History.* New York: Union of American Hebrew Congregations, 1973.

Evans, Eli N. *The Provincials.* New York: Atheneum, 1973.

Fein, Isaac M. *The Making of an American Jewish Community.* Philadelphia: The Jewish Publication Society of America, 1971.

Feingold, Henry L. *Zion in America.* New York: Hippocrene Books, Inc., 1974.

Feldman, Abraham J. *The American Reform Rabbi.* New York: Bloch Publishing Company, 1965.

Fishman, Priscilla, Ed. *The Jews of the United States*. New York: Quadrangle/The New York Times Book Co., 1973.

Gaer, Joseph and Siegel, Ben. *The Puritan Heritage: America's Roots in the Bible*. New York: New American Library, 1964.

Goren, Arthur A. *New York Jews and the Quest for Community: The Kehillah Experiment, 1908–1922*. New York: Columbia University Press, 1970.

Handlin, Oscar. *Adventure in Freedom*. New York: Kennikat, 1954.

———. *The Uprooted*. Boston: Little, Brown & Co., 1952.

Himmelfarb, Milton. *The Jews of Modernity*. Philadelphia: The Jewish Publication Society of America, 1973.

Howe, Irving. *World of Our Fathers*. New York: Harcourt, Brace and World, 1976.

Janowsky, Oscar I., Ed. *The American Jew*. New York: Harper and Brothers, 1942.

———, Ed. *The American Jew: A Reappraisal*. Philadelphia: The Jewish Publication Society of America, 1972.

Kaplan, Mordecai M. *Judaism as a Civilization*. New York: Thomas Yoseloff, Inc., 1934.

Korn, Bertram W. *American Jewry and the Civil War*. New York: Atheneum, 1970.

Learsi, Rufus. *The Jews in America: A History*. Cleveland and New York: The World Publishing Company, 1954.

———. *Fulfillment: The Epic Story of Zionism*. New York: Herzl Press, 1951 and 1972.

Lebeson, Anita Libman. *Jewish Pioneers in America, 1492–1848*. New York, 1950.

Levin, Marlin. *Balm in Gilead*. New York: Schocken Books, 1973.

Levinger, Lee J. *A History of the Jews in the United States*. Cincinnati: Union of American Hebrew Congregations, 1931.

Liebman, Charles S. *The Ambivalent American Jew*. Philadelphia: The Jewish Publication Society of America, 1973.

Lipsky, Louis. *Memoirs in Profile*. Philadelphia: The Jewish Publication Society of America, 1975.

———. *A Gallery of Zionist Profiles.* New York: Farrar, Straus and Cudahy, 1956.

Marcus, Jacob Rader. *Early American Jewry.* Philadelphia: The Jewish Publication Society of America, 1951.

———. *Memoirs of American Jews.* Philadelphia: The Jewish Publication Society of America, 1955.

———. *American Jewry: Documents, Eighteenth Century.* Cincinnati: Hebrew Union College Press, 1959.

———. *The Handsome Young Priest.* Cincinnati: Hebrew Union College-Jewish Institute of Religion, 1970.

Meyer, Michael A. *The Origins of the Modern Jew.* Detroit: Wayne University Press, 1967.

Miller, Alan W. *God of Daniel S.* New York: Dell Publishing Co., Inc., 1969.

Moise, L. C. *Biography of Isaac Harby.* The R. L. Bryan Company, 1931.

Morris, Robert, and Freund, Michael, Eds. *Trends and Issues in Jewish Social Welfare in the United States, 1899–1958.* Philadelphia: The Jewish Publication Society of America, 1966.

Neusner, Jacob. *American Judaism, Adventures in Modernity.* Englewood Cliffs, N.J.: Prentice Hall, Inc., 1972.

———. *History and Torah.* New York: Schocken Books, 1965.

Orinstein, Hyman. *The Rise of the Jewish Community in New York.* Philadelphia: The Jewish Publication Society of America, 1945.

Plaut, W. Gunther. *The Case for the Chosen People.* Garden City, New York: Doubleday and Company, Inc., 1965.

———. *The Growth of Reform Judaism.* New York: The World Union for Progressive Judaism, Ltd., 1965.

———. *The Rise of Reform Judaism.* New York: The World Union for Progressive Judaism, Ltd., 1963.

Ribalow, Harold U., Ed. *Autobiographies of American Jews.* Philadelphia: The Jewish Publication Society of America, 1973.

Rosenberg, Stuart E. *America Is Different.* London, New York, Toronto: Thomas Nelson & Sons., 1964.

Rosten, Leo, Ed. *Religions in America.* New York: Simon and Schuster, 1963.

St. John, Robert. *Jews, Justice and Judaism.* New York: Doubleday, 1969.

Schappes, Morris U., Ed. *Documentary History of the Jews in the United States, 1654–1875.* New York: Schocken Books, 1971.

Schwartzman, Sylvan D. *Reform Judaism in the Making.* Philadelphia: The Union of American Hebrew Congregations, 1962.

———. *Reform Judaism Then and Now.* New York: The Union of American Hebrew Congregations, 1971.

Sidorsky, David, Ed. *The Future of the Jewish Community in America.* Philadelphia: The Jewish Publication Society of America, 1973.

Sklare, Marshall. *America's Jews.* New York: Random House, Inc., 1971.

Urofsky, Melvin J. *American Zionism from Herzl to the Holocaust.* New York: Anchor Books, 1976.

Yaffe, James. *The American Jews.* New York: Paperback Library, 1969.

RELIGIOUS AND PHILOSOPHIC ASPECTS OF JEWISH HISTORY

Agus, Jacob Bernard *The Evolution of Jewish Thought.* London, New York: Abelard-Schuman, 1959.

———. *The Meaning of Jewish History.* 2 Vols. London, New York: Abelard-Schuman, 1963.

Baron, Salo W. *Modern Nationalism and Religion.* New York: Meridian Books, Inc., 1960.

Buber, Martin. *Israel and the World.* New York: Schocken Books, 1948.

Cahn, Zvi. *The Philosophy of Judaism.* New York: The Macmillan Company, 1962.

Cohen, Arthur A. *The Natural and the Supernatural Jews.* New York: Pantheon, 1962.

Cohen, Morris Raphael. *Reflections of a Wandering Jew*. Boston: The Beacon Press, 1950.

Dubnow, Simon. *Nationalism and History*. Philadelphia: Jewish Publication Society of America, 1958.

Efros, Israel Isaac. *Ancient Jewish Philosophy: A study in Metaphysics and Ethics*. Detroit: Wayne University Press, 1962.

———. *Studies in Medieval Jewish Philosophy*. New York: Columbia University Press, 1974.

Fackenheim, Emil L. *Encounters Between Judaism and Modern Philosophy*. Philadelphia: The Jewish Publication Society of America, 1973.

Glatzer, Nahum N. *Judaic Tradition*. Boston: The Beacon Press, 1969.

Goldin, Judah, Ed. *The Jewish Expression*. New Haven: Yale University Press, 1976.

Goldman, Solomon. *The Ten Commandments*. Chicago: The University of Chicago Press, 1956.

Guttman, Julius. *Philosophies of Judaism*. Philadelphia: The Jewish Publication Society of America, 1964.

Hailperin, Herman. *Rashi and the Christian Scholars*. Pittsburgh: University of Pittsburgh Press, 1963.

Herberg, Will. *Judaism and Modern Man*. Philadelphia: The Jewish Publication Society of America and Meridian Books, 1959.

———. *Protestant, Catholic, Jew*. New York: Doubleday and Company, 1955.

Jacobs, Louis. *Principles of the Jewish Faith*. New York: Basic Books, Inc., 1964.

———. *Studies in Talmudic Logic and Methodology*. London: Vallentine, Mitchell. 1961.

Katzman, Jacob. *Jewish Influence on Civilization*. New York: Bloch Publishing Company, 1974.

Konvits, Milton R., Ed. *Judaism and Human Rights*. New York: W. W. Norton and Company, 1972.

Kertzer, Morris N. *What Is a Jew?* New York: Collier Books, 1961.

Klausner, Joseph. *The Messianic Idea in Israel.* London: George Allen and Unwin Ltd., 1956.

Kohn, Hans. *The Idea of Nationalism.* New York: The Macmillan Company, 1961.

————, Ed. *Nationalism and the Jewish Ethic.* New York: Schocken Books, 1962.

Lewittes, Mendell. *The Nature and History of Jewish Law.* New York: Yeshiva University, 1966.

Montefiore, C. G., and Loewe, H., Eds. *A Rabbinic Anthology.* New York: Meridian Books, 1938.

Newman, Louis Israel. *Jewish Influence on Christian Reform Movements.* New York: AMS Press, Inc., 1966.

Noveck, Simon, Ed.: *Great Jewish Thinkers of the Twentieth Century.* New York: B'nai B'rith Department of Adult Jewish Education, 1963.

————, Ed. *Great Jewish Personalities in Modern Times.* New York: B'nai B'rith Department of Adult Jewish Education, 1960.

————, Ed. *Contemporary Jewish Thought.* New York: B'nai B'rith Department of Adult Jewish Education, 1963.

————, Ed. *Great Jewish Personalities in Ancient and Medieval Times.* New York: Farrar, Straus and Cudahy, 1959.

Rosenbloom, Noah H. *Studies in Torah Judaism.* New York: Yeshiva University, 1965.

Rudavsky, David. *Modern Jewish Religious Movements.* New York: Behrman House, Inc., 1967.

Schechter, Solomon. *Studies in Judaism.* 3 Vols. Philadelphia and New York: 1908, 1924, 1958.

————. *Aspects of Rabbinic Theology.* New York: Schocken Books, 1961.

Scholem, Gershom G. *Major Trends in Jewish Mysticism.* New York: Schocken Books, 1946.

Silver, Abba Hillel. *A History of Messianic Speculation in Israel.* Boston: Beacon Press, 1927.

————. *Moses and the Original Torah.* New York: The Macmillan Company, 1961.

Strack, Herman L. *Introduction to the Talmud and Midrash.* New York: Meridian Books, Inc., 1959.

Unterman, Isaac. *The Talmud.* New York: Record Press, Inc., 1952.

Waxman, Meyer. *A History of Jewish Literature.* 5 Vols. New York: Thomas Yoseloff, 1960.

    Especially chapters 2, 3, 4, 5 on the development of Halachic literature to the development of Mishna and Gemara and its culmination in the Talmud.

Wiener, Max, Ed. *Abraham Geiger and Liberal Judaism.* Philadelphia: Jewish Publication Society of America, 1962.

Zinberg, Israel. *A History of Jewish Literature.* Vols 1, 2, 3. Philadelphia: Jewish Publication Society of America, 1972.

Aspects of American and European History

A highly selective bibliography designed to emphasize philosophies of history rather than its chronology.

Arendt, Hannah. *The Origins of Totalitarianism.* New York: Meridian Books, Inc., 1958.

Beard, Charles A. *An Economic Interpretation of the Constitution of the United States* (1935 edition). New York.

Beard, Charles A., and Mary R. *Basic History of the United States.* New York: Garden City Books, 1944.

———. *The Rise of American Civilization.* New York: The Macmillan Company, 1927.

Bober, M. M. *Karl Marx's Interpretation of History.* New York: W. W. Norton and Company, 1965.

Boorstin, Daniel J. *The Americans: The Colonial Experience.* New York: Vintage Books, 1958.

Cantor, Norman F. *Medieval History.* New York: The Macmillan Company, 1963.

Cheyey, Edward Potts. *European Background of American History* 1300–1600. New York: Frederick Ungar Publishing Co., 1966.

Cohn, Norman. *The Pursuit of the Millennium.* London: Mercury Books, 1957.

Degler, Carl N. *Out of Our Past.* New York: Harper Colophon Books, 1959.

DeVoto, Bernard. *The Course of Empire.* Boston: Houghton Mifflin Company, 1952.

Durant, Will. *The Story of Civilization.* New York: Simon and Schuster.

    Vol. 4: *The Age of Faith,* 1950

    Vol. 5: *The Renaissance,* 1953

    Vol. 6: *The Reformation,* 1957

    Vol. 7: *The Age of Reason* (by Will and Ariel Durant), 1961

Grob, Gerald N., and Billias, George Athan. *Interpretations of American History.* 2 Vols. New York: The Free Press, 1967.

————. *American History: Retrospect and Prospect.* New York: The Free Press, 1970.

Haring, C. H. *The Spanish Empire in America.* New York: Harcourt, Brace and World, 1947.

Heer, Friedrich. *The Medieval World, Europe 1100 to 1500.* Cleveland: The World Publishing Company, 1961.

Higham, John, Ed. *The Reconstruction of American History.* New York: The Humanities Press, 1962.

Hoffer, Eric. *The True Believer.* New York: New American Library, 1951.

————. *The Ordeal of Change.* New York: Harper Colophon Books, 1952.

Hofstadter, Richard. *The American Political Tradition.* New York: Vantage Books, 1954.

————. *The Progressive Historians.* New York: Vintage Books, 1970.

McMaster, John Bach. *The Political Depravity of the Founding Fathers.* New York: Noonday Press, 1964.

Merk, Frederick. *Manifest Destiny and Mission in America.* New York: Alfred A. Knopf, 1970.

Monroe, Elizabeth. *Britain's Moment in the Middle East,* 1914–1956. London: University Paperbacks, 1963.

Myers, Gustavus. *History of Bigotry in the United States.* New York: Random House, 1943.

Nevins, Allan, and Commager, Henry Steele. *A Pocket History of the United States.* New York: Pocket Books, 1967.

Parrington, Vernon Louis. *Main Currents in American Thought,* Vol. 1—*1620–1800: The Colonial Mind.* New York: Harcourt, Brace and Company, 1930.

Sherman, Richard P. *Robert Johnson: Proprietary and Royal Governor of South Carolina.* Columbia, S.C.: University of South Carolina Press, 1966.

Talmon, J. L. *The Origins of Totalitarian Democracy.* New York: Frederick A. Praeger, 1960.

———. *The Unique and the Universal.* New York: George Braziller, 1965.

———. *Political Messianism: The Romantic Phase.* New York: Frederick A. Praeger, 1960.

Toynbee, Arnold J. *A Study of History.* Vol. I. New York and London: Oxford University Press, 1947.

———. *A Study of History.* Vol. II. New York and London. Oxford University Press, 1957.

———. *Reconsiderations.* New York and London: Oxford University Press, 1961.

Turner, Frederick Jackson. *The Frontier in American History.* Krieger, 1976.

———. *Rise of the West.* Peter Smith, 1959.

INDEX